W9-AOE-733

Buried from the World

Inside the Massachusetts State Prison, 1829–1831

1

Joseph Purchase age 31
Natick, he says, is as much
his home as any place Edn
poor-can read & write some
Parents put him out when 7 or 8
ys. old work'd at farming till
18 or 19 ys. old was steady till
about 15 - then got uneasy and
restless - left the man he lived
with & lived with another man
In 25th year committed his first
offence Sentenced for Man
slaughter for 3 ys & was 3
ys in jail before he came
here served out his time and
was out about a year - then
Sentenced again for attempt
to murder for 6 years been
here 41 months
A very hard case - unfeeling
and utterly destitute of moral
feeling or sense of obligation
An Infidel has no idea
of ever trying to be any thing
March 10th 1829

BURIED FROM THE WORLD

INSIDE THE MASSACHUSETTS STATE PRISON, 1829–1831

The Memorandum Books of the Rev. Jared Curtis

EDITED BY
Philip F. Gura

Published by the
Massachusetts Historical Society
BOSTON, 2001

Distributed by
Northeastern University Press
BOSTON

HV
9475
.M42
M373
2001

© 2001 Massachusetts Historical Society
ALL RIGHTS RESERVED
Published at the Charge of the Publication Fund

Editing of this book was made possible in part by the proceeds of an endowment fund created with the assistance of a Challenge Grant from the National Endowment for the Humanities, a federal agency that supports research, education, and cultural programming in the humanities.

Designed by Steve Dyer

Library of Congress Cataloging-in-Publication Data
Curtis, Jared, 1777–1862.
Buried from the world : inside the Massachusetts State Prison, 1829–1831 : the memorandum books of the Rev. Jared Curtis / edited by Philip F. Gura.
p. cm.
Includes bibliographical references and index.
ISBN 0-934909-79-2
1. Massachusetts State Prison—History—Sources. 2. Prisons—Massachusetts—Boston—History—19th century—Sources. 3. Prisoners—Massachusetts—Boston—History—19th century—Sources. 4. Prisoners—Massachusetts—Boston—Biography. 5. Curtis, Jared, 1777–1862—Notebooks, sketches, etc. 6. Chaplains, Prison—Massachusetts—Boston. I. Gura, Philip F., 1950– II. Title.
HV9475.M42 M373 2002
365'.9744'6109034–dc21

2002000732

48871672

CONTENTS

ILLUSTRATIONS

6. Photographic view of prisoners at Massachusetts State Prison, c. 1860s. *("Prison yard at dinner time," uncredited and undated stereograph, Massachusetts Historical Society.)*

7. "View of the Massachusetts State Prison, from Prison Point Bridge," c. 1859. *(*Ballou's Pictorial Drawing-Room Companion *16, no. 12 [Mar. 19, 1859]: 184. Photograph courtesy of the Boston Public Library.)*

8. An entry from volume 2. *(Jared Curtis notebooks, Massachusetts Historical Society.)*

The illustrations appear at the end of the introduction.

INTRODUCTION

In 1831 the young French magistrate Alexis de Tocqueville traveled across the Atlantic Ocean primarily to examine "the theory and practice of the penitentiary system in the United States," a subject of interest to Europeans because of the country's purported success in reducing crime and rehabilitating prisoners. After the political upheavals in France in 1830, Tocqueville, like many other petty officials, had sworn allegiance to Louis-Philippe and the House of Orléans. But because of his family's close association with the recently deposed Bourbon monarchy, he was uncomfortable with a regime that naturally regarded him with some suspicion. He traded on what good will he had and received governmental sanction for his mission, and with his friend Gustave de Beaumont he crossed the Atlantic to begin his historic tour.[1]

On their arrival in the United States the two Frenchmen diligently pursued their inquiries. They examined the voluminous reports about prisons that since the early nineteenth century had been issued for the benefit of state legislatures, as well as other relevant publications,

[1]Gustave de Beaumont and Alexis de Tocqueville, *On the Penitentiary System in the United States, and Its Application in France* (Philadelphia, 1833), xlvii. For information on their visit, see André Jardin, *Tocqueville: A Biography*, trans. Lydia Davis with Robert Hemenway (New York, 1988), chapter six.

such as those of the Prison Discipline Society of Boston, formed in 1825 to advocate enlightened penal reform in Massachusetts and other states. They interviewed wardens, other prison employees, and public officials involved in the heated debates concerning the means and end of incarceration. And like many other foreign visitors, they toured the more famous of the institutions—at Cherry Hill in Philadelphia, at Auburn and Ossining (Sing-Sing), New York, and at Charlestown, Massachusetts—that were run on disciplinary principles very different from those long established in Europe.[2] True to their stated purpose, within a year of their return to France they published a lengthy treatise, *Du système pénitentiare aux États-Unis et de son application en France* (1833), available later the same year in an English translation by Francis Lieber. Only then did Tocqueville turn his attention to his epochal meditation on democratic institutions.

For the most part, Beaumont and Tocqueville wrote approvingly of the American prisons, but modern readers may need to have the reasons for their praise explained. Taken at face value, many of the things they saw might

[2]Interest in the prisons was so strong that some of the institutions even charged admission to visit the grounds. See John F. Sears, *Sacred Places: American Tourist Attractions in the Nineteenth Century* (New York, 1989), 87–93, 96–99. The Reverend Jared Curtis (discussed below), who served a few years as the prison chaplain at the Auburn penitentiary, wrote his son that in the winter of 1827 they had had "plenty of visitors." "Probably the number who will have visited the Prison at 25 Cts each during the last and present months will not fall far short of Three Thousand," he continued. Jared Curtis to Moses Ashley Curtis, Feb. 7, 1827, Folder 2C, Moses Ashley Curtis Papers, in Southern Historical Collection, University of North Carolina at Chapel Hill. The same admission fee was charged at the Massachusetts State Prison at Charlestown; see William Crawford, *Report on the Penitentiaries of the United States* (1835; Montclair, N.J., 1969), 58–59, where the author, an English philanthropist officially charged with visiting the United States prisons, notes that visitors were only allowed to walk in the yard and as far as the doors of workshops.

seem cruel. Consider, for example, what they remembered of such an institution at nightfall. "When the day is finished," they wrote of the Auburn penitentiary, and

> the prisoners have retired to their cells, the silence within these vast walls, which contain so many prisoners, is that of death. We have often trod during night those monotonous and dumb galleries, where a lamp is always burning: we felt as if we traversed catacombs; there were a thousand living beings, and yet it was desert solitude.

Another foreign visitor, the Englishman Capt. Basil Hall, had virtually the same reaction when he visited the new prison at Sing-Sing shortly after it was opened in 1828. "I do not remember in my life," he wrote, "to have met before with any thing so peculiarly solemn as the death-like silence which reigned, even at noon-day in one of these prisons, though I knew that many hundreds of people were close to me." "At night," he continued, "the silence was really oppressive." A warden at the Auburn penitentiary put it more succinctly. When you enter this prison, he explained to new inmates, "you are to be literally buried from the world."[3]

The situation was the same at Philadelphia, the Massachusetts State Prison, the Connecticut State Prison at Wethersfield, and other state penitentiaries. Of their visit to the prison at Philadelphia, for example, where the two Frenchmen received the unusual privilege of interviewing the inmates, they wrote that virtually every prisoner with whom they spoke could not reply "without being agitated, and shedding tears." Another inmate, when asked if he looked forward to talking to the warden, waxed eloquent

---

[3]Beaumont and Tocqueville, *Penitentiary System*, 32; Basil Hall, *Travels in North America, in the Years 1827 and 1828* (Edinburgh, 1829), 1:56; Gershom Powers, *Letter of Gershom Powers, Esq. . . . in relation to Auburn State Prison* (Albany, 1829), 14.

about the joy he felt at encountering *any* living creature. He reported that when a cricket entered his yard, "it looked to me like a companion," and "if a butterfly, or any other animal" entered his cell, he never did it "any harm."[4] Given such evidence of what we would consider the psychological debility visited on inmates by their incarceration, why did Beaumont and Tocqueville consider these institutions models of penal reform?

The answer lies in the culture-wide transformation of the penal system, so brilliantly adumbrated by Michel Foucault in his *Discipline and Punish*, occurring in the early nineteenth century. At that time, Foucault explains, Western societies settled on new ways to understand the criminal and his behavior. Subsequently, they experimented with how to mark and separate him from those whose behavior they regarded as "normal" and socially responsible, and shifted the emphasis from physical to moral discipline.[5] Prior to the late eighteenth century, for example, serious offenses usually incurred corporal punishment, with jails or prisons used primarily to hold the accused through their trials and until sentence was administered. But faced with an increase in crime (particularly against property) that paralleled the rise of the market economy, by the 1820s public officials had to find more effective ways to deter criminal activity.[6] Toward this end, they developed an elaborate system of discipline administered in

---

[4]See, for example, Prison Discipline Society of Boston (hereafter, PDSB), *Seventh Annual Report, 1832* (Boston, 1833), 13–14; and Beaumont and Tocqueville, *Penitentiary System*, 189.

[5]Michel Foucault, *Discipline and Punish: The Birth of the Prison*, trans. Alan Sheridan (New York, 1977), *passim*, but esp. 249–252.

[6]See David J. Rothman, *The Discovery of the Asylum: Social Order and Disorder in the New Republic* (Boston, 1971), 30–56. But Adam Jay Hirsch argues that Rothman over-emphasizes the novelty of the reforms. As he puts it,

newly established penitentiaries where the state controlled every aspect of prisoners' lives.

These initiatives were tempered further by a variety of humanitarian concerns that characterized the period. Nowhere was this more true than in the United States, where after 1820 reformers reorganized the criminal justice system around the belief that penal institutions, in addition to deterring citizens from crime, should contribute to the criminal's rehabilitation.[7] Hence, the increasingly common use of the term "penitentiary," a place where someone should become penitent or sorry for his actions and where his salvation could be promoted. An individual came to a life of crime, reformers argued, because of failures in his upbringing and problems stemming from his environment.[8] Thus, rather than relying on the prolonged incarceration, made as uncomfortable and unprofitable as possible, that characterized European prisons, they built institutions where various personal deficiencies engendered by family and society might be counterbalanced or overcome, even as inmates came to understand and regret the error of their ways. In such institutions inmates would

---

"what the Jacksonians had to offer was not fresh theories about what the penitentiaries could or should accomplish but fresh suggestions for the implementation of old paradigms." *The Rise of the Penitentiary: Prisons and Punishment in Early America* (New Haven, 1992), 12.

[7]The best studies of this transformation are Rothman, *Discovery of the Asylum,* chapters three and four; Orlando L. Lewis, *The Development of American Prisons* (New York, 1922); Blake McKelvey, *American Prisons: A History of Good Intentions* (Montclair, N.J., 1977), 1–63; and Mark Colvin, *Penitentiaries, Reformatories, and Chain Gangs: Social Theory and the History of Punishment in Nineteenth-Century America* (New York, 1997), especially 73–108 on prisons in New England. On English penal reform, see Michael Ignatieff, *A Just Measure of Pain: The Penitentiary in the Industrial Revolution, 1750-1850* (New York, 1978).

[8]Louis P. Masur, *Rites of Execution: Capital Punishment and the Transformation of American Culture, 1776–1865* (New York, 1989), 82, discusses the use of the term "penitentiary."

be reduced to an utter equality of condition—dressing alike, eating the same food, working at the same labor—the better to understand their degraded condition. The prisons thereupon instilled the strict discipline missing from an inmate's upbringing, made him work long hours at hard labor for the profit of the state, and offered him moral instruction to rebuild his character.

First came the emphasis on discipline, particularly attempts to halt the prisoners' corrosive influence on each other, within and without the prison walls, that led to high rates of recidivism. To combat such social contamination, reformers severely limited interaction among inmates and enforced this injunction through constant surveillance. In 1821, for example, New York took the radical step of placing all prisoners in solitary confinement without labor, a course Pennsylvania followed in 1823; however, this resulted in such physical and psychological trauma that they had to revise the regimen. Refusing to abandon the notion that solitude (and the reflection and eventual penitence it presumably engendered) was central to their humanitarian project, Philadelphia reformers in 1829 pioneered the "separate" system: solitary confinement day and night, but with labor in the cells and with instruction in religion on the Sabbath.[9]

Smarting from its own abortive experiment with total isolation of the inmates, the prison at Auburn, New York,

[9]On New York's penal system, see W. David Lewis, *From Newgate to Dannemora: The Rise of the Penitentiary in New York, 1796–1848* (Ithaca, N.Y., 1965); and Lewis, *American Prisons*, 43–63 and 77–106. On Pennsylvania's see Michael Meranze, *Laboratories of Virtue: Punishment, Revolution, and Authority in Philadelphia, 1760–1835* (Chapel Hill, N.C., 1996); Negley K. Teters and John D. Shearer, *The Prison at Philadelphia, Cherry Hill: The Separate System of Prison Discipline, 1829–1913* (New York, 1957); and Lewis, *American Prisons*, 118–129, 217–252. Beaumont and Tocqueville discuss the two systems in *Penitentiary System*, 19–26, as does Crawford in his *Penitentiaries*, 9–18.

moved in a slightly different direction. Here reformers developed an elaborate "congregate" system in which criminals worked and met together for worship but like their brethren in Pennsylvania were prohibited from any communication, verbal or otherwise, with any other person, officials as well as fellow convicts.[10] As Basil Hall observed, this system allowed just the right amount of that "cheerfulness" necessary to keep inmates from becoming deranged. To be sure, prisoners could not "interchange thoughts, or hold any sociable intercourse whatsoever," but they still saw "the human face divine" and thus felt that they were not altogether abandoned, as they did under the Philadelphia system.[11]

These two competing systems of discipline were at the center of heated national debates about prison reform that were followed across the Atlantic. Beaumont and Tocqueville, like many others, visited the penitentiaries specifically to assess the strengths and weaknesses of each method. In retrospect, however, the similarities between the Auburn and Philadelphia systems seem obvious, for under both the principle of silence reigned supreme. In both, too, prisoners were disciplined claustrophobically to compensate for the presumed absence of order in their earlier years. Prison officials also added hard and incessant labor to overcome the inmates' presumed habits of idleness, for while incarcerated their time belonged fully to the state. Finally, in American prisons all temptations to vice were removed and a chaplain was often appointed to instruct the inmates in moral virtue. Controlling all aspects of prisoners' lives, reformers believed that the stringent daily

---

[10]Rothman, *Discovery,* chapter four *passim;* Lewis, *American Prisons,* 77–106; Emerson Davis, *The Half-Century; or, A History of Changes that Have Taken Place . . . in the United States between 1800 and 1850* (Boston, 1851), 171–172.

[11]Hall, *Travels,* 1:79.

routine, unmitigated hard labor, and religious education that characterized American penitentiaries would rehabilitate criminals.

In 1826 Massachusetts decided to reorganize its state prison at Charlestown, two miles up the Charles River from Boston, according to the Auburn plan. Built in 1804–1805, the original building did not allow for the degree of separation of its three-hundred-odd male convicts that the Auburn system demanded, and so at the same time the legislature appropriated funds for new construction.[12] Within three years the state, at a cost of $86,000, had built an imposing granite edifice, two hundred feet long and forty feet wide, with 304 individual cells in four stories. Each cell was only seven-and-a-half feet long, three-and-a-half feet wide, and seven feet high, and had a wrought iron door with grating at the upper part, "to enable the convict to read" by whatever light penetrated the area.

But this was just one part of the large prison complex. William Crawford, an Englishman who visited virtually all the American penitentiaries in the early 1830s, left a

---

[12]Massachusetts was unusual in not having cells for women at its state prison. Instead, they were incarcerated in local jails; see Estelle B. Freedman, *Their Sisters' Keepers: Women's Prison Reform in America, 1830–1930* (Ann Arbor, Mich., 1981), 11. There were women at Auburn, and Beaumont and Tocqueville point out that in the prison population as a whole in the U.S., women constituted about a tenth, virtually the same proportion as in France; see *Penitentiary System*, 269. When Jared Curtis arrived at Auburn late in 1825 to serve as chaplain, he found 428 inmates, 8 of who were women. Jared Curtis to Moses Ashley Curtis, Nov. 11, 1825, Folder 2B, Moses Ashley Curtis Papers, Southern Historical Collection, University of North Carolina at Chapel Hill. General details about the prison in Charlestown are drawn from Gideon Haynes, *Pictures from Prison Life: An Historical Sketch of the Massachusetts State Prison* (Boston, 1869); Crawford, *Penitentiaries*, 57–67; Lewis, *American Prisons*, 68–76, 158–174; and Michael Stephen Hindus, *Prison and Plantation: Crime, Justice, and Authority in Massachusetts and South Carolina, 1767–1878* (Chapel Hill, 1980), 162–181.

detailed description of the entire compound. "The walls," he wrote,

> Which are 18 feet high[,] enclose a quadrangular space, about 500 feet in length and 240 feet in width, and are bounded on the northern and western sides by a creek and river. Adjoining the prison on the south side is a commodious wharf. The buildings of the old prison . . . consist of two wings, with the warden's apartments and guard-room in the centre. In the rear of the buildings is a garden, and a warehouse next the wharf. Along the top of the prison walls is a platform on which several watch-boxes for sentinels are placed at convenient distances. On the west side a basin has been constructed for admitting canal boats, by which, stone, wood, &c are conveyed to the prison through an opening, which is secured by strong gates. Near this dock is a large shed, 130 feet long and 60 feet wide, open to the roof, in which the convicts are employed in cutting and working stone. There are also several workshops occupied by cabinet makers, tailors, shoemakers, brushmakers, coopers and blacksmiths.

The new prison building, he explained, had been constructed on the east side of this quadrangular space. Within its complex were the cookery and the chapel, "conveniently warmed by steam emitted from the boiler in the cookery." When he first saw the compound at Auburn, Jared Curtis, later the chaplain at the Massachusetts State Prison, wrote his son that "The prison is like the old castles of Romance, full of passages—intricacies—dismal places & dungeons."[13] His description would serve as well for Charlestown.

The entire new cellblock was surrounded by three-foot-wide galleries on each floor from which prisoners were

---

[13]Crawford, *Penitentiaries*, 57; Jared Curtis to Moses Ashley Curtis, Nov. 11, 1825, Folder 2B, Moses Ashley Curtis Papers, Southern Historical Collection, University of North Carolina at Chapel Hill.

closely surveyed—from this position a sentinel allegedly could "hear a whisper from the most distant cell"—and thus the regimen of silence was pitilessly enforced. The complex also included new workshops. Prison officials proudly reported that this area was as secure as the gallery, for it was open to the eye in such a way that "a single overseer may do more to prevent evil communication between one hundred men in this shop" than ten could in the old structure. Once committed to Charlestown, no prisoner could escape the panoptic surveillance that reduced him to helpless dependency on the state and made him understand that his only hope lay in capitulation to the discipline and its moral benefits. As Basil Hall understood, the very possibility that one was being watched focused an inmate's attention. "The consciousness that a vigilant eye may at any given moment be fixed upon [prisoners]," he wrote, was "singularly efficacious in keeping the attention of all parties awake" in a way that "no visible and permanent scrutiny" had the "power of commanding."[14]

We are fortunate in having many details of the regimen at Charlestown recorded in the warden's annual reports to the state legislature and in William Crawford's *Report on the Penitentiaries of the United States* (1835). Upon arrival at the institution, for example, each prisoner was given a physical examination and a haircut and received two pair pantaloons (one "thick," one "thin"), two jackets of similar materials, two pair shoes and socks, three shirts, and two blankets. In his cell, where he spent all his time except when at hard labor or at chapel, he found a stool, a "night

---

[14]PDSB, *Fifth Annual Report, 1830* (Boston, 1831), 7; Hall, *Travels*, 1:58. Hall also notes that in the same ways the activities of the guards or "turnkeys" also could be monitored by the warden or those whom he designated, for before the prison reform of the 1820s there was much corruption by bribery among the workers.

bucket," a water can, a cast iron knife and spoon, a pot for coffee, a tin pail for food, a bottle to hold the weekly allotment of one and one-eighth gills of vinegar, a pillow and case, a cot and canvas sacking, two blankets for summer and three for winter, and "1 Bible and such School Books, Hymn Books, and Tracts, as the Chaplain and Warden may deem proper."[15] The prison allowed no personal belongings whatsoever.

The inmate's rations were specified in similar detail. He was guaranteed a daily allotment of a pound of "number one beef" or "number one pork," ten ounces of rye meal and the same amount of Indian meal, and three-quarters of a gill of molasses. For every hundred such rations he also received two-and-a-half bushels of potatoes, two quarts of vinegar, four quarts of salt, two ounces of black pepper, and "in warmer seasons" four quarts of molasses and twelve ounces of hops, presumably to flavor his water. No snuff or tobacco was permitted, and water was only occasionally supplemented by small amounts of beer.[16]

After his initial processing, an inmate was left alone in his cell for a few days to season him to the new environment. He then was placed in one of eight "Divisions" of not more than thirty-eight prisoners each, the same number as inhabited one of the "galleries" of the new prison. The first and second divisions consisted of old men and recently admitted prisoners, who together were under the supervision of a sole "turnkey"; the other divisions each had one such supervisor. An inmate also was assigned to one of the various work crews, the largest of which at Charlestown worked at cutting blocks of granite brought by water from nearby

---

[15] *Laws of the Commonwealth for the Government of the Massachusetts State Prison, with the Rules and Regulations . . . October 1829* (Charlestown, 1830),10–11, 23.

[16] *Laws of the Commonwealth,* 11.

quarries. Other assignments included duty in the cookery, the prison hospital, or at some task like tailoring or shoemaking that contributed to the maintenance of the institution and presumably gave inmates the kinds of skills they could use when they left the institution.[17]

New prisoners also had to learn the myriad rules by which the prison operated. The Auburn plan, for example, proscribed all intercourse with the outside world, a prohibition that extended not only to visitors but also to the writing or receiving of letters, even from immediate family.[18] Prisoners could not speak to anyone in prison, even to officers (save, as we shall see, for the chaplain), "except for purposes of instruction, or to ask for orders and make necessary reports." Nor were they allowed to stand or move two abreast unless their work demanded it. This discipline, a hallmark of the American prisons, quickly reduced inmates to the kind of dependence on the institution that led to introspection and eventual contrition.[19] Such isolation also prevented the contagion of corruption commonly

---

[17] *Massachusetts Senate Documents, January 1830*, 16. A report from 1827 indicates that 105 inmates were occupied in cutting stone, with another 21 acting as "lumpers" who transported the same. There also were 35 cabinetmakers, 26 brushmakers, 6 whitesmiths and tinsmiths, 3 shoemakers, 1 copperplate printer, and 7 coopers, all of whom were "let to contractors"; 10 weavers and 13 tailors, to make inmates' clothes; 10 washers and waiters in the cookery; 10 hospital workers; 9 cooks; and 3 barbers. PDSB, *Second Annual Report, 1827* (Boston, 1828), 59.

[18] When Jared Curtis (see below) first assumed his position at Auburn, he noted that "A few years since it was the custom . . . to permit convicts to write their friends once in three months & also to receive letters from [them]." These "were all submitted to the inspection of the Keeper [warden]," he continued, and "were recorded by the Clerk in a Book." Curtis told his correspondent that he had been "amusing" himself by reading through these copies and had found "some wonderful specimens of Genius among them," examples of which he excerpted in his letter. Jared Curtis to Moses Ashley Curtis, May 10, 1826, Folder 2B, Moses Ashley Curtis Papers, Southern Historical Collection, University of North Carolina at Chapel Hill.

noted earlier in the prison's history when many inmates had slept together in common spaces, had frequent opportunities to socialize, and were allowed privileges that led to vice.

Just as the silence pushed an inmate further into isolation, so the invariable and humiliating prison routine wore down his potential rebelliousness. A loud bell awakened the prisoner, at daybreak in winter and a half-hour before dawn in summer. After roll was called he joined other inmates in his division, all dressed alike in striped clothing, and marched from his cell to the yard where he emptied his waste pail and washed his hands and face. Twice a week he also was allowed to shave, and on the same days in warm weather he could bathe for ten minutes in a canal built into the prison area for the delivery of quarry stone on barges. There were no provisions for exercise or recreation of any kind. Everywhere he went, he moved in lockstep, shuffling, right hand upon the shoulder of the man in front, head turned toward the right, a quasi-military discipline popularized at Auburn. As one person observed, the workshops were "a great curiosity when the convicts are on Duty" and "to go throughout the prison & view it in all its parts—its employments—its principles &c. &c. is worth a journey."[20]

His toilet completed, the prisoner walked in formation with the others to his respective shop to labor for two hours until breakfast, which (as with all meals) an inmate on kitchen duty handed to him and he ate alone in his cell. Twenty-five minutes later he returned to hard labor, but

---

[19] *Massachusetts Senate Documents* 2 (1829), 8; Foucault, *Discipline and Punish, passim.*

[20] Jared Curtis to Moses Ashley Curtis, Nov. 11, 1825, Folder 2B, Moses Ashley Curtis Papers, Southern Historical Collection, University of North Carolina at Chapel Hill.

not before he made a brief stop at the chapel, where he attended prayers led by the chaplain. At noon he ate dinner and then returned to work until six, when he again went to the chapel to hear the chaplain read from the Scriptures and offer another prayer. Supper followed after the prisoner returned to his cell for the night. All told only twenty-five minutes elapsed from the time his labor ended until lock up. No further activities were allowed, save silently reading the Scriptures; as the reformers hoped, prisoners had much time for thought. Night watchmen extinguished the lights at 9 P.M. and made their rounds through the night to prevent any surreptitious communication. "This is the history of a day at Charlestown," the warden wrote, "and the history of a day is the history of a year." The only variation came on Sunday when the authorities dispensed "with the hours of labor" and substituted "the hours of instruction in the Sabbath School, and the hours for public worship."[21]

The prison enforced this strict regimen with an elaborate set of rules whose infraction brought immediate chastisement, corporal or otherwise. At Charlestown, as at Auburn, for example, any prisoner who broke the cardinal rule of silence faced a series of graduated punishments. With the first infraction he was placed in solitary confinement for a day or two. After a second offense, the warden added "greater severity" to his confinement, "such as entire privation of light, and diminution of food; sometimes, also his bed is taken from him." If such punishments did not dissuade the troublemaker, he finally was whipped publicly. In cases of misconduct—which usually consisted of inattention to work, disobedience, or talking—the offender was left out of the evening muster and

[21] PDSB, *Fifth Annual Report*, 7.

reported to the warden, who would determine the level of admonition or punishment. In cases of assault by a prisoner against an inmate or a prison employee, the sentinels on the walls had orders to use their firearms immediately.[22]

Charlestown's discipline, however, was moderate in comparison to that at its sister institution, Sing-Sing. In the former institution, for example, an inmate was never flogged in front of prisoners or without the warden or his deputy present, and recourse to this punishment was infrequent. At Sing-Sing, however, Warden Elam Lynds made the prison notorious for his frequent recourse to corporal punishment, particularly the lash. His actions needed no apology, he commented, because "it was necessary to begin with curbing the spirit of the prisoner, and convincing him of his weakness." Faced with such stringent punishments for crossing prison discipline, inmates had little choice but to accept the rules and so live in a frightening, but presumably salutary, degree of isolation. "They are united" in their fate, Beaumont and Tocqueville observed, "but no moral connexion exists among them."

> They see without knowing each other. They are in a society without any intercourse; there exists among them neither aversion or sympathy. The criminal who contemplates an escape, or an attempt against the life of his keepers, does not know in which of his companions he may expect to find as-

---

[22]Beaumont and Tocqueville, *Penitentiary System*, 41. In 1833, for example, Moses Curtis, son of Jared Curtis, chaplain at Charlestown (see below), noted in his diary that "a couple of poor fellows" were "confined in darkness this morning for playing in meeting." They "are to remain solitary & alone," he continued, "with only a board & blanket," until the next day. Moses Curtis, Sept. 13, 1833, in Personal Diary, vol. 6, Moses Ashley Curtis Papers, Southern Historical Collection, University of North Carolina at Chapel Hill.

> sistance. Their union is strictly material, or, to speak more exactly, their bodies are together, but their souls are separated; and it is not the solitude of the body that is important, but that of the mind.

Through such "solitude of the mind," of course, each prisoner presumably contemplated his fate, reflected on how he had reached this end, perused the Bible left in his cell, and began, under supportive moral guidance, to find his way back to society.[23]

As the daily regimen in Charlestown indicates, the employment of chaplains for the religious edification of the prisoners was an integral feature of the American prison system.[24] Usually an ordained Protestant minister, the chaplain was an essential member of the permanent staff—along with the warden, a clerk, turnkeys, overseers, night watchmen, and a physician. If the experience of Jared Curtis, who served at both Auburn and Charlestown, is any indication, this individual sometimes lived within the penitentiary, as did the warden.[25]

Visitors to the prisons recognized the chaplain's distinctive role in the rehabilitation of prisoners. After visiting Sing-Sing, for example, and meeting its chaplain, Gerritt Barrett, Basil Hall described the great satisfaction attendant on such labors. "The pleasure of such work," he wrote, arises "from those incipient buddings of sympathy" among

---

[23] Beaumont and Tocqueville, *Penitentiary System*, 203, 24.

[24] Lewis, *From Newgate to Dannemora*, 102n., indicates that Curtis, who later would go to the Massachusetts State Prison in Charlestown, was the first full-time resident chaplain in the United States.

[25] When Curtis arrived at Auburn in November 1825, for example, he boarded with the "Superintendent." When his wife and daughter joined him half a year later, however, they boarded in a farmhouse outside the walls but not far away. Jared Curtis to Moses Ashley Curtis, Nov. 11, 1825, and June 14, 1826, Folder 2B, Moses Ashley Curtis Papers, Southern Historical Collection, University of North Carolina at Chapel Hill.

the prisoners which constantly sprang up in his path and, concomitantly, from knowing that God's work was being done among the outcast. Beaumont and Tocqueville also testified to the importance of such selfless labor. "The progress of the reform of prisons has been of a character essentially religious," they wrote, for religious instruction guided by the chaplain provided "one of the fundamental elements of discipline and reformation" in the penitentiaries.[26]

At first the chaplain in Charlestown performed only part-time work, receiving $250 a year for preaching at noon on the Sabbath and occasionally visiting the hospital.[27] But by 1827 prison officials realized that such minimal work was "not the thing demanded in such an institution," for "if there is a place on earth, where a minister of the Lord Jesus Christ may contend with sin, it is in a great Prison." They had heard of the positive results a full-time chaplain achieved at their sister institution in New York and wanted "no better illustration of what *may be done*" than "in what *has been done* by Mr. Curtis, at Auburn."[28] The following year Massachusetts remedied the situation by luring away that very individual to assume similar duties as its new prison neared completion.[29]

The Reverend Jared Curtis (1777–1862), a native of Stockbridge, Massachusetts, brought a rich personal his-

---

[26] Hall, *Travels*, 1:70; Beaumont and Tocqueville, *Penitentiary System*, 93.

[27] When Curtis assumed the chaplain's position at Auburn in 1825, he was paid $500 a year. The following year, however, he negotiated with Louis Dwight, head of the Prison Discipline Society of Boston that paid his salary, and agreed to "return for Nine Months more—at the rate of Six Hundred Dollars a year." Jared Curtis to Moses Ashley Curtis, Feb. 28, 1826, Folder 2B, Moses Ashley Curtis Papers, Southern Historical Collection, University of North Carolina at Chapel Hill.

[28] PDSB, *Second Annual Report*, 58–59.

[29] PDSB, *Third Annual Report, 1828* (Boston, 1829), 13. Curtis had served at Auburn for three years when Massachusetts hired him away. As noted

tory and solid training to the Charlestown prison. After graduating from Williams College in 1800, he had studied theology with the Reverend Charles Backus (1749–1803), a well-known Congregationalist minister who trained young clergymen at his home in Somers, Connecticut. After his mentor's death Curtis reconsidered his ministerial plans and, after serving a term as a tutor at Williams in 1803–1804, returned to Stockbridge. He became a successful merchant, first with his father, Isaac, and then with Elisha Brown. This occupied him until 1817, when he dissolved the partnership. He returned to teaching, in 1820 assuming the role of preceptor at the newly formed Stockbridge Academy, a position he held for the next five years. But in 1824 Curtis again heard his call to the ministry and began study with the local minister, David Dudley Field. Within a year (in part because Williams College already had granted him an M.A.), he received his license to preach, and as we have seen, in the fall of 1825 the Prison Discipline Society placed him in New York's penitentiary. After his move to Charlestown in 1828, he worked with the prisoners there until 1852.[30]

Curtis's extant letters indicate his deep commitment to evangelical religion. While his son Moses was at Williams

---

above (n. 27), his salary at Auburn had been paid by the Prison Discipline Society, which actively lobbied to place clergy in the new penitentiaries. He stayed at Charlestown through the 1840s; see Moses Ashley Curtis Papers, Southern Historical Collection, University of North Carolina at Chapel Hill.

[30]For Curtis's biography, see Calvin Durfee, *Williams Biographical Annals* (Boston, 1871), 228; and Edmund Berkeley and Dorothy Smith Berkeley, *A Yankee Botanist in the Carolinas: The Reverend Moses Ashley Curtis, D.D. (1808–1872)* (Berlin and Stuttgart, 1986), chapter one. Also William S. Powell, *Moses Ashley Curtis, 1808–1872: Teacher—Priest—Scientist* (Chapel Hill, 1958), 9; and Electa F. Jones, *Stockbridge, Past and Present; or, Records of An Old Mission Station* (Springfield, Mass., 1854), 233. For general background on his Stockbridge years, see Sarah Cabot Sedgwick and Christina Sedgwick Marquand, *Stockbridge, 1739–1939: A Chronicle*

College, for example, he often wrote to inquire about the boy's spiritual life and was particularly excited when, during a revival at the college, Moses seemed to be among the converted. While at Auburn, Jared applauded the revival labors of Charles Grandison Finney in the town: Curtis described him as "'sui generis' but very pointed & very powerful." To forward his own evangelical goals within the prison, Jared sought to augment his Sabbath preaching: he convinced the warden to allow the inmates to attend chapel twice daily, when they heard Scriptures and prayers. He also organized a voluntary Sabbath School, which in its first year had fifty participants. It consisted primarily of inmates with very little education who wanted to hear scriptural lessons and to learn to read, write, and cipher. In addition to his other responsibilities, the chaplain also visited the sick in the infirmary and took other opportunities to "instruct the convicts in their moral and religious duties." In October 1829, with the new prison building completed and the full transition to the congregate system effected, Curtis's various duties were written into law.[31]

([Great Barrington, Mass.], 1939). His son, Moses Ashley Curtis (1808–1872), became a prominent botanist and lived most of his life in North Carolina; his papers are in the Southern Historical Collection, University of North Carolina at Chapel Hill. There are 30 letters from father to son between 1823 and 1827, the period when Jared was still in Stockbridge and at Auburn, and 19 more between 1841 and 1856, when he was in Charlestown. Unfortunately, unlike his letters from Auburn in 1826 and 1827, the Massachusetts materials do not go into detail about life at the prison. Part of Moses's diary for 1833 relates to a visit to his father in Charlestown, where Moses, as a budding clergyman, filled in for Jared when he was away on other business. See Personal Diary, vol. 6, Moses Ashley Curtis Papers, Southern Historical Collection, University of North Carolina at Chapel Hill. Also, in Curtis's interviews with Isaac Jackson and Seth Hamilton (below), the chaplain mentions that he knew these convicts because they were from his hometown.

[31]Jared Curtis to Moses Ashley Curtis, Dec. 7, 1825, and Aug. 28, 1826, Folder 2B, Moses Ashley Curtis Papers, Southern Historical Collection,

The state was particularly impressed by Curtis's Sabbath School, which, though no convict was obliged to attend, grew by leaps and bounds. Indeed, inmates regarded it so highly that "they consider[ed] it as a favour to be admitted." Preceding the Sunday morning service, instruction consisted of a brief sermon by the minister in which he abstained "from every dogmatical discussion" and "treat[ed] only of religious morals." He followed this with a similarly ecumenical catechism, "as fit for Catholics as for Protestants, for the Unitarian as for the Presbyterian."[32] Attendees also received instruction in the rudiments of reading and writing, essential skills if they were to integrate themselves into society successfully when they had served their sentences.

As the school grew larger—to one hundred participants in 1832—Curtis, like the chaplains at Auburn and the Wethersfield, Connecticut, prison, enlisted local help to teach the prisoners in groups of four or five.[33] In the annual report for that year he noted the remarkable fact that "Probably not less than five hundred of the most moral and respectable citizens of Boston, Charlestown and Cambridge have been teachers in this Sabbath school within the past year." This participation, he noted, had the unforeseen result of greatly increasing knowledge of and sympathy for the inmates in the surrounding communities. The chaplain proudly observed that the inmates frequently reciprocated "the kind and heartfelt regard

University of North Carolina at Chapel Hill; PDSB, *Fourth Annual Report, 1829* (Boston, 1830), 10; *Laws of the Commonwealth*, 6–7, 23–24. Curtis's notebooks indicate that most who went to the Sabbath School were virtually illiterate.

[32]Beaumont and Tocqueville, *Penitentiary System*, 49–50.

[33]At Auburn the prison chaplain enlisted the help of members of the Auburn Theological Seminary, a Presbyterian institution in the same town. See Beaumont and Tocqueville, *Penitentiary System*, 54.

manifested by this operation." Prisoners who benefited from these volunteers no longer "cherish[ed] malignant feelings toward their Sabbath school teachers," he noted, and in some cases even felt that in these volunteers they had found "sincere friends." To Curtis, appreciative that in the same year the state government had "by law" provided for his full support, all this was proof that God's work was going forward within the prison's walls.[34]

The chaplain also took very seriously the state's injunction to visit with prisoners after the Sunday service and, at his discretion, at other times during the week, a privilege he did not have at Auburn, where pastoral visits were restricted to the Sabbath. Beaumont and Tocqueville, who made "repeated visits" to Charlestown, reported that at these times the clergyman strove "to touch [the inmates'] hearts by enlightening their consciences." William Crawford's report also lauded Curtis's success in this work. "The attention which is paid to the moral and religious improvement of the convicts is highly creditable to the State," he wrote, "and to the excellent chaplain to whose care they are confided."[35]

The astute visitors, however, also understood the most important thing about these interviews: the prisoners were encouraged to talk freely with their chaplain, and they usually felt "pleasure when they see him enter their cell." "He is the only friend left to them," they continued, and thus the inmates "confide in him all their sentiments." Through his solicitous visits Curtis soon enough became "initiated into all the secrets of their previous life, and knowing the moral state of all, he endeavors to apply to each the proper

[34]PDSB, *Seventh Annual Report*, 12.

[35]Crawford, *Penitentiaries*, 18; Beaumont and Tocqueville, *Penitentiary System*, 54; Crawford, *Penitentiaries*, 59.

remedy for his evil." The regulations at Charlestown put it plainly. Prisoners were "recommended to approach the Rev. Chaplain as their best friend, to disclose to him all their troubles and sorrows, and to rest assured that the instructions he will afford them, if followed, will point the way to virtue and happiness."[36]

The psychological relief these visits afforded must have been immense. As Basil Hall noted, "the only voice, except that of stern authority," which a prisoner "is ever allowed to hear, is that of the friendly chaplain," whose "duty and pleasure" was to lead the inmate's thoughts "into virtuous channels." And the import of these visits increased because the chaplain was also the prisoners' only link to the outside world. "On proper occasions," for example, Curtis could "write to the families of the convicts" and in turn receive letters from these relatives. Thereupon he was free to communicate to the prisoners such family news "as he may deem consistent with humanity and the laws, and necessary to produce useful impressions on their minds and conduct." One of the inmates who spoke to Beaumont and Tocqueville in Philadelphia testified to the importance of the chaplain's ability to humanize the painful monotony of his sentence. It was "a great happiness" to talk to the chaplain, he told them, for the minister sometimes stayed with him as long as "a whole hour." Moreover, he anticipated that Curtis would soon bring him "news of my mother and father." "I hope that they are alive," he added, because "for a whole year I have not heard of them."[37]

Aware of the dependency that could develop through

---

[36] Beaumont and Tocqueville, *Penitentiary System*, 54; Crawford, *Penitentiaries*, 59; *Laws of the Commonwealth*, 69–70.

[37] Hall, *Travels*, 1:69; *Laws of the Commonwealth*, 69–70; Beaumont and Tocqueville, *Penitentiary System*, 188.

such interviews, prison authorities realistically worried that some prisoners might fabricate facts to win their chaplain's sympathy and, eventually, his support for a pardon. Thus, if in speaking with the minister any convict was "proved guilty of telling lies, or giving an unfaithful and untrue account of his history, feelings or intentions, with a view to deceive," he would be punished "in accordance with the rules of the prison for lying."[38] Prisoners had to understand that their conversations with the chaplain were to effect their spiritual rehabilitation and thus that they should deal faithfully with him.

In 1829, before the new prison, and thus the transition to the congregate system, was completed, the Reverend Curtis undertook an additional task at Charlestown. On March 10, he began systematically to interview each inmate to learn his background and recorded these biographies in two elaborate notebooks, only recently discovered.[39] For whatever reason, he began with inmates whose last names began with "P" and interviewed several prisoners a day, three or four days a week, for five months. When he com-

[38] *Laws of the Commonwealth*, 69. The matter of pardons was hotly debated during this period. Some critics, for example, argued that the prerogative was exercised so frequently that it impaired the effectiveness of the law. See, for example, Crawford, *Penitentiaries*, 7, where he claims the rate of pardons at Auburn between 1825 and 1835 was one in four. Also see Beaumont and Tocqueville, *Penitentiary System*, 233–239, and Hindus, *Prison and Plantation*, 105.

[39] Another important source of information on the inmates at Charlestown is the Commitment Register for the prison, held at the Massachusetts State Archives. Organized chronologically, the records provide a brief physical description of the criminal, where he was convicted and for what crime, whether he had previously been incarcerated at Charlestown, and the disposition of his sentence. I have selectively used these records below in my discussion of some of the prisoners and am indebted to Edward Hanson of the Massachusetts Historical Society for alerting me to this valuable resource.

pleted this alphabetical canvass on August 3, he began over again, over the course of a month recording information from all new prisoners. From late September until the spring of 1830 he made no new entries, perhaps because that period marked the prisoners' move to the new facility, which actually occurred October 3–6, 1829. On March 1, he again began adding biographies, still working alphabetically, and continued to do so sporadically (presumably as new inmates arrived at the penitentiary) until April 19, 1831, when the second book was filled.[40]

Curtis probably used this material, which was unedited, organized chronologically, and alphabetically indexed at the end of each volume, in two ways. The first was personal and practical: to ascertain, given each inmate's backgrounds and prior history in the prison, how he might respond to the new, congregate system under which he soon would live, and thus to help Curtis counsel him. The second was statistical and public. That is, with his contemporaries Curtis shared a faith in numeracy to identify and eradicate the kinds of evils that brought hitherto-law-abiding citizens to prisons like Charlestown.[41] He and other prison officials, in other words, conducted their interviews

---

[40] Crawford (*Penitentiaries*, 59) notes that because there were only one-third as many prisoners at Charlestown as at Auburn, Curtis had a much better opportunity to "gain a knowledge of the hearts and minds" of the prisoners.

[41] The Unitarian clergyman Joseph Tuckerman, for example, who in the late 1820s began a "ministry-at-large" to Boston's poor, issued quarterly reports on his labors that included statistical information about the city's poor and delinquent. See Daniel T. McColgan, *Joseph Tuckerman: Pioneer in American Social Work* (Washington, D.C., 1940), 134–153; and Conrad Edick Wright, "Saving a Soul: Joseph Tuckerman and the Final Days of Sylvester Colson," *Proceedings of the Massachusetts Historical Society* 104(1992):110–122. On the general interest in numeracy at this time, see Patricia Cline Cohen, *A Calculating People: The Spread of Numeracy in Early America* (Chicago, 1982), 169; and Mary Poovey, "Figures of Arith-

in order to discern common denominators among the inmates that they then organized statistically for their own use and the use of those who promulgated moral reform in the republic at large.

In the introduction to his translation of Beaumont and Tocqueville's book on American prisons, Francis Lieber described the kind of statistical information valued by "the politician, the public economist, the criminalist, the divine, the promoter of discipline," and all others "who have the welfare of the nation at heart." "It is among other things important to know," he continued,

> The sex, age, and education of the convict, whether the latter was bad, common, good, or polite his trade, colour, the trade of his parents, whether he lost them, and at what age, in what month the crime was committed, (*whether it is a first, second, third, &c. crime,*) the crime was premeditated or not, the causes of the convict's bad habits, (intemperance, lottery, women, gambling, &c. bad example of parents or masters;)—if the convict is a female, whether a prostitute, (which is generally the case) if they are emigrants, how long in this country; whether married or not, whether he or she has children, how many, when and where convicted, nature of the crime, sentence, how long imprisoned before the trial; how long after the crime the trial took place, &c.; general state of health, what religion, at least, in which educated; whether the term expired, or was abbreviated by pardon or death, behaviour in prison, &c.[42]

---

metic, Figures of Speech: The Discourse of Statistics in the 1830s," in *Questions of Evidence: Proof, Practice, and Persuasion Across the Disciplines,* ed. James Chandler, Arnold I. Davidson, and Harry Harootunian (Chicago, 1994), 401–421.

[42]Francis Lieber, preface and introduction to *Penitentiary System,* by Beaumont and Tocqueville, xxvii-xxix.

Lieber presumably knew that such inquiry was not unprecedented in American prisons but wanted to encourage its more systematic pursuit. At Auburn in the late 1820s, for example, Warden Gershom Powers himself had interviewed his prisoners, but he did so only at the conclusion of their sentences, literally in the hours just prior to their release. As he reported, at the termination of each prisoner's incarceration Powers sought "to enter into a free and friendly conversation" and sought through a purposely "desultory course of inquiry" to get answers to the kinds of queries Lieber enumerated. In addition, Powers tried to elicit facts about the inmates' confinement at Auburn to establish what parts of prison discipline had been most effective and how the officers had treated them. His reason for waiting until the penultimate moment for conducting his interrogations was simple. During their confinement, Powers noted, prisoners had "so many motives for concealment" that he felt as though their testimony might not be fully credible.[43]

It seems likely that Powers and Curtis, who had worked together at Auburn, discussed the need for such interviews before the latter left for his new position in Massachusetts. Perhaps because he had more faith in his efforts to counsel and morally educate his charges, Curtis chose to conduct the interviews differently, in many cases at the beginning of an inmate's incarceration or in others without regard to how long a prisoner had served. Further, unlike the warden at Auburn, who redacted his interviews in reports to

[43]Gershom Powers, *Report of Gershom Powers, Agent and Keeper of the State Prison at Auburn* (Albany, 1828), 50. His interviews appear in "Annual Report of the Auburn Prison" and "Abstract of Brief Biographical Sketches as Taken from Convicts When Discharged from This Prison," *New York Senate and Assembly Documents, 1829*, I, nos. 15:32–63 and 38:37–54.

the New York legislature between 1829 and 1831, Curtis kept the substance of his notes private.[44] He used them publicly only as the raw material from which he assembled statistical information for his own legislature and others concerned with penal reform, and to explain and justify his and other prison officials' work at Charlestown.

In 1831, for example, after he had interviewed the entire prison population, he reported to the state some of the "results, obtained from inquiries lately made of the convicts." He presented statistics, assembled from talks with 256 prisoners, in categories such as these:

> Did not know the alphabet when they came to Prison, 20
> Could read only in easy lessons for children, 21
> Could not write, 64
> Had been accustomed, though not in general, intemperately to the use of ardent spirit, before the age of 16 years, 127
> Acknowledged that intemperance led them to crime, 156
> Brought up without any regular trade or employment, 82
> Had, before coming to prison, lived in habitual neglect and violation of the Sabbath, 182
> Number of colored persons, including Indians, 48
> Number of those born without the limits of the United States, 48

The following year he extended his analysis, reporting on 220 inmates, a reflection of a decline in the prison population that he and other officials at Charlestown believed to be a result of their reforms. Now Curtis added statistics

---

[44]Interestingly, while Powers provided much biographical material in his reports, he kept each criminal anonymous. He may have done so to insure less bias against the individual who, after all, was being released to try to make his way again in society.

under such rubrics as when each of a prisoner's parents died in relation to his age, how many siblings he had, and whether he had served as an apprentice or had associated with "lewd" women.[45]

To be sure, Curtis's amateur—or shall we call it pioneering?— sociology transparently displays his preconceptions about the causes of criminal behavior, for he obviously framed questions that related to the origins of crime as he understood them. But the very survival of the notebooks in the form in which he kept them makes them significant. Through them we not only have access to the hard biographical data that the chaplain used to prepare his statistics, but we also can put a face and a story to virtually every inmate in the Massachusetts State Prison between 1829 and 1831. Thus, while the general thrust of Curtis's questions is apparent in all his interviews, the overwhelming specificity, the very individuality, of the answers, is stunning. Originally intended to provide quasi-scientific statistics to those who made laws and directed public policy, Curtis's notebooks are the sole memorial of hundreds of inarticulate prisoners who lived in the vast silence of the Charlestown prison. His words, surrogate for theirs, reveal the contours of prison experience in Jacksonian America—in Massachusetts as well as in other state penitentiaries—which hitherto have been understood only in the vaguest, most impersonal outline.

To illustrate how Curtis's statistics tell only the barest story we need only compare their stark impersonality to the sociological and psychological richness of the full biographical sketches recorded in his notebooks. Consider, for example,

---

[45]PDSB, *Seventh Annual Report, 1832*, 17; PDSB, *Eighth Annual Report, 1833* (Boston, 1834), 59.

his category, "Number of colored persons, including Indians—48," and then his biography of John Gibson, a "Black man" born a slave in Schodack, New York, who did not know his age but thought that he was about thirty-eight.[46] When Gibson was still a boy his master sold him to a "gentleman" in New Haven, Connecticut, where he was put aboard a schooner, taken to New Orleans, and sold again, for $800. He lived there for a decade but then ran away. He found his way to Charleston, South Carolina, and shipped as a sailor for Liverpool. After several other voyages, Gibson decided to live for a while in Boston before going to sea again, this time to Canton in China. He told Curtis that from all this work he managed to save the considerable sum of $700 but upon his return to Boston spent it so "freely" that most of it was quickly gone. Thus, he "took to stealing," and was caught and sentenced to four years at Charlestown. After his release, he worked steadily and "honestly" for nearly three years, but he ran into another African American, one William Riley (now in prison with him), and together they broke into a store. Gibson was then serving his third year of a fourteen-year sentence.

Francis Mitchell, alias Henry Francis, was a twenty-nine-year-old mulatto who told that he was born free on Cuba (p. 137). At the age of seven he came to Charleston, South Carolina, and went into service for a wealthy family. But he could understand no English, and they "knock'd him

---

[46]Curtis's entry for John Gibson appears on p. 95 below. Subsequent references to passages in Curtis's notebooks as published here are in parentheses.

Some of the information on Gibson in the Commitment Register for the prison differs from what he told Curtis. In one entry, for example, he is listed as being born in New Haven but in another, in Maryland. He also is listed as dying at the prison in 1833, while serving his 14-year sentence. See Commitment Register, Charlestown State Prison, 1818–1840, nos. 173 and 774, Massachusetts State Archives.

about pretty hard & being a child he knew not what to do." After two years he "went away" and was befriended by an "Italian Gentleman" who could speak Spanish and with whom he lived until the older man died a few years later. They lived in Wilmington, North Carolina, where his sponsor had placed Mitchell with a barber to learn the trade. Mitchell later moved to Boston and, having "as much business as he could do," took in a partner who "prov'd a bad man." The shop lost customers and Mitchell fell into crime. He first came to Charlestown when he was twenty, and on his release he was "led away by an old rogue" into burglary. Now he was in for life. "Very frank & intelligent," Mitchell was the principal barber at the prison. He received a pardon in 1830.[47]

Dyer Vespasian (or "Obediah Vespatio," as he was called in one of the prison's registers) was the same age as Gibson, and his story, while less dramatic than these other two, speaks as powerfully of the matter of race in Jacksonian America (p. 28). A thirty-eight-year-old, "almost full blood" Indian of the "Pequod" tribe, virtually extirpated by the Massachusetts Bay Colony Puritans in the Pequot War of 1637–1638, Vespasian had been born in Michigan.[48] He had learned no trade and while young worked as a servant in a "Gentleman's family." Like many other men trapped at the lower end of the economic ladder, he went to sea,

[47]Prison records have him born in "Port-au-Prince, West Indies." See Commitment Register, Charlestown State Prison, 1818–1840, nos. 242 and 527, Massachusetts State Archives.

[48]Entries in various registers for the prison have him born in New York City and Westfield, Massachusetts. It is unclear what an inmate would gain by lying about his birthplace, though there are many such discrepancies between Curtis's manuscript entries and the official prison records. See Entries of Convicts in the State Prison, Charlestown, Mass., 1805–1818, nos. 534 and 801; and Commitment Register, Charlestown State Prison, 1818–1840, no. 339, Massachusetts State Archives.

where he soon began drinking "too much." This habit ruined him, he told Curtis; after a third offense for larceny, he found himself in Charlestown for life. He had a wife and child, and he admitted to being "very sick of crime & prison." He finally received a pardon in 1834. In its account of the poverty and degradation he faced, Vespasian's narrative uncannily resembles that of his more famous kinsman, the Methodist minister and writer William Apess.[49]

Not coincidentally, these prisoners of color fell at the lower end of the socioeconomic scale, but Curtis's notebooks also reveal that the vagaries of the market economy brought hard times on many who previously had been quite wealthy and fit no statistical category save "native born." Forty-eight-year-old John Russell, for example, was a successful saddle- and harness-maker who, having inherited $4,000 upon his father's death, married into one of the most respected families in West Cambridge, Massachusetts (p. 9). He then took up the butchering business and, at about the same time, joined one of the city's "independent Militia Company," an activity that cost him "a good deal of money on equipping, &c." But his new work did not go well, and as his business and personal debts accumulated, he experienced another blow, his wife's death. He then fell into a "great depression of spirits & sort of mental alienation" that brought him to drinking and gambling, and he was so embarrassed by his situation that he changed his name, so "that his friends [might]not know of his condition." The story of fifty-two-year-old Jacob Russell, from Milton, Massachusetts, was less detailed but no less moving

[49] See Barry O'Connell, introduction to *On Our Own Ground: The Complete Writings of William Apess,* ed. Barry O'Connell (Amherst, Mass., 1992), xxvi-xxxviii.

(p. 5). He described himself as a "man of some property" who had lost it through "misfortune." He was convicted for assaulting his wife with intent to murder but remembered nothing of it, he told Curtis, because just prior to the purported event he had gotten "melted in the heat while working hard."

Consider, too, G. F. Weems, twenty-six, a native of Virginia, with home and property in the District of Columbia (p. 36). He had entered Princeton when he was fourteen but left in his junior year. He "read Physic" with a doctor but also began to associate with some older men "who moved in the gay and fashionable circle" in Philadelphia. Thereafter he "lived to a great length what is termed a life of Pleasure" until some concerned friends "removed him" to live with an uncle in Maryland. His habits again got the better of him and he began "travelling about, a sort of Gentleman at large," a course he followed until the death of a dear brother "stop't him in this new episode of dissipation." He thereupon began study with two clergymen in New York and then enrolled at the Andover Theological Seminary, one of the country's premier religious institutions. After only a half-year there, and with the blessing of Dr. Leonard Woods, Andover's president, he began to supply other ministers' pulpits, in Boston and elsewhere. Engrossed in Weems's story, Curtis never specified why the aspiring clergyman now languished in Charlestown, but the commitment register indicates it was for a second charge of stealing.[50] Had he been allowed to talk to other inmates, Weems would have found among his fellows

[50] Weems was pardoned Aug. 31, 1829, not long after Curtis interviewed him, and in this case the facts recorded in the chaplain's narrative accord with those in the official prison records. Commitment Register, Charlestown State Prison, 1818–1840, no. 889, Massachusetts State Archives.

George W. Harvey, a fellow Princetonian imprisoned for forgery (p. 110), and a West Point graduate who had served as a second lieutenant (p. 132).

For a remarkable adventure story one can turn to the odd tale of Melzar Hatch, from Scituate, Massachusetts (p. 100). Raised by his father, he apprenticed with a ship carpenter in Charlestown. His training completed, Hatch followed his trade at sea, where he was captured by Barbary pirates and made a slave for four years to a wealthy Algerine. Closely guarded, he despaired of regaining his freedom, but eventually one of his master's daughters took pity on him and expedited his escape. Hatch cautiously made his way to the city harbor, swam to a British ship, and made his way to London via Gibraltar. But his troubles were not over. He was impressed on a British man-of-war and detained in England's military service for fifteen years! Wounded several times, he served at the legendary Battle of Trafalgar at which Lord Nelson was killed. With the ensuing peace, Hatch finally received his discharge and returned to the United States. Now he was in Charlestown serving six years for an attempted rape of a child, a charge he denied. Curtis described him as a "clever old fellow, a strange sort of man," and his tale is as remarkable as that of the young Israel Potter whose similar account of hardship and adventure Herman Melville would transform into a novel. Prison records show Hatch pardoned late in August 1829.[51]

These are among the more unusual stories that the prison chaplain heard, but even the simplest narratives have their interest and poignancy. Thirty-year-old Rhode

[51] Commitment Register, Charlestown State Prison, 1818–1840, no. 529, Massachusetts State Archives. Ann Fabian recently has discussed such tales of misfortune in her "Beggars and Books," *Proceedings of the American Antiquarian Society* 108, pt. 1 (1998):67–112.

Islander Joseph Davis, for example, who also used the alias "Hopkins," had been raised by his father, an attorney, until his death when the boy was only eight (p. 74). By his early teens Davis was in Boston and quickly fell in with bad company. He went in and out of prison for larceny; after his last conviction, for passing counterfeit money, he had drawn a life sentence. In Charlestown Davis stood out because he was an avowed deist, brought to his beliefs by reading manuscripts that his father had left behind. In prison he fed his interest by studying Thomas Paine and Voltaire, to whom he had been introduced, he claimed, through volumes available at the local "circulating Library." He was only one of several prisoners who confessed their infidelity to Curtis, who thereupon strove to win them back to Christ. Presumably as a result of conversations with the chaplain, Davis found that his mind had been so "taken on the subject" of religion that he wanted "to get at the truth" of it.

If Davis was unusual for his beliefs, others were so for their talents. Twenty-five-year old John Jourdan, for example, who had been raised in nearby Medford, demonstrated a flair for art (p. 114). His father had sent him to an academy for two years so that "he might fit himself to command a vessel," but five months after Jourdan's enrollment, the preceptor of the school died. The teenager thereupon enlisted aboard a privateer until the end of the War of 1812. At sea he became "very wild & vicious" and soon found himself in and out of prison for crimes ranging from horse theft to counterfeiting. At Charlestown he had earned a reputation for being disruptive, and he had made up his mind, he told the chaplain, to be "the bully of the prison." Surprisingly, though, within the last two years he "had turned his thoughts to painting, & practiced some in rough sketches, finding that he had some talent in it, was led to think whether he might not yet be something in the world & get respectable & honest living by pursuing it." Because this interview took place before the change to the congregate system, prison officials permitted him "to devote some of his time" to his newfound skill because of its "happy effect" on his behavior.[52]

Some of the prisoners' stories verge on the humorous, if one could forget the conditions under which these men served their sentences. Most of forty-year-old Alexander Palmer's story, for example, reads like countless others (p. 149). Orphaned at five, he was a "wild boy" who was put out to labor in his hometown of Hebron, New York. Following the War of 1812 he took up weaving for a while and then was in and out of prison for burglary. After a pardon he went to Boston and followed the trade of upholstery, which he had learned in prison, but then was caught breaking into a store again. He returned to Charlestown and to his trade. But he escaped "by concealing himself in the Box or seat of a Sofa, which he had made & prepared" for a tradesman outside the prison. When the sofa was sent for, "he slyly got into it, & his fellow convicts took it up & put it on the cart & he was carried out without suspicion." After this ingenious escape he made it to Philadelphia, but there an old convict who recognized him turned him in. He thereupon was returned to Charlestown yet again.

Another particularly engaging tale came from twenty-

[52]There are many discrepancies between what Jourdan told Curtis and what is recorded in the prison's commitment registers. One entry has him born him at Cape Elizabeth, Maine, another in Boston, with his parents then living in Medford. He was conditionally pardoned in 1830, but under the name Samuel was recommitted Jan. 21, 1834, for burglary in Cambridge, Massachusetts, under a 20-year sentence. He escaped in September 1838. Entries of Convicts in the State Prison, Charlestown, Mass., 1805–1818, no. 461; 1805–1824, no. 456; Commitment Register, Charlestown State Prison, 1818–1840, nos. 534, 1481, Massachusetts State Archives.

nine-year-old David Bills (p. 58). He told Curtis that he was born in Manchester, England, and came to America with "Sir Ed. Packinham at the time of his attack upon N. Orleans." But Bills deserted on the day of battle and surrendered to Gen. Andrew Jackson, "who used him well." After peace was declared, he went to Canada and worked as a countinghouse clerk, but he then returned to the United States and enlisted in the army. While stationed in Boston in Capt. David Perry's company, he again deserted and ran to the backcountry to become a peddler. Soon enough he was convicted of forgery and of "getting a girl with child" without marrying her. His saga continued and finally ended in Charlestown, with Curtis noting that some at the prison thought Bills to be "partially derang'd." But that was not the chaplain's final judgment of this inmate, for he subsequently learned that most of Bills's story was a fabrication! Written vertically over the whole page of this interview were these words: "Whole Story Humbug—never was in England nor with Gen. Packenham." Here the commitment register provides parts of his real story. Bills was actually born in Suffield, Connecticut, and was serving his third sentence for stealing, all convictions in Northampton, Massachusetts.[53] Another inmate had similar delusions of grandeur. Lewis Fazey, born in Paris, France, and a resident of New Orleans for many years, "palmed himself off as General Jackson" before he came to prison! (p. 171)

But Bills and Fazey are unusual, for while there are often slight discrepancies between information in the commitment registers and Curtis's biographies—usually with regard to places of birth—most of the men he inter-

[53]Bills died in prison Nov. 12, 1831; see Commitment Register, Charlestown State Prison, 1818–1840, no. 969, Massachusetts State Archives.

viewed seem not to have fabricated their stories. Consider the richness of these biographies of individuals hitherto lost to history but now recovered through Curtis's diligence. Jacob Richmond, a free Black from Wilmington, North Carolina, who became a whaler, was convicted of perjury and sentenced to two years (p. 11).[54] Charles Rivers, a "shipper of goods" from England to America, was at one time worth $80,000, but got involved in selling stolen material (p. 12). Seventy-two-year-old Job Thayer, a shipbuilder accused of attempted murder, was a native of Braintree, Massachusetts. He was "full of fire & venom" and insisted that "Federals & Jews ought all to be driven from the face of the earth" (p. 24). He died in prison February 1, 1830.[55] The farrier Josiah Veasey of Boston, in prison on burglary charges, complained that "infidel Books" provided by some of the prison guards had "poisoned his mind" (p. 29). Thirty-year-old Ira Warren, a poorly educated Bridgewater, Massachusetts, native, told Curtis that he "liv'd well with his family except when in liquor" (p. 43). He was serving a seven-year sentence for bestiality.[56] Jonas Ball, born in Newton but employed for the last thirteen years by the American Fur Company in the "North West of N. America," was serving a sentence for larceny (p. 60). John Danby, born at the "Cape of Good Hope," South Africa, was educated in England and Holland, and had "been to all parts of Europe, the East Indies, & in most of the great communal places in the

[54]Commitment Register, Charlestown State Prison, 1818–1840, no. 1023, Massachusetts State Archives.

[55]Entries of Convicts in the State Prison, Charlestown, Mass., 1805–1818, no. 894; Commitment Register, Charlestown State Prison, 1818–1840, no. 366, Massachusetts State Archives.

[56]Commitment Register, Charlestown State Prison, 1818–1840, no. 1013, Massachusetts State Archives.

world" (p. 78). John Daily, thirty-eight, from Liverpool, England, impressed into the British navy, taken prisoner in Canada, someone who "spent his money as fast as he earned it," had his four-year sentence extended because he was "a prime mover in a rebellion" that took place at the prison (p. 79). For their sheer variety, these narratives deserve a wider audience.

Beyond their intrinsic interest in providing vivid portraits of the inmates, Curtis's interviews also increase our understanding of the prison at Charlestown at the moment when it was about to adopt Auburn's congregate system. We might begin with the light they shed on the interview process itself. For one thing, Curtis recorded the prisoners' tales with all their twists and turns even as he tried to lead inmates to reflect on how the paths they traveled led inexorably to the state prison. No doubt the richness of these interviews resulted in part from their timing, for as we have seen, unlike Auburn's warden, who conducted his at the conclusion of an inmate's sentence, Curtis spoke to his men without regard to how much of their sentences they had served. This probably accounts as well for the high degree of emotion frequently recorded in Curtis's interviews: many inmates "wept freely" when they spoke of their pasts. As forty-year-old David Balkam, for example, spoke of his wife and child in nearby Boston, Curtis reported, "the tears rolled very freely down his face" (p. 53).

We also learn of the frustrations and joys inherent in such work. On one occasion, for instance, when Curtis clearly wished to continue his discussion with one David Remick, his work was cut short by prison discipline. "Did not see him as long as I wished," the chaplain wrote. "The Bell had rung for prayer" (p. 3). Another prisoner, Alpheus Spring, presented a different problem: Curtis "could not make him talk a good deal" about himself (p. 20). Indeed, this inmate just "sat smiling all the time," and "his air and meanness told me that I might talk as much as I would & be none the wiser for him & he neither not to be made wiser by me."

Other prisoners, however, particularly when they learned of the comfort Curtis could provide, actively sought his help. Jesse Bradbury, for example, called on him "in distress of mind for his sins as he said" (p. 30). Bradbury "had been a good deal troubled for six weeks," Curtis wrote, and thus he "talk'd with him & gave him such advise & instruction as [he] thought his case required." Henry Harvey, a native of New London, Connecticut, the only prisoner actually to write his own biography (which Curtis duly copied into his book), best summed up the inmates' response to the time Curtis spent with them (p. 106).[57] He was willing to share his history with the chaplain, he wrote, because "you are the only person, (prisoners excepted), since my estrangement from home, who has spoken kindly, or seemed to have the least sympathy for my misfortunes." He was pardoned in the spring of 1831.

In terms of the services Curtis performed for the inmates, random notations at the end of the first volume of his notebooks are particularly informative and moving. Josiah Harris, for example, hoping for a pardon after serving a year of his five-year sentence, asked the chaplain to write the selectmen of St. George, Maine, to get their recommendation of his good conduct and to ask other townspeople to do the same (p. 231). "They all know him in town," Curtis wrote, and "know that his character has been good." Elijah Cole, who obviously had problems with his eyes, asked Curtis to help procure "a Bible with plainer

[57] Commitment Register, Charlestown State Prison, 1818–1840, no. 691, Massachusetts State Archives. Harvey's first arrest and conviction was at the age of 18. Charles T. Reed had promised that he would give Curtis a brief sketch of his life "in writing" but evidently never did so.

print than the one he has" (p. 231). Others wanted him to contact family. An inmate with the last name of Freeborn, "lying at the point of death," asked him to send "what money is due him on the Books of the prison" to his sister Sarah Dick, of Dartmouth, Massachusetts (p. 232). Another inmate in the hospital, Alfred Clark, needed a letter sent to his relative Israel Clark because Alfred had "long been feeble, & in the Hospital" ever since he came to Charlestown (p. 233). Nehemiah Hughes wanted Curtis to contact a Mr. Gile of Walpole, Massachusetts, to come and see him, and to ask Gile "if father & mother have not moved out of Walpole to write & let him know it & where they have gone" (p. 233).

We also learn some of the prisoners' responses to the impending switch to the Auburn system, details of which they might have heard from prisoners who had been there (there were several such at Charlestown) or the prison officials themselves. Interestingly, those who commented on the matter favored the switch, primarily because it would curtail their contacts with inmates who tried to corrupt them. James Kidder, for example, explained to Curtis that he could not wait for the completion of the new prison so "that he may be alone" (p. 124). James Brumsden promised that "when the new prison is done & he can be alone," he would "try as hard as he can to establish better habits of feeling & action" (p. 51). Solomon Russell told Curtis that "he thought his mind had been corrupted here" (p. 7). He was "very sorry," he continued, that he "could not have been confin'd alone" and wished that "he could be so now."

Conversely, several inmates openly expressed their disgust at the corruption rampant in the prison, and some even took reform into their own hands. William Bradley, for example, a hatter from Roxbury, Massachusetts, in

Charlestown on his first offense, said that to cope better with prison he had joined "the Singer's room." Possibly named for the fact that these inmates constituted a choir for services, the singers allowed "no swearing" because they themselves had "made a law against it & have agreed to report to the Warden every violation" (p. 58). Other inmates were particularly distressed that in prison their Christian principles were constantly undermined. Moses Thompkins told the chaplain that "he got his infidelity in prison by reading infidel books" (p. 26). Josiah Veasey echoed his remarks but put the blame elsewhere—the books that had "poisoned his mind," he said, came from the prison officers themselves, who could be bribed to provide them or other supposedly contraband goods (p. 29).[58] J. T. Torrey seconded this report (p. 207). He told Curtis that prior to the prison's reorganization one "could get into the prison through the officers, just what he wish'd." Some of the officers, he continued, were "as bad as the prisoners."

Vesey alerts us to another fact about Charlestown before its reformation: the widespread corruption among prison officials themselves. Prior to penal reform, for example, the labor of some prisoners was contracted outside the penitentiary. They had to perform a certain amount of work per day, their "stint," before the contractors would pay the state for the work. But inmates also were allowed and even encouraged to go "over stint," which meant that they themselves received some payment and were allowed personal goods in their cells (hence inmate Freeborn's request, *supra*, to have money due him sent to his sister after his death). Obviously, this made possible the corruption of

[58]Such episodes are also mentioned in PDSB, *Fourth Annual Report*, 11. Also see Hirsch, *Rise of the Penitentiary*, 98–100.

prison employees through bribery, something that the Charlestown prison's reorganization on the Auburn plan would virtually eradicate.[59]

Curtis's interviews also suggest some general observations about the criminal population in the nation's state penitentiaries, ones that in some cases corroborate earlier scholarship and in others considerably expand our understanding of who was in prison and why. Most importantly, these biographies reveal three common denominators among many of the prisoners in Charlestown. First, an overwhelming number of convicts acknowledged that intemperance had led them down the road to crime. Second, a large proportion of the prison population reported difficult childhood situations, which they escaped by leaving home early of necessity, sometimes involuntarily because one or both of their parents had died or voluntarily without their approval or consent. Third, many inmates, for a variety of reasons, had received poor educations and had had no training in any skilled trade or employment, facts that often led to grinding poverty and attendant desperation. Such individuals clearly were at a liability in the market revolution that was transforming both the nature of work and the way it was compensated.

Even in an age in which alcohol was freely and widely used in the population, Curtis's statistics on drunkenness are eye opening.[60] In 1831, for example, the chaplain calculated that 156 of the total population of 256 inmates acknowledged that intemperance had led them to crime. But the details of how alcohol abuse defeated many of those

[59] See the broadside *Annual Report of the Number of Convicts in the Masachusetts State Prison, Their Employment, &c.* (Boston, 1828), where it remarks about prisoners who "none now are let out to contractors."

[60] See, for example, W. J. Rorabaugh, *The Alcoholic Republic: An American Tradition* (New York, 1979).

sentenced to Charlestown provide a rich texture to this stark figure. We find twenty-six-year-old John Quiner, an ex-seaman who admitted that his "intemperate habits" had produced a state of "partial insanity" in which he committed more and more serious crimes (p. 1). Stephen Symms, about the same age, "drink'd some—gambled—went to the theater and often the girls" (p. 18). From there, Curtis notes, he went "from step to step to crime." Gardner Fox, a "hard labouring man," was convicted of stealing a silver teaspoon (p. 91). He has "plenty of rum blossoms on his face," Curtis noted.

Other stories are more psychologically complex. George Watkins, from Douglass, Massachusetts, had been doing fine, "steady & industrious," until the parents of a woman he loved "opposed his marrying" (p. 40). To make matters worse, the young woman died soon thereafter. This sent Watkins into a tailspin, first to gambling and drinking, then to forgery. Antoine Johnson, from the Canary Islands, "a yellow man, about as dark as a common Indian," drank "hard" (p. 114). This "led him to almost everything else that was bad." John Jones, a ship carpenter in for larceny, said that he was "ruined by Rum" and "resolved a great many times never to drink any more, but some temptation has drawn him away" (p. 181). William Dunbar, sentenced for shooting at and wounding his wife, had "no recollection" of the act and could not even remember "whether he had been drinking or not" when he did it (p. 80). Henry Himleer, from Berkshire County, Massachusetts, told Curtis that his "grand failing" was intemperance (p. 181). He "us'd to have Sprees," he reported, when he "would stop work for several months without taking a drop, then would have a high, & would keep high till he [had] spent all his wages, & then would go to work again."

Even when, under his insistent prodding, inmates admitted only that they drank "some" but not to excess, the chaplain recorded the fact. Robert Blaney, for example, told Curtis that he was "never addicted to drinking so as to hurt him" (p. 201). He just "drink'd a glass or two a day like other folks." Curtis obviously was eager to link the criminals' rehabilitation to the temperance movement outside the prison's walls and thus encouraged prisoners to consider how likely it was that many of their miseries stemmed from demon rum.

But as these vignettes suggest, many of the prisoners' difficulties with alcohol were related to other causes, one of the most prevalent of which might best be described as a breakdown of family control in an inmate's earlier years. The most extreme examples concerned enslaved Africans like Dick Richards, literally seized as a child from his home village and brought across the Atlantic (p. 2). African Americans fared only slightly better, if at all: Prince Henry, a native of Bridgetown in Barbados, in his teens ran away to Maine (p. 98); William Lyons, born a slave in Dutchess County, New York, as a small boy was taken to Vermont to serve an "infidel" (p. 129). Henry was first committed when he was only twenty and served three different terms, for assault and larceny, before he was finally sentenced to life. He died in prison in April 1832.[61] Freedmen, too, described difficult circumstances from which they tried mightily to escape. Thomas Watson, for example, had "no parents" and as a child was "bound out" to people who promised to give him schooling but did not (p. 35). Sixteen-year-old George Lincoln "could not read at all" and told Curtis that "he does not wish to learn to read" (p. 177). He had no other education at all. Charles Cooper ran off to sea at the age of ten (p. 69). Pious parents

[61] Entries of Convicts in the State Prison, Charlestown, Mass., 1805–1818, unnumbered entry and nos. 73 and 36; Commitment Register, Charlestown State Prison, 1818–1840, no. 333, Massachusetts State Archives.

raised Charles Nichols, of Boston, until they died (p. 146). Thereupon he was "left in a great measure, without advice & salutary discipline."

Such unfortunate situations, however, were common throughout the prison population regardless of race. Twenty-four-year-old Augustus Colburn was brought up by an uncle in Dracut, Massachusetts (p. 71). His father had died before he could remember it, he reported, and his mother lived in Maine, "he does not know where." Erastus Danforth's father died when he was twelve and never spoke of a mother (p. 81). He "had no guardian and took care of himself." Forty-five-year-old William Freeman was an illegitimate child raised by his grandfather (p. 91). Jesse Gould's father died when he was a child; after his mother remarried, his stepfather "put him out to a trade" (p. 92). At fourteen he ran away. Lewis Gray, now forty, grew up on Boston's streets (p. 93). His father died when he was young and no one "exercis'd care" over the boy. He "wandered about the streets" until an uncle finally took him in. Joseph Hanson's parents both died when he was young, and "he had no one to bring him up" (p. 103). The result, as Curtis wrote, was that he "always has had his own head & done what he saw best." Seventeen-year-old Charles Wallis, orphaned when a child, "was thrown unprotected upon the world" (p. 191). Of nineteen-year-old William Seymour, Curtis wrote a similar appraisal: "Thus being in ignorance & being thrown upon the world have probably destroy'd him" (p. 21).

To be sure, many inmates reported a more stable upbringing, although few could match forty-three-year-old Samuel Merrill's story, that he was one of eighteen children by the same mother (p. 142). Further, unlike others whose childhoods had been fractured by the deaths of parents or siblings, he had "seen the whole family, father, mother, & the 18 children," he told Curtis, "seated at the same table," raised in exemplary piety. More often than not, though, the haunting phrase Curtis had used for Wallis's situation, "thrown unprotected upon the world," best described an inmate's early years. And when an absence of affection and supervision was coupled to a young person's lack of education and training in any skilled labor, the result was often a downhill slide to the penitentiary.

Alexander Palmer, whose father died when he was five, was typical (p. 149). Early on he was put out to service, but the man "did not use him very well & he ran away—learned no trade, worked here and there." Erastus Plumbley, only eighteen and serving time for stealing a pocketbook, could "scarcely read at all" and was "brot up to farming & tending ferry" (p. 168). Alonzo Chase, who could "read and write poorly," only found work at taverns, and "tended stable, drove stage, and worked at blacksmithing some" (p. 168). And thirty-year-old John Blann, who had lost his parents when he was nine and since then had had no home, could read but not write (p. 48). He "wandered about different states" for a decade and then finally went to sea. So obstreperous was he that by his own admission he had been confined to his cell for misconduct for over a hundred days. In many of these cases Curtis's shorthand told the story: "Can read, but not write" and "has but few advantages," often with the addendum "Is now in our Sabbath School," where volunteers from the surrounding community tried to remedy the inmates' educational deficiencies. Increasing in number in society as a whole, such impoverished and ill-equipped individuals were becoming the focus of other reformers as well, most notably of the new urban ministry typified by the Reverend Joseph Tuckerman, who in the late 1820s began a "ministry at large" to Boston's poor.[62]

[62]See note 41, *supra.*

Here then is a general profile of a typical inmate at Charlestown early in the nineteenth century. Raised in an unstable household, lacking any formal education or apprenticeship, a young man found himself on the bottom of the economic ladder. To find employment he moved to a larger town or city where temptations to vice (particularly drink) increased and where, given his desperate economic condition, he fell in among bad company. What happened then? Curtis's notebooks also reveal several other common denominators, demographic and otherwise, that distinguished the inmates at the Massachusetts State Prison.

For one thing, most of the prisoners—around 90 percent—were serving time for crimes against property, particularly larceny and burglary. The comparatively lower rate of violent crimes may have been due to the fact that in Massachusetts, as in most other states, most of these crimes still carried the penalty of death by hanging.[63] But what reformers perceived as an increase in crime also suggests that the much-heralded prosperity attendant on an expanding economy brought as much disappointment and desperation as success. In a report for 1829, for example, prison officials noted 164 sentences for "store-breaking" and theft. Counterfeiting or, more specifically, the passing of bogus bills (not their actual manufacture) was mentioned in seventeen cases, a statistic that suggests that individuals down on their luck took to it to remedy unfortunate circumstances. Forgery was less common and generally favored by individuals from more affluent backgrounds, presumably conversant with mercantile ways. Against this background of crimes involving money or goods, sentences for violent acts—sixty-two-year-old Joseph Durfee,

[63]On changing attitudes toward capital punishment during this period see Masur, *Rites of Execution*, 88–92, and chapter five, *passim*.

for example, assaulted his wife when he was "in Liquor & in an irritable state of mind"—were uncommon, the most serious of them leading to capital punishment (p. 77). The report for 1829 noted only twenty-one sentences for assaults and two for murder.[64]

The examples of counterfeiting and forgery are interesting for their illustration of how small an amount of money often was involved in crimes that brought people to state prison. Ebenezer Shannon, for example, had been in and out of the prison and at the time of Curtis's interview was serving a sentence for possessing counterfeit money (p. 19). He claimed that "an old Scoundrel tried to get him to take or buy some." After Shannon refused, the old man convinced him to allow him to hide some of it in his house "where it would keep dry." Somehow (probably because Shannon used some of it), the small cache was discovered and linked to him. Reuben Blood, a cooper, had never been in any trouble before passing three counterfeit bills the previous winter (p. 62). The $50 in "Bad money" in his possession he had procured in New Hampshire.

More unusual is the story of thirty-year-old Charles Perry, a copperplate printer in Boston (p. 149). He lived in a boardinghouse "where a number of Stage players belonging to the Theatre" also stayed, and they introduced him to both the theater and drink. After completing a two-year sentence for a small forgery, "being out of money, he borrowed five Dollars of an old convict he came across." He should have known better, for when he tried to use the money to pay for some article, he was "apprehended for passing bad money." Within a few hours of leaving Charlestown he was put in the Boston jail and then

[64] The full statistics appear in the prison's report in *Mass. Senate Documents . . . January 1830*, 15.

sentenced again to Charlestown! Charles Reed, whom Curtis called "a young man of fine talents and Ed[ucation]," received a three-year sentence for forgery committed in Boston (p. 13). Of Varnum Powers, who forged a will and also took false oaths in court, Curtis wrote: "In this business he lost all he had & was tempted to pass some counterfeit coin" (p. 153). He evidently owned a "dye for stamping" coins.

Another fact that leaps from Curtis's pages is the large number of crimes committed by two groups associated in the popular mind with a general lack of moral restraint: immigrants (particularly the Irish) and seamen. In 1834, for example, Curtis singled out an "unusual influx of unprincipled foreigners " (as well as "natives from other states") as a leading reason for an increase of the prison population that year, and he clearly had in mind the Irish.[65] With the Germans, they comprised the largest group of immigrants to the United States in the 1820s, and they also made up the largest non-native population in the prison. Moreover, by this time the Irish already were considered distinctive in character, the poverty and oppression under which they lived contributing to a reputation for rowdiness (the "wild Irish" was a common phrase).[66] Indeed, twenty-seven-year-old John Marlow's story was so representative that it made Curtis pen an epithet to sum up the man's case (p. 140). A native of Ireland, Marlow had been in America for nine years and had lived in Montreal, Canada.

---

[65] Massachusetts State Prison, *Annual Report for 1834* (Boston, 1835), 23.

[66] See, for example, Dale Knobel, *Paddy and the Republic: Ethnicity and Nationality in Antebellum America* (Middletown, Conn., 1986), esp. 39–67. For the complex construction of ethnicity in the antebellum period, also see Matthew Frye Jacobson, *Whiteness of a Different Color: European Immigrants and the Alchemy of Race* (Cambridge, Mass., 1998); and Noel Ignatiev, *How the Irish Became White* (New York, 1995).

He worked as a servant with various families but left the city because wages were low. He told Curtis that he "was addicted to drinking too much" and that his sentence at Charlestown resulted from stealing a coat, his first crime. "Thinks he shall do better when he goes out," Curtis noted, and then added his own prejudiced comment on his background: "Make a fish live out of water, & then an Irish man may stop drinking when once given to it."

Indeed, he had plenty of other evidence to confirm his prejudice. The Irishman Robert Riley was "stolen away" at the age of ten by a sea captain and brought to America, where he had lived for the past twenty-nine years working as a servant "in the best families in Boston" (p. 3). His drinking led him to passing counterfeit money, and he had served several terms in the prison. John Reed, in the country for fourteen years and brought up in the business of "folding cloth for market," was convicted of buying stolen goods (p. 5). Twenty-eight-year-old John Woods came from the old country to New Brunswick when he was fifteen and had been in the United States eight years, working as a shoemaker (p. 43). In a drunken rage he attacked someone and was convicted of assault with intent to kill. Thomas Duncan, a forty-five-year-old native of Dublin (and whom Curtis explicitly noted as a Catholic), ran away from his father when still in his teens and enlisted aboard an English man-of-war (p. 75). After several years he deserted, got aboard an American vessel in the West Indies, and came to Boston in 1810. Soon after he arrived in port, he told the chaplain, he "was enticed by others to go onto the Hill to see the women" and got into the habit of "drinking and excess." By the end of the year he had squandered $500, all his savings, and started committing larceny. Now he had been in prison on and off for fifteen years "and all as says from love of *rum.*" Finally, consider

John Power, brought up as a "waterman" (i.e., a laborer on the country's inland waterways) and fourteen years in the United States (p. 204). A hard drinker, in a state of intoxication he robbed two ladies in a street in Boston, "one of her veil & the other of her Work Bag." On Curtis's prompting, he admitted that he thought rum was "a dreadful thing."

If many of the state's new immigrants seemed born for trouble, so, too, its common sailors. Of course, for many, particularly the poorly educated or destitute, going to sea represented one of the few ways to make an honest living, even as it unfortunately brought one into contact with some whose depravity was notorious and, seemingly, infectious. Those effects contributed to the rise in this period of such national organizations as the American Seamen's Friend Society and such local counterparts as the Boston Seamen's Friends Society (established in 1827), which offered sailors moral guidance and support.[67] Such groups might have helped Ebenezer Shannon, for example—described above for his counterfeiting—who was born and raised in New Hampshire (p. 18). His father died when Ebenezer was six, after which he was put out to a farmer with whom he stayed for eight years, until that man's death. With no other skills, he went to sea "some" and at seventeen joined the "U.S. services," which proved his downfall. The sailors were "a very wicked set of fellows," he told Curtis, who taught him to "swear, drink, gamble, & everything else that was bad." Since then, as we know, he had been in and out of Charlestown.

[67] Perhaps the best known of those who ministered to seamen was Edward Thompson Taylor, widely known as "Father Taylor," minister at the Seamen's Bethel Chapel in Boston. See David S. Reynolds, *Beneath the American Renaissance: The Subversive Imagination in the Age of Emerson and Melville* (New York, 1988), 19–30.

Born near Cape Ann in Massachusetts, thirty-six-year-old James Chipman had lost his father when he was a child, and when he was eight his mother put him out to a sea captain (p. 64). The captain proved a hard master, and at fourteen Chipman ran away, traveling to the West Indies and thence back to Boston. He never had any education, however, and though he never drank "except for fashions sake," he began stealing and store breaking. He had been in Charlestown for seven years. Benjamin Goodrich, forty-eight, had followed the sea since he was eleven (p. 96). He told Curtis that of late he had been intemperate "whenever he has been ashore." He stole a boat in broad daylight and explained his action by claiming that his vessel was setting sail with all his things on board, and he took the boat to catch it. Twenty-nine-year-old John Willis, a "colored man" from Pennsylvania, lost his mother when he was twelve and the next year left his father and went to sea (p. 223). Intemperate, when ashore he ran after "bad girls," and he admitted to the chaplain that he had not been in a church or "Christian assembly" for twenty to twenty-five years until he came to prison. Israel Cowing, fifty-nine, went to sea half a century earlier (p. 65). He had been in prison for four years on a charge of attempted murder and admitted that he had drunk "more than need[ed] to, though he did not make a beast of himself." His life was made more miserable by his having lost a leg that was frozen at sea; as a result, he had been in the "Alms-House." Over and over, a pattern repeats itself: broken family life, no skilled training, running away to sea, and drinking heavily.

Other patterns, sociological and environmental, leap from these stories. For one thing, given the fact that the implementation of the Auburn system was only a few years old, recidivism was still very high, as though once someone tumbled into jail or prison, the slope upward and out proved slippery at best. There also were problems attendant on the increasing geographic mobility that characterized the age, for as Curtis's comment in 1834 suggests, a surprising number of inmates at Charlestown were from states other than Massachusetts. Then, too, a considerable proportion of the inmates were unmarried, a fact also noticed by B. C. Smith of the Auburn penitentiary, where the numbers of unmarried prisoners almost equaled those of the married. Further, in Curtis's notebooks we read of several inmates with obvious mental problems clearly in need of more specialized care but instead languishing in an environment that only exacerbated their condition.

Finally, a seemingly disproportionate number of inmates were very young—in their teens.[68] In sentencing such young people to Charlestown, judges, who in Massachusetts had the discretion to assign convicts to houses of correction rather than to the state prison, evidently believed that a stay in Charlestown, with its presumably enlightened regimen, would increase the chances of these young men's rehabilitation.[69] There still must have been considerable danger, though, in grouping teenagers with criminals who had spent years in prison, a fact recognized

---

[68]Some states, including Massachusetts, had "houses of refuge" for young offenders of both sexes. These were reformatories for young people (under the age of 20) who had committed crimes or were in situations (as orphans, for example, or abandoned children) that put them at risk for crime. The presence of people in their teens at Charlestown suggests that if a crime were viewed as particularly dangerous or if the youth was a multiple offender, he was sent there. See Beaumont and Tocqueville, *Penitentiary System,* 108–125; and Lewis, *American Prisons,* 293–322.

[69]Hindus, *Prison and Plantation,* 105. He points out that in Massachusetts judges also determined the length of the sentences. Ironically, in houses of correction sentences, even for the same crimes, tended to be briefer than in the state prison because penal reformers believed that the kind of rehabilitation possible in a penitentiary like Charlestown took a longer time.

by reformers who agitated for separate institutions for juvenile offenders.

In the preface to their book Beaumont and Tocqueville summarize their own views of the prison populations that they had observed. "Society, in our days," they wrote, "is in a state of disquiet, owing, in our opinion, to two causes." The first was of "an entirely moral character." They observed in men "an activity which knows not where to find an object," an "energy deprived of its proper element, and which consumes society for want of other prey," a way of describing the expansiveness, the social and psychological fluidity, that characterized the Age of Jackson. The other cause, they continued, was of "an entirely material character." Social unrest, and the crime engendered by it, related directly to the material condition of those whom the juggernaut of progress had left behind. It originated in the "unhappy condition of the working classes who are in want of labour and bread; and whose corruption, beginning in misery, is completed in the prison."[70]

Interestingly, neither the various visitors to American prisons nor the reformers themselves claimed that such material and psychological alienation was yet engendered by the conditions of industrial life, for they hardly ever mention the factory communities that within a decade became widely viewed as incubators of immorality and vice. Rather, as Curtis's interviews suggest, many of Charlestown's inmates simply were left behind in a world whose social and economic complexity had increased, placing the uneducated and unskilled, and those without strong support systems like family, at a distinct disadvantage. Like their neighbors, Charlestown's inmates wanted to better themselves, intellectually and materially, but for one reason or another they had been frustrated. Rather than

[70]Beaumont and Tocqueville, *Penitentiary System*, xlv.

awaking to the American dream, they languished in the sepulchral silence of Charlestown and other state prisons where they presumably would be made more fit to assume their places in the outside world.[71]

Finally, we owe it to the prison reformers and the prisoners who left Charlestown and turned their lives around to discuss evidence, however vague, that speaks to the success of the penal system, both in deterring crime and reforming those who served their sentences. By one measure—the number of people committed to Charlestown—prison reform seemed to work. In 1831 for example, only 71 new prisoners entered the penitentiary, compared to around 165 in 1818 and from 1815 to 1826 an average of 98. More striking, in total there were only 225 inmates in Charlestown, down from 300 the year before. The warden attributed this significant decline to several factors. He placed the "Temperance Reformation" first, followed by the system of Sabbath School instruction that had spread throughout the state. He also approvingly cited the state's recent institution of a "House of Reformation for Juvenile Delinquents," which obviously would decrease the numbers of those sentenced to the state prison, and he applauded "the reform in prison discipline" that he oversaw.[72]

On this last point we should take him at his word, for it seems clear that the situation at Charlestown had changed

---

[71] On industrialization, see, for example, David A. Zonderman, *Aspirations and Anxieties: New England Factory Workers and the Mechanized Factory System, 1815–1850* (New York, 1992); Thomas Bender, *Toward an Urban Vision: Ideas and Institutions in Nineteenth-Century America* (Lexington, Ken., 1975), esp. 19–70; and John F. Kasson, *Civilizing the Machine: Technology and Republican Values in America, 1776–1900* (New York, 1976). On the transformative effect of the market in this period, see Charles Sellers, *The Market Revolution: Jacksonian America, 1815–1846* (New York, 1991), esp. 202–236 on "God and Mammon."

[72] PDSB, *Seventh Annual Report*, 11.

greatly from what it was before the staff instituted the Auburn system. As the inspectors of the prison noted in their report of 1831, previously the

> facilities for intercourse of the convicts with each other, and even with strangers, their control of the money allowed them under the name of over-stint, and, above all, their confinement of several in the same cell, without superintendence during the night, gave them the means and opportunities for corrupting each other, for evading the regulations and defeating objects of the Prison, and for endangering the public peace.

Moreover, they continued, the prisoners had been constantly engaged in plotting not only for their own escape but also "for the perpetration of felonies without the walls, or by those of their own number who were about to be liberated." Harshly punished for all sorts of offenses and always worried about being exposed by their fellow inmates, they lived in a climate of depravity and fear, and came to regard themselves as the "irreconcilable enemies of society."[73]

A scant four years later, the results of the new system were conspicuous everywhere—in the "whole demeanour, the habits, and the health of the convicts." The inmates, the inspectors continued, were "obedient and respectful to their officers, are more cleanly, industrious and contented, sensible to kindness, accessible to feelings of compunction, and easily induced to express resolutions of amendment." Basil Hall's experience when he first saw Sing-Sing conveys some sense of the order that the Auburn system instilled. He had viewed the site when convicts themselves still were constructing it and wrote that

---

[73]PDSB, *Seventh Annual Report*, 13.

"my astonishment was great when I approached the spot, and saw only two sentinels pacing along the height, from whence I looked down upon two hundred convicts at work." There was "an air of confident authority," he continued, "about all the arrangements of this place, which gave us a perfect feeling of security, though we were walking around unarmed amongst cut-throats and villains of all sorts."[74]

One cannot deny that the new prisons were different, but we have to acknowledge without romanticism the nature of the changes reformers advocated, for as Lieber wrote, prisoners were afraid of "the order, obedience, and silence imposed upon them." "To correct a criminal radically," he continued, "more is required than an excitement of feeling: his habits must be broken; his mind must be trained." If prison discipline were working correctly, the convicts would contract "more correct views of society, and of themselves, and come to a better knowledge of their obligations to God, and society."[75] The evidence from Charlestown suggested that this was indeed happening, even if not in an environment that we would consider enlightened.

In his interviews, for example, Curtis frequently mentioned whether inmates had turned to the Bible and what degree of remorse they displayed for their actions. He noted, drawing on certain pet phrases, if prisoners "manifested some feeling" or had "tenderness of feeling," what we would term remorse. Curtis also frequently recorded whether inmates had any "sensibility" or were "sensible," again suggesting knowledge of the error of their ways. One who lacked such virtue he described as "hopeless," a

[74]PDSB, *Seventh Annual Report,* 13; Hall, *Travels,* 1:52–53.

[75]Lieber, in Beaumont and Tocqueville, *Penitentiary System,* xviii, xx.

"hard case," or "utterly lost," and such individuals obviously caused Curtis a good deal of pain.

Jason Bump, for example, who had been put to work in a cotton factory when he was only seven, seemed bent on a life of crime (p. 50). "He is a lost man," Curtis noted, "unless Divine power interpose to pluck him as a brand from the burning." The chaplain had spent more than half an hour "endeavoring to make him feel." And John Fick, one of the few other inmates identified as a factory operative, was even worse off, for he was "utterly destitute of principles usually entertained by men in regard to right & wrong" (p. 87). He did not believe in the Bible and was a fatalist, not holding that men were accountable beings, "or can help what they do, & therefore are to blame for nothing." "No wonder he is in prison," Curtis pithily added, "& it would be a wonder if he kept out long."

Others, though, gave Curtis more hope. Twenty-seven-year-old Nathaniel Giles, serving a sentence for swindling and other crimes, told the chaplain that he considered his punishment "better than thousands of Dollars" because it had opened his eyes to his potential ruin (p. 97). Another, Samuel Lombard, was "deeply affected with his condition," wept "freely" when he talked of his crimes, and seemed "a good deal concerned in regard to his everlasting peace" (p. 134). Stephen Symms told Curtis that he "believes the Bible & for 6 or 8 months past has studied & reflected upon it more than in all his life before" (p. 17). Not that Curtis was so idealistic that he believed all that he heard, though, for he acknowledged a prisoner's duplicity when he recognized it. The hardened multiple offender William Millard, for example, struck the chaplain as blatantly insincere, trying to impress him with feigned remorse (p. 137). "Thinks if he was only pardoned," Curtis wrote, "he should never forfeit any confidence placed in him & should not abuse the clemency of the government." "Most likely, he never will [be pardoned]," the chaplain concluded. "How little do we know our own hearts!"

Of course, prisoners not serving life sentences eventually were released, whether or not they were truly reformed. What do we know of them after they left Charlestown? Unfortunately, very little of a specific nature, although the prison maintained some statistics about where discharged inmates went and whether they stayed out of trouble. A report of 1827, for example, concerning seventy-nine prisoners released in the previous decade, listed nineteen as recommitted. With the advent of the Auburn system, however, this figure improved. In October 1832, Curtis wrote that "a goodly number" of those who had left the prison in the past three years "are known to be doing well" and maintaining "a fair standing in the communities in which they reside." And of the ninety-two inmates discharged since the Auburn system was implemented, he added, only two had been recommitted. Massachusetts never adopted Lieber's radical suggestion: to resettle released criminals away from cities because those who returned to urban environments quickly found other criminals and so were tempted to return to lives of crime. But judged by the criteria implicit in the annual prison reports, the state genuinely seemed to make progress toward the rehabilitation of inmates for life beyond the cellblock.[76]

Whatever one believes about the efficacy of reform undertaken at the Massachusetts State Prison in Charlestown in the late 1820s, one has to respect the reformers' sincerity

---

[76]PDSB, *Second Annual Report,* 70-71; PDSB, *Eighth Annual Report,* 59; Lieber, in Beaumont and Tocqueville, *Penitentiary System,* xx.

and the officials' diligence. Faced with an increase in crime whose origin lay in a rapidly changing economy and inheriting a penal system whose methods, if not premises, seemed erroneous, reformers sought both to dissuade people from crime and to redeem those who already had fallen into it. Not surprisingly, they organized their new prisons on the same principles—moral and otherwise—that defined the new tenor of the age and ran the engines of progress.

Basil Hall recognized this congruity. "A convict who is brought to one of these prisons," he observed, "is speedily instructed in many useful things" of which he was "in all probability" ignorant before. In the first place, he learns "habits of industry" from which, "in spite of himself, he is made sensible how much he may do by steady labour." He also is taught temperance and discovers "what it is to sleep soundly, to rise without a headache, and to look to labour as a source of health, strength, and even of enjoyment." He learns "habits of obedience, and of submission to something stronger than his own perverse will." And finally, he is "acquainted with order, cleanliness, and punctuality, all new and agreeable to him." Curtis's earlier experience at Auburn corroborated Hall's assessment. "You can hardly have an idea," he wrote his son in school at Williams shortly after arriving at Auburn, "of the neatness, order & regularity" of the prison, and of "the perfect system which prevails in every Department." "There is not a workshop or cell," he continued, "which is not neater & kept in better trim than any room you have in College." Prisons mirrored what reformers believed to be the best social arrangements beyond their walls, and thus to spend time in one would socialize inmates to the values that marked not only good citizens but also compliant workers. Massachusetts prison officials put this most bluntly in 1829 when they declared that at the new prison they wanted inmates "to move and act like machines."[77]

By 1830, resistance to these values marked one's social deviance, and those who made the rules and regulations that maintained and expanded this brave new world already were too committed to it to question its premises. A few nay-sayers did. By 1840, for example, the erstwhile Transcendentalist Orestes Brownson spoke out in moving terms for the laboring classes and predicted outright class warfare if their needs were not met. A decade later, in his short story "The Tartarus of Maids" Herman Melville pilloried the supposed fruits of industrialization by showing readers the dehumanizing horrors within the machine. And in his different but equally powerful way in *Walden* and "Life without Principle" Henry David Thoreau warned of what happened when men became merely the tools of their tools.

Though these and other critics did not know it, their arguments against an uncritical embrace of the market revolution found corroboration in the moving biographies of the inmates in Charlestown, as well as in the stories of those in other prisons now lost to history. At the least, Curtis's notebooks make us understand that, as with the imprisoned of other times and places, most people in Charlestown did not end up there because they were inherently evil. To be sure, some were depraved, but most simply lacked the resources to deal with the demands of a new social and economic order that harshly punished

[77]Hall, *Travels*, 1:68–69; Jared Curtis to Moses Ashley Curtis, Nov. 11, 1825, Folder 2B, Moses Ashley Curtis Papers, Southern Historical Collection, University of North Carolina at Chapel Hill; *Laws of the Commonwealth*, 102. On reformers and inmate socialization, see Rothman, *Discovery of the Asylum*, 107–108, and *passim*.

those who did or could not keep time to its inexorable drummer. Thus, among many other things, Jared Curtis's remarkable notebooks provide a casualty list of those falling by the way as America was transformed into a successful industrial and mercantile power. As such, they are unique and, in their revelation of the causes and explanations of that ambiguous thing called "crime," merit wide reading and consideration.

A Note on the Manuscript

In 1998 Douglas and Maureen O'Dell, proprietors of Chapel Hill Rare Books, generously brought to my attention the Curtis notebooks, which they had purchased from a book dealer in the midwest, and allowed me to transcribe and work with them. Subsequently, they were acquired by the Massachusetts Historical Society, where they now reside.

Reverend Jared Curtis labeled this manuscript his "Chaplain's Memorandum Book. Massachusetts State Prison. March 10th 1829–April 19th 1831." It consists of two volumes, each 9¾ x 17½ cm. and bound in brown leather, most likely sheep. Both spines are repaired with lighter brown leather. The dated entries are in pencil; the index and leaf numbering in black ink. There are errors in enumeration.

Volume 1. 1–176r text; [177–181r] index; [181v–184v] lined through text. Title on pastedown endpaper, first five pages, and 145v–148v in ink; all other text in pencil. Error in enumeration: first leaf numbered as pages, second leaf [numbered 3] begins enumeration as leaves.

Volume 2. 1–176r text; 176v–181v index. Error in enumeration. Leaf numbering begins with 3 [i.e., second leaf].

A Note on Editorial Method

Jared Curtis's memorandum volumes were private notebooks, not public documents, and there is no sign that he intended to circulate them, much less publish them. Although his writing throughout is legible, and internal evidence suggests that he may have composed them from notes, he did not polish his entries. He punctuated irregularly, used abbreviations frequently, and wrote in complete sentences rarely. A typesetter would find his text to be riddled with ambiguities—letters that might or might not be uppercase; punctuation marks that might reasonably be read as capitals, commas, or dashes; contractions for which alternative readings are possible; sentences and sentence fragments that either end or do not end at a given punctuation mark. In order to translate Curtis's text from manuscript to type, I have had to adopt a set of conventions for each entry.

Heading. Most entries begin with his subject's first name and family name as well as his age. I have set these elements apart from the rest of the text as a heading. Curtis usually spelled out the prisoner's first name, but he occasionally employed contractions. In two instances, he omitted the first name entirely, and he was not always systematic in his placement of his subject's age, sometimes relegating it to the body of the entry. From time to time, if a prisoner was not Caucasian, Curtis mentioned race in the introduction to the entry.

I have regularized each entry's heading. It now includes first name (if known), last name, and age. If Curtis abbreviated the first name, I have supplied the missing letters within [square brackets]. If he did not mention age until the body of the text, I have added it in [square brackets] to the heading while also leaving it in the entry proper. When Curtis inserted a comment on race between the prisoner's name and age, I have retained his remark in the heading.

Body. With the major exception of punctuation, I have ordinarily transcribed Curtis's entries as he wrote them. Abbreviations are retained except in cases where they pose the possibility of confusion. If I have supplied letters, I have done so in [square brackets]. If canceled material is legible, I have provided it in *<angle brackets and italics>*.

In the interests of consistency and readability, I have taken an aggressive approach to punctuation. I have begun each sentence or sentence fragment with a capital and ended it with a period unless internal evidence dictates connecting fragments with a comma or a dash. I have supplied a comma after the penultimate element in a series where Curtis neglected to do so.

Cross references. In Volume 2, Curtis occasionally inserted cross references to entries in Volume 1. For the most part, these cross references were not substantive, and I recognized them through a note at the end of the entry preceding. When a cross reference includes substantive information, I have added it to the initial entry as a note.

Appendix. Curtis took up half a dozen pages at the end of Volume 1 with notes on meetings with prisoners. Many of these notes are illegible; those that I have been able to recover I have presented in an appendix.

Manuscript index. I have omitted Curtis's manuscript index.

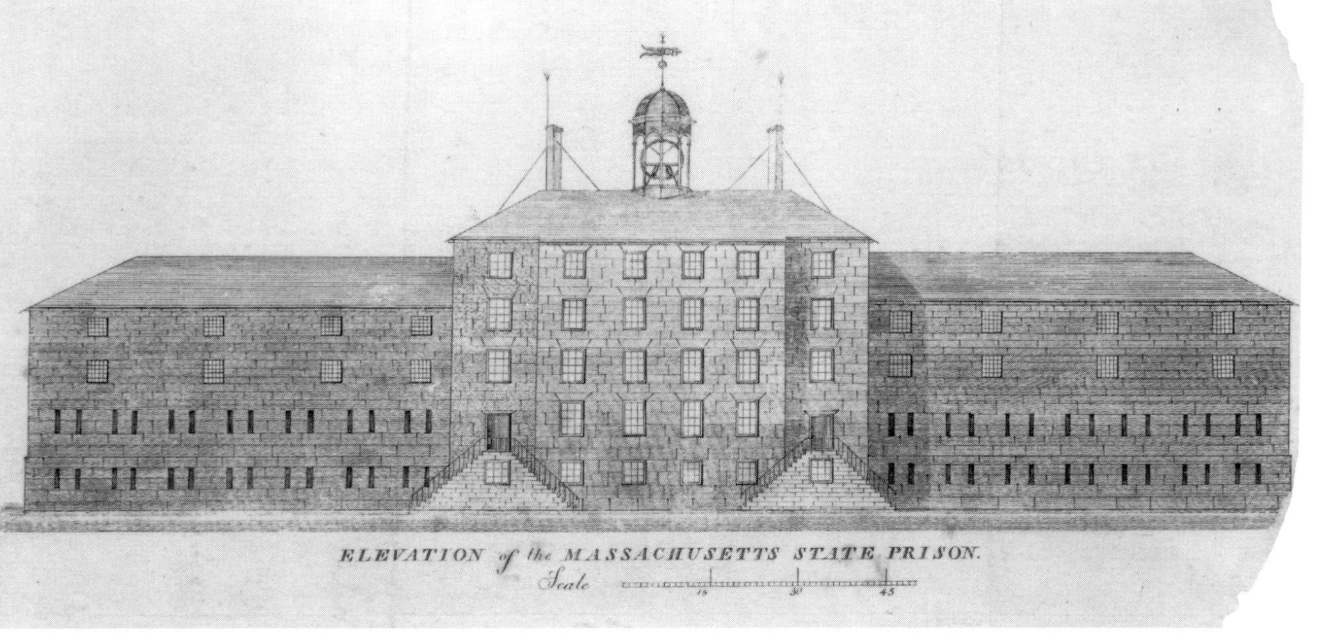

1. Front view of the Massachusetts State Prison c. 1806, illustrating the institution's basic form prior to its reorganization in the late 1820s. Its cupola and square windows identify it in subsequent depictions.
("Elevation of the Massachusetts State Prison," from An Account of the Massachusetts State Prison *[Boston, 1806]. Courtesy Boston Athenæum.)*

2. View of the prison from the Charles River, c. 1839. This image shows the prison building of 1806 in the center and, to its left, the new dormitory built during the prison's reorganization in 1829. Granite for the stone cutting works at the prison was delivered by barge.

(Original source unknown. From the "Old House File," Boston Athenæum.)

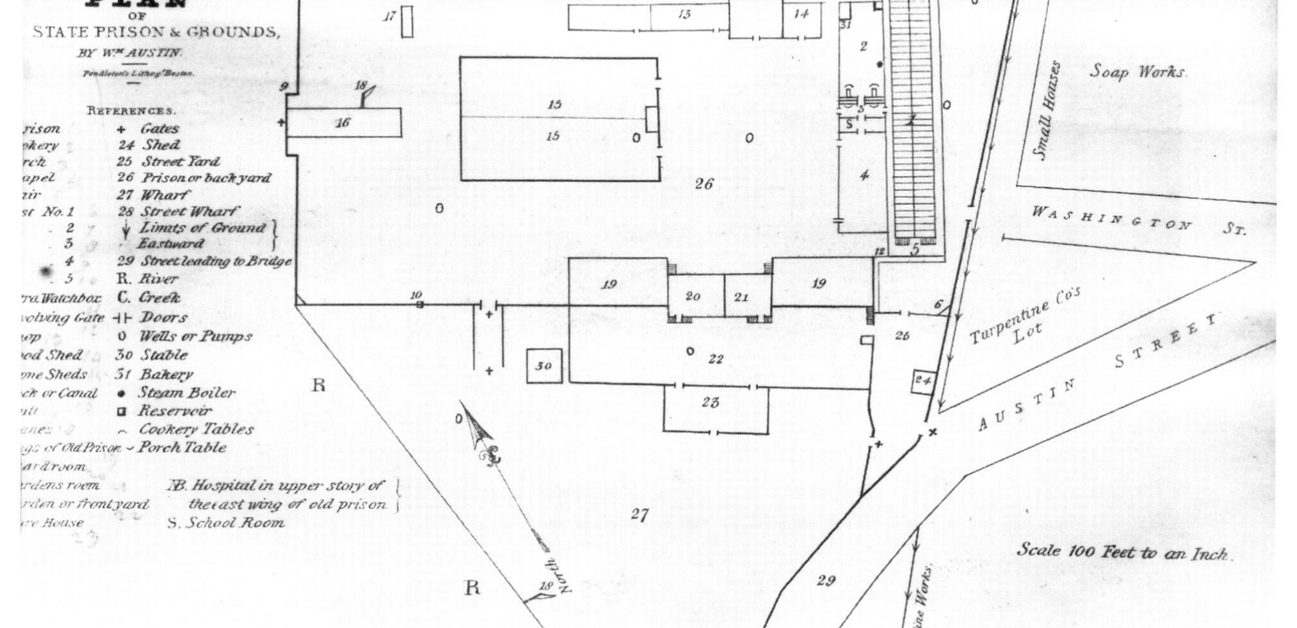

3. Plan of the Massachusetts State Prison, c. 1830. Remarkably detailed depiction of the topography, buildings, and utilities that defined the institution at the time of its reorganization during the Reverend Jared Curtis's tenure as chaplain. *("Plan of the State Prison & Grounds," frontispiece to* Laws of the Commonwealth for the Government of the Massachusetts State Prison *[Boston, 1830]. Courtesy Boston Athenæum.)*

4. View of the prison yard, c. 1830. This remarkable engraving shows the original building (with cupola and two wings) in the center. The two identical buildings on the right are the "stone sheds" where prisoners cut granite blocks. The prisoners on the left enter the cookery, a building that also housed, further to the right, the chapel. The dormitory built for the prison's reorganization on the Auburn plan is the large building at the far left, behind the cookery. *("View of Prison Yard & Buildings," frontispiece to* Laws of the Commonwealth for the Government of the Massachusetts State Prison *[Boston, 1830]. Courtesy Boston Athenæum.)*

5. Interior view, stone cutting sheds, 1853. Although this engraving dates from a later period, these sheds were part of the prison complex in 1829, when the Reverend Jared Curtis became chaplain at the institution. (*"Stone-cutting department of the Massachusetts State Prison,"* Gleason's Pictorial Drawing-Room Companion *4, no. 13 [Mar. 26, 1853]: 197. Photograph courtesy of the Boston Public Library.)*

6. Photographic view of prisoners at Massachusetts State Prison, c. 1860s. Although dating to a later period, this view shows prisoners in front of one of the original prison buildings (note rectangular windows).

("Prison yard at dinner time," uncredited and undated stereograph, Massachusetts Historical Society.)

7. "View of the Massachusetts State Prison, from Prison Point Bridge," c. 1859. This remarkable view, which documents the coming of the railroad to the area, shows the further construction undertaken at the institution c. 1850. The large building with the cupola atop dates from that period; one can just make out, tucked against its right side, the cupola of the original prison building. On the left of the image one sees Boston and the Bunker Hill Monument.

(Ballou's Pictorial Drawing-Room Companion *16, no. 12 [Mar. 19, 1859]: 184. Photograph courtesy of the Boston Public Library.)*

John Gilbert al Scroggins
2d Comm – Went from here
in June last & returned about
3 months ago – Born in England – is a Sailor – been
in U. S about 9 years –
No Education – cant read –
Intemperate – Sentenced
in New Bedford – Was here
4 yrs the first time – present sentence 2 yrs – Says
he never gets into any
difficulty here – behaves
well & should think him
a very Stupid man –

March 18

8. An entry from the second volume of Jared Curtis's two notebooks, this biography gives a thumbnail sketch of the life of John Gilbert. *(Jared Curtis notebooks, Massachusetts Historical Society.)*

Buried from the World

Inside the Massachusetts State Prison, 1829–1831

VOLUME I

March 10, 1829

Joseph Purchase[1]—Age 31

Natick, he says, is as much his home as any place. Ed[ucatio]n poor. Can read & write some. Parents put him out when 7 or 8 ys old. Work'd at farming till 18 or 19 ys old. Was steady till about 15, then got uneasy and restless. Left the man he livd with & livd with another man. In 25th year committed his first offence. Sentenced for Manslaughter for 3 ys & was 3 ys in jail before he came here. Servd out his time and was out about a year, then sentenced again for attempt to murder for 6 years. Been here 41 months.

A very hard case. Unfeeling and utterly destitute of moral feeling or sense of obligation. An infidel. Has no idea of ever trying to be anything.

John Quiner—Age 26

Born & brot up in Beverly.[2] Parents now live there. Brot up a Seaman. Went to sea at 15. Decent common Education. Says his parents were very careful to bring him up well & in good & regular habits. With the exception of one or 2 voyages, had excellent captains. Saild 3½ ys with a remarkably

---

[1] "Joseph Purchase, 35 y, prisoner in State Prison, d. there, Feb. 20, 1832." *Vital Records of Charlestown, Massachusetts, to the Year 1850*, comp. Roger D. Joslyn (Boston, 1984–1995), 2:294.

[2] John Campbell Quiner, son of Abram, Jr., a laborer, and Susanna Quiner, was born in Beverly on Nov. 1, 1802. He was "found drowned in one of the factory canals at Lowell on the morning of June 23d, 1833, a. 30 y. 7 m. 22 d." *Vital Records of Beverly, Massachusetts, to the End of the Year 1849* (Topsfield, Mass., 1906–1907), 1:273, 2:537, 538.

fine man Capt Seeley on board of which vessel was a man now Capt Odell of Boston a religious & excellent man & a good friend of his.

Made his last voyage 2½ ys ago. After quitting the Sea, became somewhat intemperate, tho not a drunkard. Says that as to anything dishonest, his character stood fair till the commission of the crime for which he is now suffering although from his intemperate habits, his reputation had suffered. Convicted of Larceny. Sentenced for 2 ys. Been here now 15½ months. Says that his intemperance produced a partial insanity & that it was in this state of mind that he committed the crime. Made his escape in Novr last & retaken the next day. Has never been in any other difficulty, & his conduct, aside from that, has been good. Says he is well treated by his officers.

Quiner is a man of sense & converses well. Speaks of his parents with deep feeling & seems resolv'd to do well but says he is afraid of his old habit of intemperance. Hopes he shall be able to resist it.

Dick Richards (Black man)—Age about 40
Does not know exactly his age. Born in Africa. Brot away in a slave ship when he was 12 or 13 ys old. Was sold in Bermuda. Liv'd there about a year, then he ran away & came on a ship to Boston where he has liv'd since—about 19 years. No education. Says he us'd to go to meeting. Loved to go to meeting. Went to sea some & lived at service some. Never given to drinking. Was led away by bad Company. 3 offender. 1st time confin'd one year, out 5 ys, went to sea. 2d time, confin'd one year, then out 9 months. 3d time, sentenc'd 4 ys. And has an additional life sentence. Been here 10 years. Says he has got along well has not been punish'd in six years & confin'd at night in the same room. Says he does not allow of any thing bad in his room. Has

made up his mind fully, never to do wrong any more. Intends to try to get pardoned & if any bad folks try to lead him away he shall shake his head at them & shall never steal again, long as he live.

Dick seems to be a good hearted, frank, clever sort of a fellow.

ROBERT RILEY—AGE 45
Born in Ireland. Says he was stolen away at the age of 10 by a sea Capt. & brot to America. Has not Education enough to read. Been in the US 29 ys. Lived most of the time in Boston. In the late war was 5 ys in US service. Has lived as a servant in the best families in Boston. Says he was not habitually intemperate, but us'd occasionally in a frolic, to get high. Second comer. First offense—3 ys—out 6 or 7 mo. 2d Sentence on 2 Indictments—3 ys on each. Been here 5 ys next June. Says he was guilty the first time, the last time not guilty. Did not know the money was counterfeit. Says he has been in Cells 3 or 4 times for misconduct. Health very feeble & says he is unable to work. Makes very strong protestations & appeals, as to his motives & resolutions. Has a good deal of Irish slang, and it is pretty difficult telling exactly what he is. Wept freely, and manifests some feeling.

DAVID REMICK—AGE 40
Born in Mass, but moved with parents to Ballston N.Y. when he was young. Was brot up there. Had good parents & was brought up to good Habits. Decent Com[mo]n Education. At 15 left parents by their consent & advice. Work'd at various things—Brick-making—Boating & follow'd lumbering 7 ys in Canada. In 6 ys made 5000 Doll. The 7th year lost most of it by speculating in lumber. Came into this state to see his friends and was prosecuted in Berkshire for an at-

tempt to Rape, & sentenced for 10 years. Stayed here 9 ys & 3 mo, & was pardoned. Was out 5 mo & then sentenced again in the same County for the same offence & sentenced for 10 ys. Been here now near 3½ ys. Says he was not guilty of attempting Rape in either case. Says he has never been in punishment since he has been here. Says he believes the Bible to be the word of God. Never profane, nor much intemperate. Sometimes drink'd a little when in company, but never made a practice of drinking. Until he got into this difficulty always sustaind a fair character for honesty, industry, & integrity. (Did not see him as long as I wish'd, the Bell having rung for prayers.)

March 11, 1829

WILLIAM PAINE (COLOR'D MAN)—AGE 36
Born in Salem & have lived mostly there & in Boston. Has always follow'd the Seas. Can read, and write some. Second time here. 1st time 4 ys—out 2—then sentenced for 6 ys. Been here 5 years. Sentenced both times in Boston. Says he never was a drunkard. Drink'd his grog as other sailors do, but never to excess. Says he was a pretty honest & a steady trusty man. Sentenced both times for Larceny. Was in the U. S. service in the Navy during the whole of late war, most of the time on the Lakes. Since in prison has never been punish'd for misconduct, either the first or last sentence. Says he reads the Bible and believes it. Appears humble. Is frank, & converses very well. Should think him a very good convict.

ROBERT RILEY 2D—AGE 34
Born in Kingston Jamaica & brot up in St Domingo. Can read & write. Born free. Always been a seaman. Was formerly steady till he lost all he had, & then he took himself

to Stealing. Drink'd some—tho not very hard. Is here for 3d time. 1st time 2 ys—out 2 mo. 2d time 7 ys & 10 mo—in cells 10 mo for misconduct. Out 14 days, then Sentenced 3d time. Been here 3 ys. Sentence 5 ys. Says he has been punish'd a good deal, sometimes for fighting, & sometimes for other offences. Is very sorry. Intends now, if possible, to get along well & avoid punishment. Never means to commit any more crimes if he can but live to get out.

Probably a hard case.[3]

JACOB RUSSELL—AGE 52

Home in Milton. Family wife & 6 Children. Farmer, once a man of some property but through misfortune lost it. Can read & write tho his Education is poor. Train'd up in steady and correct habits. Never intemperate—until the present confinement. Was well esteem'd by his neighbours & friends. Has been here between 3 & 4 ys. Sentenced 10 ys. Convicted in Dedham for an assault on his wife with intent to murder.

Says he got melted by the heat in working hard, and became deranged. Made the assault, as he supposes, in this state of mind. Says he has no knowledge of it. Never been in punishment since his confinement. Says he reads the Bible a great deal. Believes it to be the word of God. Appears very well. Has considerable sensibility & I should think, not a harden'd man.

JOHN REED 1ST—AGE 37

Born in Ireland. Been in U.S. 14 ys. Brot up to the manufacturing business, principally the business of folding cloth

[3]Cross reference in volume 2 notes: "Wishes me to talk with Judge Thatcher & Lawyer Knap about his case. Says N. Guilty." Peter O. Thatcher was judge of the Boston Municipal Court. John Knapp, a lawyer, lived in Boston. *Massachusetts Register* (1829), 29, 40.

for market. Decent common Education. Wife & 3 children in Boston. Sentenced for Larceny in Boston for 7 ys. Been here 16 mo. Says that previously to this trouble was well esteem'd & sustain'd a fair character. Never intemperate. Says he is not Guilty. Bought the goods of others not knowing them to have been stolen (Says he ought to have been more careful) (probably well knew the fact.) <*Has been punished some since he come here.*> Has a brother here—Henry Reed[4] & has 2 Brothers in a Manufacturing establishment in Andover. Is a man of good natural talents. Says he has been in the cells twice for misconduct. Pleads that he did not intentionally err. I suspect he has some of the Irish grit occasionally. Nothing improper in his conversation or deportment. Was frank & pleasant.

HENRY REED—AGE 27

Born in Ireland. Been in U.S. 9 ys—in Boston. Kept Grocery Store some & Livery Stable some. Has wife but no children. Decent Education. Sentenced in Boston for forgery 5 ys. Been here almost a year. Been in cells once for not doing work enough, and once for breaking Store. Previously to this confinement was a man of fair character, as he says. Was never intemperate or given to vice.

Says he did not commit the forgery to defraud. There was no such man as the Note purported to be against. The note was made to be revenged on his Lawyer—Moore, of Boston,[5] who had mismanaged his business. He gave him the note to collect, knowing there was no such man as the signature denoted & then refus'd to pay the expence which had been caus'd by trying to find him &c &c. Not much feeling & I suspect a rather hard case.

---

[4]See next entry.

[5]Abraham Moore. *Massachusetts Register* (1829), 40.

George Rosseter—Age 23
Home in N. York. Mother lives in R.I.

Education tolerably good. Servd an apprenticeship at Saddlery business. Last 2 years before coming on to Boston, spent in Philadela. Came to Boston a year ago last October. Convicted in Boston 1 year ago. Sentence 5 ys. Larceny. First imprisonment. Has generally been industrious & well esteemed. Not vicious. Gambled some but not intemperate. A sensible young man, though I fear does not feel as much as he ought. Been in cell once for Gambling, tho he says he did not gamble. Has generally got along well since has been here.

Solomon Russell—Age 29
Home—Troy, N.Y. Education poor. Learnd shoemaker's trade. Has not lived in Troy for a number of years past. Liv'd in Providence & Boston, & has been to Sea some. Says he has been a wild youth. Convicted of Larceny in Boston & sentenced 2 ys. Been here 1 year. His first offence. Says he knows it is best for him to do right & be a good man. Sometimes he resolves to take a right course & then again his resolutions vanish. He does not know what will be the result. Thinks his mind has been corrupted here & he is very sorry he could not have been confin'd alone, & wishes he could be so now.

Says he has been punish'd some. Probably, a sorry case.

March 12, 1829

John Read—says he spells Reed—Age 30
Born & brot up in N. York. Learnd the Trade of a Tailor & followd the business for a livelihood. Had a Shop in N. York. Decent common School Education. Mother died

early, & his father had a large family & could not give him much learning, and did what he could to superintend his morals. Previously to his coming of Age, says he was not very wild or vicious. Left his master to whom he was apprenticed, 2 ys before his time was out. Went by his father's request to Jersey & liv'd 2 ys with a relative & work'd at his trade. When of Age while working at his trade as a journeyman in N. York there was a general turn out among the craft for more wages. In this way was thrown out of employ for about 3 months. In this time became idle and dissolute—gambled—ran after bad women &c &c—was suspected of crime, & thrown into Bridewell.[6] Says he was not Guilty & was acquitted. Here became acquainted with many very great rogues, & made up his mind to follow mischief with them. Soon commenced his career & has pursued it since till getting here. Anderson al[ias] Stevens now in N.Y. Prison was the man who led him away. Says he is a very great scoundrel & a very dangerous man. Found he was unwilling to answer many questions & did not press him much. He is an infidel in sentiment. Believes there is a God & says he loves him with all his heart &c &c. Is a very accomplished rogue.

Charles W. Rice—Age 21

Brot up in Boston.[7] Parents live there now & are reputable. Education good. Learn'd the Trade of House carpenter of his father. Says he was tolerably steady till about 19. Then left his father. Married 2 ys ago next June. One child. Was unsteady & wild after leaving home.

---

[6] I.e., city jail.

[7] Possibly Charles Warran Rice, born Sept. 12, 1808, in Warren, son of Charles and Annas Rice. *Vital Records of Warren (Formerly Western), Massachusetts, to the End of the Year 1849* (Worcester, 1910), 56.

Went into Worcester Co. Work'd at his trade. Hir'd a horse and Chaise to ride out with wife. Ran away with it. Was apprehended & sentenced in Ipswich to this prison for 5 ys. Been here a year next May. Got along well here.

Has some tenderness of feeling. Says he is resolved to lead a good life hereafter.

TIMOTHY RIDICAN—AGE 16

Born in Ireland. Been in U.S. three years next May. Mother was poor & he left her, he says because he thought he could help her more by going to Sea than by staying at home. Came to Boston & went fishing several voyages. Was friendless. Could not get employment as he wanted. Got into bad co[mpany]. Got to drinking, then to stealing. Sentenced once to City Prison for thieving. Afterward sentenced here for 2 years. Been here 10 months. Can read & write some. Says he has got along well here. Has some tenderness of feeling & says he shall certainly never again commit crimes.

March 13, 1829

JOHN C. RUSSELL—AGE 48

Born & brot up in N. Hampshire. Saddler and Harness maker. Has wife & 1 Child. Has liv'd some at West Cambridge. Decent common Education. Father died when he was young, & was left to care for his mother. Was a steady, industrious young man, & much respected. Married in N.H. and after a year or two moved to West Cambridge. Says his wife was from one of the most respectable families in the town & her father wealthy. When he was 21 he had a property of $4000—left him by his father. When he came to Cambridge, was in good circumstances.

Went into the Butchering business. Did not succeed well. Belong'd to an independent Militia Company &

spent a good deal of money in equipping &c &c. Between this and all his ill success with Butchering line lost most of his property. In addition to all this, lost his wife, which very much affected him. She left a son about 2 ys old which he carried to its grandparents & has not seen it since.

This was about 23 years ago. His losses & death of wife brot on great depression of spirits & a sort of mental alienation. Went to drinking to excess, to gambling & from this to other sins. Has changed his name that his friends may not know of his condition. Has been in prison a good deal—in all 9 or 10 ys. Is a man of sense. Open & frank. Conduct in prison exemplary. Says he is confident he shall, if he ever gets out, live a different life. The only bar in the way he says is intemperance & he thinks he shall be able to overcome it. Prison a horrible school of corruption.

George E. Roulstone—Age 33
Home in Charlestown. First Confinement. Decent common Education. Says he had good parents. Learn'd the trade of a Morocco draper. Work'd at that some after he was of age, and at tannery some. For the last year or two drew a hand Cart in Boston. Says he was generally steady and industrious. Convicted in Boston of Larceny & sentenced 1 year. Been here about 5 months. Says he sold a gun for another fellow supposing it to be his. The fellow it appears had stolen the Gun & ran away & he had to suffer for it. Says he has never been punishd or in any difficulty here.

Says he is determin'd fully to do well when he leaves the prison. Never much intemperate. Drinks sometimes. Appears like a rather stupid but harmless sort of man.

March 16, 1829

Jacob Richmond[8]—Age 37

North Carolina. Wife & child. Married about 5 ys ago. Born free. Cannot read. Never had any opportunity to learn. Always follow'd the Sea. Began to go to Sea at 12 ys old. Says he was generally cook or Steward & sustain'd a good character as a seaman. Says he never made a practice of swearing when at sea. Has often rebuked others for swearing. Was cast away at Sea & got into New Bedford. From there went Whaling. When he returned to N.B. got into this difficulty. Says he got into the habit of drinking while employ'd in whaling, & when he return'd was persuaded while in a state of intoxication to swear in Court that a certain man had been engaged in tearing down a building there, and was convicted of perjury. Sentenced for 2 ys. Been here about 4 mo. Says he did very wrong. Did not understand the nature & guilt of so doing, but never should have done so had he been sober.

Says he has behav'd well here & has been in no trouble. Seems to be a very good hearted, frank, & clever fellow, though ignorant. Thinks this trouble will be a good lesson to him as long as he lives. Wishes very much to get back to Carolinas.

John Rogers—Age 17

Born at Bordeaux in France. Left France when 9 ys old & has been in the Sea Services most of the time since. Came first to N.Y. Can read & write. Says this is his first difficulty & he means it shall be his last. Has, in general, he says been

[8]Commitment Register, Charlestown State Prison, 1818–1840, no. 1023, Massachusetts State Archives.

an industrious boy. Saild out of Boston 2 ys & thinks he could get as good recommendation from his captains as any body. Never was intemperate. Says he was very profane & is sorry for it. Sentenced for stealing in Boston. Sentence 3½ years. Says he did not steal the goods. Acknowledges that he had the goods in his possession, but they were brot to him by another to keep & knew not that they were stolen. Says he has got along well here & is determined to conduct well here in all things.

Appears to be a clever boy & well dispos'd. Wish for spel[ling] Book some in his room. Can't read.

CHARLES RIVERS—AGE 52

Belongs in Eng. Has a wife & 5 children in Eng. Friends and connexions very respectable & his Education good.

Has for 18 ys past been a shipper of Goods from Eng. to America. Began with 1000 pounds Sterling & says until the close of the last war was very successful. Was worth at one time 80,000 dollars. Made a very large shipment just at the close of the war and sunk a great part of it. Lost 22,000 Dol by Aaron Dana[9] in Boston. In Dec last sent some goods to an Auctioneer in Boston. Purchas'd them in Baltimore. Some of them prov'd to have been stolen in Boston before this, and he was apprehended & then tried on 2 Indictments 6 mo. on one & 1 year on the other. Has been here 8 weeks. Got along well so far.

Rivers is a man of sense & has a smooth tongue but it is fear'd that his exterior is the better part of him. Told a good story. After all I think him rather a suspicious character.

---

[9]Aaron Dana, broker, 26 State Street, Boston. *Boston Directory* (1829), 82.

Charles T. Read[10]—[Age 25?]

A young man of fine talents & Ed[ucation] lately sentenced for Forgery in Boston for 3 ys. Had a long conversation with him but did not take notes. Requested him to give me a brief sketch of his life in writing which he has promised to do.[11]

Joel Severance—Age 29

Born in Vt. Mother now lives in N.H. For the last 3 ys before getting into prison lived in Charlestown, Boston, and the vicinity. Workd as a laborer at various kinds of work. Parents poor, and his Education very scanty. Reads poorly. Livd with father till 15, then went to learn Saddling & Harness making business. Lived with this man 2 ys until he died, then return'd home & worked at blacksmithing with his father till his death which was 3 years. Says his habits in early life were good, & was well brot up. Says he never was intemperate. Was arrested in Essex Co. 7 yrs ago. Convicted in Salem 6 yrs ago last Nov. of passing c[ounterfei]t money & sentenced for life. Since here has been treated uniformly well & has never been call up for any misdemeanor. Says he believes the Bible & feels the importance & duty of living according to its precepts and is determined, if ever he goes out of prison to live an upright, honest life.

Seems to possess a good deal of softness of feeling. Mind tender, and so far as I can judge is determined to live honestly hereafter. Says he was guilty of this crime for which he

---

[10]Possibly Charles T. Reed, born in Cambridge, May 30, 1803. *Vital Records of Cambridge, Massachusetts, to the Year 1850*, comp. Thomas W. Baldwin (Boston, 1914–1915), 1:588.

[11]Curtis's memorandum books do not include a biographical sketch by or about Read.

was sentenced & appears much humbled under it. Should think much better of him than most convicts.

Jos[eph] O. Salisbury—Age 25

Born in Vt. Mother now lives in St. of N.Y. Brot up to farming. Education very poor. Can read, & can barely write his name. Had good parents.

Has a wife & 2 children in Uxbridge in Wor[cester] Co. Says his habits were not vicious. Was like other young men rather gay & wild, never intemperate. Says the cause of his trouble was that a young fellow courted a girl & he cut him out & married her. This made the fellow mad & he swore revenge. Accus'd him after a while of stealing & had him put in Jail. While there the jail was set on fire by Loomis,[12] a convict now here, & he not making it known was convicted with Loomis & sentenced also for life. For part of his time, far[e]d hard. For the last four ys has been punished but once. Never in prison before. Appears pretty well. Says he shall steer straight if he ever gets out.

March 17, 1829

John Scroggins—Age 34

Been in prison now 4 ys. Here a second time. Sentenced now for 3 ys with one year additional for being second comer. Here first time 3 ys. Out 15 months. Born in England. Been in U.S. 10 ys. Seaman. Father & mother died when he was young & he went early to sea. Never learnd to read. Never attended meeting on the Sabbath much, nor regarded the Sabbath. Was almost always at Sea. Was thoughtless & wild. When in Port, us'd to get high and run after the girls. Says he is sick of a prison & means to take a

[12]Presumably inmate James Loomis. See below, pp. 124–126

course when he goes out, altogether different. Says he has been in Cells on punishment 30 days, but has behav'd generally well. Is a frank sort of fellow, but not much sensibility.

AARON SHEPARDSON—AGE 38

Born in County of Norfolk & liv'd there till 22, then went into the Western Country, & after that came to Lee, Mass. Wife & 3 children in Lee.[13] Decent common Ed[ucation]. Parents in good circumstances & of fair character. Bred to farming. Sentenced in Berkshire Co. four years ago for stealing a horse. Sentence 7 ys. First offence. Before this character, as he says, stood fair. Had become reduced in his circumstances & was led to this act by his situation. Says he has got along well here & without trouble.

Has not much feeling. Is an infidel in sentiments and I fear has not much principle of any kind. Although he was respectful & says he is determined to conduct well in future life.

DAVID SAWYER—AGE 33

Born in N.H. Livd there the first 15 yrs of his life, then went to R.I. From there came to Mass., where he has resided for the last 8 ys. Good common school Ed[ucation]. Parents very respectable & took all due pains to bring him up well. Mother died when he was 10. Father married again. His step-mother did not treat him well & he went from home. Farmer. Says he was a strange young man & his habits correct. Never married. Been here 3 ys & 5 mo. First confinement. Sentence 5 ys. Assault to kill. Says he was not guilty of any such intent. Says he was never intemperate. Since here,

---

[13]Aaron and Lucinda Shepardson had a son, Aaron, born in Lee on Sept. 15 or 16, 1822. *Vital Records of Lee, Massachusetts, to the Year 1850* (Boston, 1903), 226.

has never been punish'd—makes it a point. Is a pleasant man & a man of sense.

W[ILLIA]M STEVENS—COL[ORE]D MAN—AGE 20
Born & brot up in Maine. The last 4 ys been in this state—the two last years in this prison. Convicted in Boston—of stealing. Sentence 5 ys. First offence. Brot up to farming. Can read & write. Says he was about as steady as boys in General. Not vicious. Us'd to attend meeting on the Sabbath. Attended Sabbath school 2 Summers. Parents dead. They were religious people & did what they could to have him well instructed. Never in any difficulty before this for any offence. Says he came from Portland to Boston with Madam Cobb. Liv'd with her & drove her carriage. Foolishly thought he could do better & left her. Liv'd here & there. Became unsteady & associated with bad company & finally got to prison.

Possesses a good deal of sensibility. Is mild & pleasant & very frank. Wept very freely. Appears much better than most prisoners.

W[ILLIA]M SMITH—AGE 29
Home for the last 15 ys in Virgil, Cortland Co., N.Y. Born in Vt. Not married. Parents living in Virgil. Brot up to farming. Never had any education. Can not read at all. Might have learn'd when a boy, but was weakly, & subject to fits & did not incline to go to school. Left N.Y. about 3 ys ago to make a visit. Was taken sick on the road. Spent most of his money. Got as far as Sheffield in this State, at a Tavern saw considerable money in the Bar & resolv'd that at night he would get it. Went away & returnd at night, but could not get into the Bar. Took a watch, Hat, & pr of Boots & decamped. Was apprehended & sentenced for 5 ys. Been here 2 ys & 9 mo. Says he has stolen some before but not

much. Appears frank but has not much feeling. Says he has got along well here & intends to behave himself when he gets out. His chance, I think, a very poor one. Drink'd some, tho not very much.

REUBEN SHAW—AGE 47

Born & brot up in Abington, Plymouth Co.[14] Wife & 5 children there. Boot & Shoemaker. Parents still alive. Education rather poor. Can read, write, and cypher. 2d Comer. 1st time 3 ys. Out 5 ys. 2d time been here 2 ys & 9 mo. Sentence 4 ys. First time Larceny—G[uilty?]. Last time adultery—not G[uilty?].

Never habitually intemperate. Cannot say that he has not sometimes drink'd more than was for his good. Never had much property, tho he got a good living. Says he has never been punished or reprimanded for any offence since he was in prison. Is a man of sense & makes very fair promises. How sincere he is is more than I can say. Professes to believe in the Bible and the binding obligation of its precepts.[15]

STEPHEN SYMMS—AGE 29[16]

Born & Brot up in Roxbury. Learn the trade of Sailmaking. Work'd considerably in Boston. Father is now living in Rox-

[14]Ruben Shaw, son of Joseph and Molley Shaw, was born in Abington, Jan. 11, 1781. He married Abigail Josselyn of Pembroke, Sept. 30, 1811. *Vital Records of Abington, Massachusetts, to the Year 1850* (Boston, 1912), 1:201–208; *Vital Records of Pembroke, Massachusetts, to the Year 1850* (Boston, 1911), 344.

[15]Cross reference to Shaw in volume 2 notes: "Recollect to ask Judge Putnam whether he has any recollection of giving Shaw, convicted at Plymouth, of Adultery in 1826, May term, a longer sentence on account of his having been [illeg.] before in State Prison. Shaw says a witness was sworn at his trial to prove this fact. Sentenced for 4 ys."

[16]Roxbury records list James Symmes, son of Stephen and Hannah, born Mar. 1, 1799. *Vital Records of Roxbury, Massachusetts, to the End of the Year*

bury. Never married. Can read & write. Ed[ucatio]n poor. 3d Comer. 1 time 2 ys. Out 6 mo. 2d time 4 ys. Out 3 ys. 3d time here 2 ys. Sentence life for Being 3d comer. All for Larceny. 1st 20 Doll. 2d 5 Doll. 3d 60 Doll.

Says he has generally got along well in prison. Ascribes his misfortunes primarily to running away from his father. Had committed some offence and expected to get a flogging from his father & would not go home. Was away 3 ys. In this time was led away by loose companions. Drink'd some, gambled, went to the theatre and often the girls, & from step to step to crime. Is frank and manifests some sense of his follies & crimes & feels that his situation is a very hopeless one. Says he believes the Bible & for 6 or 8 months past has studied & reflected more upon it than in all his life before. Is a ruined man, most probably. Is a waiter in stone shed. Lungs affected & says the stone-dust hurts him very much.

March 18, 1829

EBEN[EZE]R SHANNON[17]—AGE 36

Born & brot up in N.H. Came from that State to this 3 ys ago. Father died when 6 ys old, then put out to a farmer. Liv'd with him till 14. He then died, when he left the place & shirked for himself. Workd at farming some. Went to sea some. Education poor. Can hardly read & write. Habits good while young. At the age of 17 was persuaded by a cousin to enlist as a sailor in the U.S. services where he continued 2 ys. This, he says ruind him forever. The sailors were a very wicked set of fellows. There learnd to swear,

---

1849 (Salem, 1925–1926), 1:337. "Stephen Symmes, 32 y, prisoner in State Prison, d. there July 18, 1831." *Vital Records of Charlestown*, 2:305.

[17] "Ebenezer Shannon, 47 y, convict in State Prison, d. there Sept 21, 1835." *Vital Records of Charlestown*, 2:287.

drink, gamble, & everything else that was bad. 3d Comer. 1st time Larceny—2 ys out—part of a year only. 2d time here 4 ys. Out 8 ys. 3d time Life. Been here 2 ys.

Says he is very miserable & is sensible that his heart is exceedingly corrupt & hardened. Knows that vice must make a man wretched. Says that the last time he was sentenced he was not Guilty. Convicted of having C[ounterfei]t money in possession. Says an old scoundrel tried to get him to take or buy some & he refus'd utterly. Says the fellow declared he would leave some & stuck it away in the wood house, where it would keep dry. This was found & he had to suffer.

Says he has got along well & has behaved well here. He is frank & talks sensibly but has, I fear, very little sense of his real condition.

CHARLES W. SPAULDING[18]—AGE 23

Born in Tyngsboro.[19] Liv'd there til 13. Father then moved. Livd with him till he died. Was then 18. Learnd no trade. Work'd on farm. Decent com[mo]n Education. Well brot up. Parents strict in the discharge of their duty. Says he was an industrious & steady young man, & was never in any difficulty till he came here. After father died, went to Lowel. Tended Stable, drove Hack &c. Continued very steady till within 3 or 4 months of the time of the arrest. Sentenced in Boston for passing c[ounterfei]t money for 4 ys. Been here 15 months. Got along uniformly well here. Appears like a very clever good hearted young fellow. Says he went from Lowel to Waltham on a visit, there wishing to get a horse to take a ride. He went to a man by the

---

[18] "Charles W. Spaulding, 24 y, convict in State Prison, Charlestown, d. there, Feb. 2, 1830." *Vital Records of Charlestown,* 2:303.

[19] Charles Wesley Spaulding, son of Josiah and Betsey Spaulding, was born in Tyngsborough, Jan. 4, 1804. *Vital Records of Tyngsborough, Massachusetts, to the End of the Year 1849* (Salem, 1913), 31.

name of Andrews who keeps a stable. Says that Andrews provided him to take 30 Dollars of C[ounterfei]t money. He did so. Came to Boston, bespoke a suit of clothes, paid 15 Dollars of this money. Was apprehended & sentenced as above.

Is determined fully, as he says, never again to do a wrong act.[20]

Alpheus Spring—Age 30

Born in Hampshire Co. Ed[ucatio]n good. Single man. For a considerable number of years past work'd as a machinist. 2d Comer. Here the first time near 2 ys. Pardoned out. Was out 8 ys, then sentenced for store breaking 10 ys. Been here near 2 ys.

Is one of the most hardened, insensible, & incorrigible fellows I have seen here. A confirm'd infidel. Could not make him talk a great deal. Sat smiling all the time I conversed with him, & his air and meanness told me that I might talk as much as I would & be none the wiser for him & he wishes not to be made wiser by me.

Should think him a shrew'd, hardened, & determined knave.[21]

John Snow[22]—age 67

First confinement. Been here 10 months. Sentence 7 years for burning a Barn. Says he is not Guilty & knew nothing about it. Home—West Bridgewater. Was born there. 6 chil-

[20] Cross reference in volume 2 describes Spaulding as "Mild, pleasant, and humble."

[21] Cross reference in volume 2 calls Spring "Sour crabbed & reserved. Should think him very bad tempered."

[22] "Died Oct. 12, 1831, in 70th year." *Vital Records of West Bridgewater, Massachusetts, to the Year 1850* (Boston, 1911), 217. Snow was still incarcerated in the state prison and died in Charlestown; see *Vital Records of Charlestown*, 2:305.

dren—4 living. 2d wife living. Comfortable property. Can read & write. Ed[ucatio]n not very good. Says he sustained a fair character all his life. Says he has always believed the Bible & now believes firmly. Health poor. Very bad eyes. Says he never drink'd much. Appears to be a harmless sort of an old man, but fear he has not chosen that good part which will make his old age happy.[23]

W[illia]m Seymour—Age 19

Born & brot up New Haven Cn. Mother lives in Hartford Con. When quite young was put out to be a farmer in the country. No Education. Cannot read. Livd with the man 4 ys, then went to Hartford & livd 2 ys. Tended Stable. Then went to New London & livd 6 mo. Then back to Hartford, & from there to this state & work'd on Canal.[24]

2d Comer. Convicted first in Springfield—for stealing watch. Sentenced one year. Out one month, then sentenced in Boston for stealing for 3 ys been here 5 months. Says he behaves well & gets along well. Says he was generally steady—not intemperate. Rather a stupid young man, and yet appears clever & dispos'd to do pretty well. His being ignorance & being thrown young upon the world have probably destroy'd him.[25]

Jonah Spaulding—Age 19

Home in Fitchburg. Can read, not write. Father dead. Mother lives at the East.[26] Has not seen her for 12 ys. Sen-

[23] Cross reference to Snow in volume 2 reads: "Sore eyes, & very infirm."

[24] I.e., the Middlesex Canal. Constructed between 1793 and 1803, the Middlesex Canal provided a waterway between Concord, N.H., and Charlestown, Mass. The last trip on the canal was completed on Nov. 25, 1851. Carl Seaburg et al., *The Incredible Ditch: A Bicentennial History of the Middlesex Canal* (Cambridge, Mass., 1997).

[25] Cross reference in volume 2 notes: "Black man—ignorant."

[26] I.e., in Maine.

tenced in Worster for burning a Carpenter's Shop for 3 ys. Says a parcel of drunken fellows set the shop on fire & because he was out that night they swore he did it. Says he did not do it the [that] he knows of—expects he did not. Is a non compos and a strange genius—seems clever & that is all there is of him. Has been in the cells for quarrelling. The convicts love to [illeg.] upon him.[27]

GEORGE SMITH—AGE 38
Born England. Glassmaker always work'd at that business. No Education. Cannot read. Been in U.S. 5 ys. Says he never was before in any prison. Been here a year & 5 mo. Sentence 2 ys. Not a drunkard. Sentenced of entering a Store. Says he had the goods in possession, but did not take them or know them to be stolen. They were delivered to him by a countryman to carry to Cragie's Bridge.[28] Educated a Catholic. Says he gets along well & is well us'd.

A stupid sort of man tho he does not appear bad.

March 20, 1829

THO[MA]S SNYDER (BLACK)—AGE 25
Born in Worster.[29] Brot up in Boston. Liv'd as waiter 16 ys with Jonas Stone. Can read a little. Cannot write. First con-

[27] Cross reference to Spaulding in volume 2 gives his first name as Jonas and notes: "So much of a non compos that I thought it useless to call him."

[28] Andrew Craigie (1743–1819), apothecary general in the Continental Army, became a financier and land speculator after the American Revolution. Craigie's speculations included the first bridge across the Charles River between Boston and Cambridge. *American National Biography*, 5:657–658.

[29] Thomas Snyder, son of Thomas and Kata-Rodman Snyder, "All Blacks," was born in Worcester on Mar. 12, 1805. *Worcester Births, Marriages and Deaths*, comp. Franklin P. Rice (Worcester, 1894), 238.

finement. Been here 5 mo. Sentence 2 ys & 10 days. Says that until a year ago he was steady & his habits good. Was then led away by bad Co. Never Intemperate. Sentenced for stealing—hat & silver spoons. Says he makes it a point to behave well. Appears like a pretty clever fellow.

Says he recollects my boarding with Mr. Stone 10 years ago.

JOSEPH <*Steavens*> SEAVERNS[30]—AGE 33

Home in Western.[31] Born & brot up there. First offence. Been here 4 mo. Sentence Life. Counterfeit money. Good Com[mon] Ed[ucation]. Follow'd butchering & driving cattle. Says he always sustained a fair character, & never addicted to vice. Us'd to drive cattle to Providence Market. There received seven Hundred Dollars of a man by the name of Lucius Smith, mostly for money he had lent him. Six hundred of which was C[ounterfei]t. Had no suspicion of the fact. Tried & sentenced in Taunton. Has wife & five children—wife a religious, good woman. Got along well, & is determined to behave well at all times. Hopes to get pardoned ere long by the exertions of friends.

Believes the Scriptures and the importance of its truths. Appears like a sensible man, well bred, and of some feeling.

W[ILLIA]M STARKWEATHER—AGE 20

Born & brot up in Norwich Ct. Been here 3 mo. Sentenced 2 years. Decent education. Says he has been tolerably steady & industrious. Livd with his father who is now living in Norwich. Went last fall to the Eastward with a Capt. Kim-

---

[30] Spelled Seaverns in volume 2, where a cross reference notes: "Appears very well."

[31] Joseph, son of Joseph and Elizabeth Seaverns, was born in Weston, Apr. 15, 1796. *Town of Weston: Births, Deaths and Marriages, 1717–1850* (Boston, 1901), 178.

ball. Return'd as far as Boston. There bought 40 dollars worth of Goods of 2 fellows who came to the vessel with some trunks of Goods. Names of the men Davis & Brooks. Strangers to him, but who he afterwards learn'd had both been in this prison. Carried the goods to the house where he boarded. As he was going from Boston by land in Stage & there the goods were recognis'd & he apprehended. Says he was never addicted to drinking at all. Is a young man of sense. Does not seem to have as much sensibility as some. Still converses well. Says he has no Bible or Testament in his room & should be glad of one.

JOB THAYER[32]—AGE 72
Says most of his ancestors & family have liv'd to a great age. An uncle, who was his next neighbour died lately aged 102.

Good com[mon] Education. Farmer. Also work'd a good deal at ship-building. Married when 30. Wife now dead. Died since he came here. 3 Children. Says he has been an industrious, hardworking man. Says he was respected by some & by some he was not. Says that Old Harry could not live on good terms with them.

2d Comer. Sentenced for an attempt to murder the first time—1 year. 2d time for a similar crime. Sen 15 ys. Been here between 7 & 8 years. Says he has always behavd well here, & got along well. A very strange old man. Very passionate. Full of fire & venom. Hates the old testament. Says the new will do. No man shall ever impose on him. He will

[32]"Job Thayer, 73 y, convict in State Prison, Charlestown, d. there Feb. 1, 1830." *Vital Records of Charlestown*, 2:303. See also Entries of Convicts in the State Prison, Charlestown, Mass., 1805–1818, no. 894; Commitment Register, Charlestown State Prison, 1818–1840, no. 366, Massachusetts State Archives. These records indicate that he was born in Braintree, Massachusetts.

have his revenge. Prison the best place for him. Health feeble. Says that Federals & Jews ought all to be driven from the face of the earth.[33]

Benj[ami]n Thompson—Age 31

Born & brot up in Maine. Before coming to prison had no learning. Can now read. 3d Comer. 1st time 2 ys. 2d time 2 ys. 3d over 8 ys. Sentence Life.

Left parents when young. Went into US Army & was in the Army during the whole war under Gens Brown[34] & Wilkinson.[35] Says he had been very wild & dissipated & livd a wicked life. Bad women did more to corrupt & ruin him then anything else. Says he has been a hard character here & behav'd bad. Is sensible that he has been very foolish & wicked in so doing. Is determin'd hereafter to take a different course & behave well. Hopes he shall sometime or other get pardoned. Is frank & has good natural talents.[36]

Moses Thompkins—Age 39

Home in Adams, Berkshire Co. Wife & 3 children there. Poor man. Work'd at shoemaking. Been here 3 ys & 9 mo.

---

[33]Cross reference to Thayer in volume 2 indicates: "The most incorrigible and God-forsaken man that I ever yet found—malicious, impudent, saucy, defying God & man."

[34]Gen. Jacob Brown, New York militia officer and commander of an attempt to invade Canada in 1814. Francis F. Beirne, *The War of 1812* (New York, 1949), 166–167, 225–229, 250–263.

[35]Gen. James Wilkinson, who commanded a failed American invasion of Canada during the War of 1812. *American National Biography*, 23:400–402.

[36]Cross reference to Thompson in volume 2 speculates: "Suspect he has a brother, John, in Auburn prison. Both are from Maine, and resemble each other, and this man says he has a brother John who went West. I know John well if it be the same & a very hard fellow, as this Benjn, I fear, is also. 3d comer."

Sentence 7 ys. Here once before. Confin'd then 2 ys & 8 mo. Can read & write. Education Poor. Says he was a steady young man. After he was married lost what little property he had. This afflicted him a good deal & he took to drinking which was the cause of all his subsequent misfortunes. Says he has never been in any trouble here for misconduct.

Is an Infidel in sentiment. Says he got his infidelity in prison by reading infidel Books. Never read any Books in favour of Religion. Thinks religion a good thing to regulate human conduct. Does not believe that God governs the world, or there would not be so much evil & confusion in it. Should think him a man of not much mind. Is very feeble in health and appears like a harmless sort of a man.

March 21, 1829

JACKSON TREADWELL—[AGE 16]

Says his name is Treadwell Jackson. Age 16. Born & brot up in N.Y. Has follow'd the sea. Has been to school. Can read, not write. Attended Sab[bath] school in N.Y. 2 or 3 mo. Mother is living in N.Y. Father is dead. Says he has been a wild boy. Went with bad Co. In Bridewell once for Stealing. Been here 2 ys. Sentence 3 ys. Been punish'd once. Has got along in general well. Mother us'd to bind him out, but he would run away. Says he has been a very bad boy, & is sorry for it. Intended hereafter to do well. He is very open hearted & frank & professes considerable sensibility.

SAM[UE]L T. THAYER—AGE 41

Home in Plainfield, Hamp[shire] Co. Wife & 8 children. Comfortable property. Farmer. Workd at shoemaking some.

Decent common Ed[ucation]. Character always good till 5 ys ago. Has been a leader of singing in the Congregation—a tything man in the Town &c.

Been here 2½ ys, Sentence 3. Convicted of Larceny at <*N.H.*> Northhampton. Intemperance led to it. Has never been call'd up or reprimanded since he has been here. Leads the singing in Chapel. Says he is fully determin'd on a correct course after he goes from here. Says he was well brot up & his parents did their duty to him. The fault is his own wholly. He is a sensible man & talks with much propriety.[37]

George C. Thompson, alias Towsley—Age 63
Home in Canada. Born & brot up in Salisbury Ct. Livd in Canada 15 ys. Is a farmer. Never married. Lives with a brother in Can[ad]a. No property. Decent com[mon] Ed[ucation]. Says he was always steady & industrious till within a few years, then began to drink too much. 2d offence. 1st time here 1 yr. Out 20 mo. 2d time been here 9 mo. Sen[tenced] 1 year.

Larceny both times. Says he is ashamed of himself & hopes he shall never repeat his bad practices. Says he is formerly persuaded of the truths of the Bible & is sensible that he has abus'd Gods goodness, & violated his commands. No difficulty here. Never call'd to an account for any thing.

Is a sensible man and converses well, and it is probable that if he would avoid intemperance that he would do well. Think he shall, but it is to be fear'd he is too old & too far gone to reform.

[37] Cross reference to Thayer in volume 2 notes: "Term expires Oct. 15 [1829]."

March 23, 1829

Dyer Vespasian—Age 38
Born in Michigan. Indian, of the Pequod Tribe, almos[t] full Blood. Brot up in Westfield, Mass. Ed[ucation] poor. Read some, not write. Learnd no trade. When young livd as servant in a Gentleman's family. Afterwards went to sea. Always wild. Got to drinking too much & that ruin'd him. 3d Offence. 1st time 1 year for Larceny. Out 1 year. 2d time—3 years. Out 1 year. 3d time—sentence 3 ys. with an additional sentence for life. All for Stealing. Married. Has wife & 1 child. Has been here the last time 8 ys. Says he gets along well here & is never punish'd. Appears like a good hearted fellow. Says he is very sick of crime & a prison.[38]

Calvin Spelman—Age 47
Home—Granville. Born & brot up there. Decent common Ed[ucatio]n. Brot up to farming. Wife dead.[39] Has had 11 Children—7 living. Contracted a habit of Intemperance pretty early in life.

Sentenced for an attempt to rape, for 10 ys. Says he never made such an attempt. Acknowledges that he was to blame in making a base proposition to the girl, but he offered no violence. Was partially intoxicated at the time. Never before accused of crime. Been here almost 2 years. Got along well here. Believes the Bible to be the word of

---

[38] Cross reference in volume 2 confirms: "Indian." See also Entries of Convicts in the State Prison, Charlestown, Mass., 1805–1818, nos. 534 and 801; and Commitment Register, Charlestown State Prison, 1818–1840, no. 339, Massachusetts State Archives. These records show two different birthplaces: New York City and Westfield, Massachusetts.

[39] Calvin Spelman and Catherine Steward indicated their intention to marry, Apr. 20, 1801. *Vital Records of Granville, Massachusetts, to the Year 1850* (Boston, 1914), 157.

God. Is a sensible man and converses well. Has, I am told, been rather a troublesome man in society on account of his Intemperate habits. Ruin'd by intemperance and is no doubt *Guilty*.

JOSIAH VEASEY[40]—AGE 24

Born & brot up in Boston. Parents both living. Education good. Never learn'd a trade. Work'd 2 ys with father at Horse-shoeing. When he was 14 his father faild in business. Run into intemperate & vicious habits. Neglected his family. Got into the house of correction &c &c. This threw him on the world without a guide. He got into bad Co. & bad habits himself & finally to this place. Was pardoned out. Went home to his mother, but soon got with old prison associates, one of whom broke a store and because he boarded with him & was found in his Company, he was apprehended & sent back to prison. Was out only about 6 weeks. Says he was not Guilty. Acknowledges that his associating with bad Co. brot him here. Is a young man of fine personal appearance and good mind, but his mind has been much corrupted. Says infidel Books have poisoned his mind. Could formerly get as many as he pleas'd through some of the officers. Not so now. Is sensible of his folly. I fear a ruin'd young man.

JOSIAH WALLIS—AGE 46

Born & brot [up] of Con. Home in Gen[essee] Co. N.Y. Says he is *partly* married. Did not mean to be. Can read & write. Ed[ucatio]n poor. Farmer & Shoemaker.

Says he was always pretty steady & industrious, & never had a lazy hair of his head. Went into State of N.Y. in 1805. Convicted in Springfield 1824 in May for Larceny. Sen-

[40] "Josiah Vesey, Jr., prisoner in State Prison, d. there, Aug. 4, 1831." *Vital Records of Charlestown*, 2:313.

tence 5 years. Been in Cells 15 days or about that, for smoking. Is a strange fellow. Mighty innocent, and yet as full of revenge as he can be & as proud spirited as Lucifer. Came into this State to see his friends. Probably is an old State Prison character.

JOHN WILLIAMS—AGE 19
Sentenced in Cambridge for Stealing for 2 ys been here 17 mo. Ed[ucation]n poor. Born in Portland. Father moved a good many ys ago to State of N.Y. He went with him has not liv'd with him much. Has been wild & unsteady. Set out to go to Portland from St of N.Y. to see a Brother. Stole some watches for which he was sent here. Is a hard boy. Stupid. Does not believe the Scriptures, & seems to have very little sensibility. Fear he is a ruin'd boy.

JAMES WATERMAN—AGE 29.
Born in Eng. Been in U.S. 11 ys. Seaman. No Education. Left parents early. Bound to Sea Capt. Was ignorant, wild, headstrong, & vicious. Drink'd to excess.

2d Comer. In 1822, Sept, convicted Boston of Larceny. Sentence 2 ys. Out about 3 months, then Sentenced again for 14 ys for Larceny. Been here 4 ys. Says he was a hard character when here the first time. Last time has got along well & means to behave well in future. Is frank & open, but probably from old habits, a hopeless case.

JESSE BRADBURY—call'd on me to day in distress of mind for his sins as he said. Had been a good deal troubled for 6 weeks. Talk'd with him & gave him such advise & instruction as I thought his case required.

JOHN WILLIAMS (BLACK MAN) ALIAS—KIAR—goes by the name of Kiar here. Came here by that name the first time—[Age 33]

2d Of[fence]. First time 2 ys. Out 11 days at liberty. 3 months before he return'd here. Been here now 9 ys. Sentence out next month then has 120 days to serve for having been in the cells. Age 33 ys. Home N. Hampshire.

First conviction says he was not guilty. Got him for being in bad company. Last time guilty. Good character when young & was steady till 18, then went to sea got bad habits & by bad co[mpany] led to this prison. Here became still worse. Is now sick of vice & is fully determind never to commit another crime. Says he went away the first time as wicked & savage as a person could be. Did not care what he did. Can read, write a little. Wishes me to speak to the Warden to take off some of his 120 days. Fear he is a hard case.

March 24, 1829

W[ILLIA]M C. TODD—AGE 21

Been here 5 mo. Sentence 15 mo. Convicted in Boston. Born there. Has liv'd mostly in Reading. Learn'd trade of Carpenter. Can read & write. Ed[ucatio]n poor. Mother died when he was 4, father when he was 7. Had step mother, & when his father died, his step-mother turned him out of house & he had to shirk for himself. His Guardian bound him out. Says he was pretty steady till 16 or 17, then left his master & became unsteady. Convicted for stealing Rigging in Charlestown. Says he never committed but one theft before—was not detected in that. Promises fair as to the future—says he is determind on a correct life. Is frank & does not appear hard.[41]

---

[41]Cross reference to Todd in volume 2 gives his name as William E. Todd.

Joseph Whipple—Age 26

Born & brot up in Boston. Parents dead—no relations nearer than cousin. Can read a very little—cannot write. No trade. Had no regular business & livd a very unsteady life. 2d Com[er]. 1st time 2 ys. At Liberty 8 days. Sentenced 2d time for 5 ys. Been here 4. Says that at about 15 he run into all sorts of mischief & gave himself up to it. Has been punish'd a good deal here—mostly the first part of his confinement.

Is, I fear a very hard case—though frank & pleasant. Says he thinks he shall never get to prison again.

Henry Woods—Age 54

Born & brot up in Acton in this County.[42] Has not lived there since 21. Never married. Has follow'd the Sea most of the time. Can read, write, & cypher. Says that until he came here the first time, he had been a pretty steady man. Was not guilty. Being here the first time fitted him for subsequent wickedness & villainy. 3d Comer. 1st time Highway robbery, pardoned in consequence of its being made certain that he was not guilty. Says the man who swore against him afterwards confess'd that he swore falsely. Confin'd first time 11 mo. Out about 6 mo. Then sentenced again in Boston 6 mo out then 1 year. 3d time 7 ys. Been here 4 ys. Was here another time besides 6 years. Says he has got along with little or no punishments for the whole time. Says he has been confind 14 ys in the whole. He must then have been here once more than he states. Suspect him to have very little feeling and is most likely a thoroughly corrupt & hardened man.

---

[42]Henry Woods was born in Acton, Feb. 18, 1777, the son of Moses and Kezia Woods. *Vital Records of Acton, Massachusetts, to the Year 1850* (Boston, 1923), 121.

Says Esq Jarvis[43] once put him into the Cells 77 days for an unnatural Crime of which he calls God to witness he was innocent.

Register says he is a fifth comer.

MARK WINSLOW—AGE 48

Born & brot up in Barre Worster Co. Left there 1810. Has been a respectable man in Society. Been Capt. in the Militia. Handsome property. Good Com[mon] Education. Wife but no children. <*Lef*> Lived some in N. Orleans, traded there. His partner went off with $7000. Was owner of some vessels. Was very unfortunate & lost most of his property. Let to Gambling some, tho he says he did not lose property in this way. Not intemperate. <*Here 2d time*> Once in Boston Jail for counterfeiting. Says—N.G.

Been here 2 ys & 7 mo. Sentence on 2 Indictments 3 ys each for counterfeit money. Got along well here. Believes in the Bible & in future rewards & punishments. Is a man of good sense & attainments & might be a very useful man. Says his mind is fully made up to be a virtuous man, as he knows that no other course can make him happy. His past aberrations have always made him miserable & he knows that vice must, from its very nature, make man so.

ORRIN WEBBER—AGE 27

Born & brot up in Brimfield.[44] Farmer. Parents both alive. Mother in St of N.Y. Father & mother separated when he was quite young. He was bound out. The man with whom he lived was very profane. When he was 6 ys old the man

---

[43] William C. Jarvis, Esq., a director of the prison. *Massachusetts Register* (1828), 162.

[44] Orlin [sic] Webber, daughter [sic?] of Nabby Bement, was born in Brimfield, Feb. 26, 1802. Oren Weber and Relief Harper of Sturbridge published their intention to marry on Feb. 20, 1838. *Vital Records of Brimfield, Massachusetts, to the Year 1850* (Boston, 1931), 146, 254.

died. He was then thrown upon the town. Select men bound him out to a man <*who abused him*>. Father & mother both married again. The man to whom he was last bound abused him and he usd to run away.

Learning poor—read & write poorly. Says he was good to work but unsteady & wild. First confinement been here 3 ys & 10 mo. Sentence 4 ys. Sentenced in Springfield for Larceny. Says he believes in the truth of the Bible, & feels its importance. Says he is sensible of his folly is determin'd to do well hereafter.

Says he was never intemperate. Says he has got along well in general.

Appears soft & tender & I think is now fully resolvd on a correct course. How far he may carry his resolutions into actions time will show. He attributes all his misfortunes to being thrown on the world as he was when a child, without father or mother to watch over & [illeg.] him.

March 25, 1829

Amos Warren—Age 51

Born in Charlestown and brot up in and about the Town.[45] Education good. Father & Mother both living in Medford, in good circumstances. Educated to Shoemaking. Says he was an industrious young man & respectable. Livd in West Cambridge till near 30 ys of age. 3d Comer. First time for forgery 8 ys. Out 2 years. Then sentenced 4 ys. Then out 3 or 4 mo. Then sentenced 5 ys. Been here 3 ys.

Has been married 3 times. 1st wife got Bill from him. 2d wife dead. 3d wife living. 5 Children. During the last con-

[45] Amos Warren, Jr., son of Amos and Elizabeth (Whittemore) Warren, who published his intention to marry Susanna Frost of Cambridge, Oct. 31, 1802. *Vital Records of Charlestown,* 1:514; Thomas Bellows Wyman, *The Genealogies and Estates of Charlestown* (Boston, 1879), 2:997.

finement has been punish'd only 2 days. Formerly punished goo[d] Deal. Deacon Warren of Charlestown is his Uncle.[46] I should expect him to be a hard case though he converses very well.

Jacob Whitmarsh—Age 32

Born & brot up in Plymth Co.[47] Decent com[mon] Ed[ucation]. Father died when he was 4. Lived with mother most of the time till he was of age. She is now living. He has wife & 4 Children.

2d time. 1st time 8 mo. Out 12 ys. Been here last time 2½ ys. Sentence Life for C[ounterfei]t Money. Talks like a man of sense. Says he has never enjoy'd any thing in such a life as he has liv'd & is thoroughly convinced that a life of vice is a life of misery. Was a wild young man. Has dealt considerably in C[ounterfei]t money, but says that the man who swore against him testified falsely. He did not have the money of him although, previously to this he had let him have bad money.

March 26, 1829

Tho[ma]s Watson (Blk)—Age 17

Born & brot up in Providence R.I. Brot up to farming. No parents. Bound out. Person to whom bound agreed to give him schooling but did not. No learning. Cannot read. Left Providence about 2 ys ago & came on to Boston. Was enticed away.

Says he was pretty steady and never got into any trouble

---

[46]Deacon Isaac Warren. Wyman, *Genealogies and Estates of Charlestown*, 2:995; Timothy T. Sawyer, *Old Charlestown: Historical, Biographical, Reminiscent* (Boston, 1902), 107.

[47]Jacob Whitmarsh, son of Levi and Hannah Whitmarsh, was born in Abington, Dec. 24, 1796. He married Betsy Crooker, probably of East Bridgewater, on Jan. 29, 1818. *Vital Records of Abington*, 1:246, 2:231.

till he came onto Boston. There got into bad company & was led to stealing. Been here about 2 ys. Sentence, Life. Burglary. Led on by man much older than he was. Got along well here. Been in cells once 5 days. Appears to be a tolerably clever boy.

Joseph Wells—(Blk)—Age 23

Born in Connecticut. About 12 ys ago, parents moved into Franklin Co. Mass. Parents been dead one 3 & the other 5 ys. Generally work'd at farming. Has been to sea some. Education poor. Can read a little. Cannot write. Says he was rather wild. Liked a frolick now & then, but he had never before the crime which brot him here, been guilty of any crime. Been here almost 2 ys. Sentenced in Lennox for life. Burglary. Been confined in Cell once. He says for breaking stone. Rather a stupid black. Discover nothing particularly bad. Hopes he may some time or other get pardon'd if he behaves well.

G.F. Weems—Age 26

Native place, Virginia. Home & property in District of Col. Mother living. Father not. Collegiate Ed[ucation] at Princeton N.J.[48] Entered very young at 14. Left during Sen year. Read Physic. Became associated with those older than himself & who moved in the gay and fashionable circle. Became very dissipated. Lived to a very great length, what is termed a life of Pleasure in Philadelphia, till his friends removed him. After staying a considerable length of time in Maryland with an Uncle engaging in politics and travelling about, a sort of Gentleman at large he came up to N. York.

[48]George Weems attended Princeton with the class of 1817 but dropped out his junior year. Princeton University Archives. See also Commitment Register, Charlestown State Prison, 1818–1840, no. 889, Massachusetts State Archives.

There ran a grand round of dissipation also. After a time lost a Brother whom he lov'd most tenderly. This event stopt him in his dissipation. Became gloomy. Turned his mind to Religion. Got acquainted with & studied some with Two clergymen there. Finally resolved to come to the North. Had first rate recommendations from several gentlemen of high standing. Came on to this State & joined the Theological institution at Andover. Was there 1½ year. Was urged to supply a Clergyman's pulpit one Sabbath. Had the consent of Doct Wood.[49] After this preach'd several times elsewhere—in Boston once. His purpose was ever to become an Epis[copa]l Clerg[yma]n. This is but a very imperfect sketch of his relation.

JOHN WEST—AGE 30

Born in Maine. Has resided in this state about 12 ys. Trade a Machinist, and a first rate workman. Dec[en]t com[mon] Ed[ucation]. Until about 2 or 3 ys, habits good, & character respectable. Married at 21, in Boston. Wife lives there now—2 children. Ascribes all his misfortunes to Intemperance—got into this habit in R. Island. Liv'd in a very dissipated place. Got along well here.

Says he has no doubt of the truth of Bible. Sentenced in Boston 14 mo ago, for 3 ys. Since in prison, has got along well and had no difficulty. West is a man of sense, and of great mechanical ingenuity and might be one if the most useful men in Society. He thinks, were he to regain his freedom, he should never drink any more. He doubtless feels so now. And could he be temperate, I doubt whether he would run again into crime. But such cases are almost hopeless ones. Is very frank & appears well.

---

[49] Leonard Woods (1774–1854), Congregational clergyman, moderate Calvinist, professor of theology at Andover Theological Seminary, 1808–1846. *American National Biography*, 23:813–815.

Charles White[50]—Age 24

Home in Easttown, Mass. Born & brot up there. Work'd some on farm & some in furnace. Never married. Decent com[mon] Education. Parents brot him up well. Steady & <*and*> industrious till a short time before he committed the crime for which he was sentenced. Stole a horse. Sentence 3 ys. Been here 13 mo. Had become intemperate in some measure. Has had no difficulty here. Says he never observed Sabbath as he ought.

March 27, 1829

Josiah White Jr—Age 24

Brother of Charles White on the preceding pages.[51] Brot up in the same manner as his brother. Never intemperate. Workd in furnace & therefore never was in the habit of going to meeting on the Sabbath much or regarding Sabbath. Otherwise, says his habits were generally good. Says, not guilty. Indicted with & for the same offence as his brother. Says his brother took the Horse, but he himself has no hand in the transaction. Sentence 2 years. Got along well here. Not much feeling or sensibility.

John W. Wilson—Age 29

Born in Scotland but parents moved to Eng when he was very young. Was brot up there. Always follow'd the sea. Decent com[mon] Education. Says that he had been respectable & had commanded a vessel 4 ys for a Merchant in Trinidad. Never intemperate. Went into the Naval service of the Republic of Venezuela in S. Am. Was brot into

[50] "Charles White, convict in State Prison, Charlestown, d. there, d. Sept. 19, 1834." *Vital Records of Charlestown,* 2:287.

[51] See the preceding entry.

Boston in the charge of piracy. Lay in prison 2 ys. Spent his all. Was acquitted and thrown moneyless among strangers except the deprav'd inmates of his prison. Sentenced for passing C[ounterfei]t money.

Has wife & one child in S. America. Intends going there as soon as discharged. Is a man of intelligence. Being among strangers & moneyless & having formed an acquaintance with rogues in prison, he was led away & landed in this prison as a result.

JOHANNES VAN VAUGHT—AGE 42
Born in Holland. Been in U.S. 6 ys. Seaman. Can read & write Dutch. Been in prison 4½ ys. Sentence 7 ys. 3 indictments for stealing clothes, from 3 diff. people. Got along well here. Works with team outside.

Seems to be a clever sort of fellow. Talks broken. Thinks he shall steer his bark differently if ever lives to get out.

March 30, 1829

JOEL WHITTIMORE—AGE 31
Born in N.H., but had livd in Boston 17 ys. Has kept Grocery store some time & followed Trucking some. Married. Wife & 4 Children. Decent Education. Father a christian man, & brot up his children well. Says his habits were always good. Never intemperate, and always industrious. Bot a watch of a young fellow now here, which he had taken from a Jewellers Store. Did not know the watch was stolen. After the things were advertised, suspected that the watch had been stolen, and ought to have made it known but did not & Nash[52] having told where the watch was, he was arrested, and Sentenced for 3 ys. Been here 1 year. Had no trouble here for misconduct.

---

[52] Presumably inmate Elias Nash. See below, p. 145.

Appears to be more than ordinarily serious and thoughtful, & his mind tender on serious subjects. Appears humble & on the whole very well. Mr. Whitney, No. 1 Dock Square, his prosecutor, wishes I would see him.[53]

George Watkins—Age 27

Born & brot up in Douglass.[54] Read poorly, but cannot write. Education very poor. Parents liv'd a good ways from school. He was subject to fits, & did not go to school much. Brot up to farming till 20, then worked at Carpenter's business. Married—2 Children.

Says he was steady & industrious till 18. Lovd a certain young woman very much. Her parents opposed his marrying her but thinks he should have succeeded if she had liv'd. Her death affected him very much & he did not much care what became of him. Went off into the state of N.Y. & wandered about a spell, then returned. Continu'd unsteady. Gambled & drink'd some. Got married finally. After a while another man claim'd his wife as his. Found that he had a right to her. Drinkd then harder. Finally passed a note drawn by another man, which was a forgery & sent here for 3 ys. Been here near a year.

Thinks this will cure him of his wildness.

March 31, 1829

John Wilson—Age 29

Born & brot up until 11 ys old in Scotland. Servd an apprenticeship <*on*> in the sea service. Served in that busi-

---

[53]Moses Whitney, watchmaker, 1 Dock Square, Boston. *Town Directory* (1829), 284.

[54]George Augustine Watkins, son of Zacheus and Susanna Watkins, was born in Douglas, July 1, 1802. He published his intention to marry Mehaley Kelley, Mar. 11, 1820, and Ophelia Stearns, Jan. 14, 1832. *Vital Records of Douglas, Massachusetts, to the End of the Year 1849* (Worcester, 1906), 68, 157, 158.

ness 8 ys. Ed[ucatio]n poor. Can read & write a little. Got into habit of drinking & was led away by bad Co. Been in prison 10 mo. Sentenced in Boston for 1 yr. Time expires in May. First offence. Seems to a very clever, honest hearted fellow, & thinks he shall never get into any more trouble if the Lord spares his life to get out. Has never been called up here for any misconduct.

EBEN[EZE]R WHITTEMORE—[AGE 40]
Born & Brot up in Worster Co. Age 40. Ed[ucatio]n rather poor. Can read & write some. Farmer. Never married. Father died when 4, mother when he was 3 ys old. After their death, lived with a sister who was married & continued with her till 15, then went to live with Mr Laws till 21. Since then have liv'd in various places. Got rather unsteady. Says he threw an axe <*into*> at a horse which got into his Lot. Was mad, & had been drinking some or should not have done it. Wounded the horse dreadfully & for this was sentenced to this prison. Been here about 6 mo. Sentence 18 mo. Never in prison before. Gets along well here. Says he has not regarded the Sabbath or attended public worship as he ought before he came here. Attended sometimes.

Is a singular sort of a man. Appears good natured & frank, but ignorant & odd.

STEPHEN WAIT—AGE 18
Born in England, but came to US with parents when 6. Went to Vt, where he was brot up & where parents now live. Ed[ucatio]n pretty good. At 14 <*got wild lo*> got wild & left father, thinking he would do better. Went first to Canada & from there to N.Y. Went to sea & followed this till near the time of getting into this difficulty. Says he was not intemperate. Had been cast away & had lost most or all he had. Wanted some clothes to go to Sea, and took some

without leave. Sentenced in Boston. Been here 5 mo. Sentence 1 year.

Should think him rather stupid, & careless. Thinks, however, that he shall be a steadier man here after.

<*Stephen Wait*> MALACHI WICKSON—AGE 23
Born & brot up in Bristol Co. Ed[ucatio]n decent. Has follow'd the sea most of the time since he was 14. Been rather wild but not particularly vicious. Never intemperate. Sentenced for running away with a Schooner belonging to his uncle. Uncle ow'd him & would not pay him & to be revenged, run off with his vessel, & left it when he had accomplish'd his end. Sentenced 18 mo. Been here 11 mo. Got along well here. Should think him rather wild, thoughtless & stupid.

W[ILLIA]M WATERHOUSE—AGE 32
Born & brot up in Rutland N.H.[55] Decent com[mon] Ed[ucatio]n. Servd an apprenticeship of 7 ys in Albany at the coachmaking business. Married. Wife & 2 chil[dre]n in Rutland. First offence. Never in prison before. Sentenced in Oct. last for 1 year. Got along well in prison. Never reproved for misconduct. Says he was a man of general good habits & character & has work'd hard. Went with some unsteady fellows to keep 4th of July & contrary to his usual habits got too much drink & committed a Larceny. Next morning when he was sober, repented of the act, gave up the money voluntarily, & settled it. But was prosecuted & pleaded guilty. Appears very humble & deeply sensible of his offence & few prisoners appear as well. I think he is determined to do well.

[55] Presumably Rutland, Vermont.

April 1, 1829

JOHN WOODS—AGE 28

<*has*> Born in Ireland. When 15 came here with father to N. Brunswick. Been in U.S. 8 ys. Brot up a Shoemaker. Decent common Education. Says he never gambled and rarely drank too much. Has been steady, honest, & industrious. Married. Has 2 children. Wife lives in Franklin.[56] Says that getting *too much liquor* was the source of his getting here. Convicted of an assault to kill. Says he had no such intention. Sentence 20 years. Been here 5 mo. Does not appear to be a hard fellow. Talks very well.

IRA WARREN[57]—AGE 30

Born in Bridgewater, Mass. When about 6 father moved down to Maine. Continued with him till 20, then his father gave him his time & he came back to his native place & has since lived there & in the vicinity. Brot up chiefly to farming. Married. Has 1 child. For 5 or 6 ys past has been intemperate—some part of the time very much so. This has been the cause of all his misfortunes. Education poor. Can read, write very poorly. Says he has been a pretty hard working man. Says he has livd well with his family except when he was in liquor, then was abusive. Says his wife is a clever good woman. Sentenced for 7 ys in Dedham. Been here near 5 mo. Had no difficulty here.

Says he has determin'd to drink no more as long as he

---

[56]John Woods married Persis Johnson in Franklin, Mar. 10, 1825. *The Record of Births, Marriages and Deaths in the Town of Franklin from 1778 to 1872*, ed. Orestes T. Doe (Franklin, Mass., 1898), 102.

[57]Commitment Register, Charlestown State Prison, 1818–1840, no. 1013, Massachusetts State Archives.

lives. Denies being guilty. Convicted of Bestiality. Appears decently.

Edward Butler—Age 27

Parents died when he was 5 ys old. Was bound out. No education of any consequence. Can read but not write. Born in Boston & has lived there and in vicinity most of his life. Work'd at Brickmaking, teaming, &c &c. Never married. Says he has always work'd hard. First offence. Been here 2 months. Sentence 9 months.

Says he has drink'd too freely & that has brot him here. Stole 3 pints of Rum. Wept very freely. Says he can now see his folly and hopes this confinement will be a warning to him. Appears very well.

Emory Delano—Age 23

Born & brot up in Randolph <*has*>. Is an illegitimate son. Never knew his father. His mother is living, but never took any care of him. Was thrown upon the Town. When he was 6 ys old, was bound out. Learned shoemaker's trade. Did not stay with man to whom he was bound till 21. Has work'd a little while at a time here & there. Education very poor. Early in life began to drink too much. One day quarrelled with a man with whom he work'd. Both of them had drink'd to[o] much. In the affray he stabb'd him. Sentenced for 1 year. Been here about 1 month. Is not usually a bright young man. Ruined by ardent spirits. Says he ought to be here & he hopes it will cure him of drinking.

G.W. Langdon—Age 33

Born & brot up in N. Hampshire. Carpenter by trade. Decent com[mo]n Ed[ucatio]n. Never married. Liv'd in this state about 5 ys, mostly in Boston. Before coming to Boston was pretty shady. After he came there began to run after bad women and after a while to stealing. Says he never stole anything till within 3 years. Been confind in the city prison once before for 6 mo. Never in State prison before—any where. Is a man of good sense & some little feeling.

F.W. Adlington—[Age 38]

Been here a little more than a month. Sentenced in Dedham for stabbing a man with a penknife for 18 mo. Age 38. Born in Boston, & has lived there & in the neighboring counties a great portion of his time. A Tailor by trade. Has kept a shop in Boston & in one or two other places. Also kept an Eng. goods store about a year in Cornhill-Boston in Co. with one Larkin. Decent Ed[ucatio]n. Father died when he was 5. Mother been dead 18 years. Large family 13 children. Was poor. When 14 went to serve an apprenticeship with a tailor, & continu'd with him till 21. Then left & set up Business for self. Succeeded very well. Left this business & engaged in the Dry goods business. This was about the close of the late war. Failed in business & since that time has been very unfortunate—in everything he has engaged in. Soon after starting in business married. Had 5 Children. Wife & 4 children dead. One daughter, 14 is living. His troubles led to intemperance & this to his present situation.

Is a man of sense & some feeling, but I fear, utterly a lost man.

W[illia]m M. Freeman—Age 44

Born & brot up in Wrentham & that his home. Farmer, Nailer, & has worked a good deal as a Machinist. Good common Ed[ucatio]n. Never married. Never in State prison before. Says he has been rather an unsteady man. Travelled about a good deal & been to sea some. Has been intemperate & ascribes his misfortunes to this cause. Convicted of stealing 4 lbs of cheese. Says he has no doubt he took it but being in liquor he has no knowledge of the fact. Sentence 1 year. Been here a little more than a month. Is a man of good sense, pleasant, but has not much sensibility.

REUBEN BLOOD—AGE 26

Born <*& brot up*> in the State of N.H. Cooper by trade. Has work'd at farming considerably. Lived in this State since he was 7. Can read, write, & cypher. Has been a steady hard working man. Never in any trouble before this. Says he never pass'd a counterfeit Bill till last Winter. Pass'd only 3 Bills. Had 50 Doll of Bad money. Got it in N.H. Sentenced in Boston to 3 ys & 20 days confinement here. Been here about 19 days.

Should think him rather a novice in crime & not very hard, tho he has not all the sensibility that could be wishd.

May 1, 1829

ABNER ANDERSON—TRUE NAME—HE SAYS IS ATHERTON—AGE 24

First confinement. Home Dedham.[58] Parents live there. Decent education. Workd at Black & White Smithing till in his 20th year.

Parents poor. Says he was brought up well. Us'd to attend church regularly. Attended a Sab[bath] School one winter. Habits as good as those of most young men. Been in this prison 22 mo. Sen. 3½ ys for taking a pocket Book. Sentenced in Boston. For 3 or 4 ys before coming here was at the Southard most of his time. What first led him astray

[58]Abner Atherton, son of Abner and Catharine Atherton, was born in Dedham, Oct. 23, 1804. *The Record of Births, Marriages and Death . . . in the Town of Dedham*, ed. Don Gleason Hill (Dedham, 1886), 148.

was his being led away by some unprincipled young men in Boston to go after lewd women. From this to the crime which brought him here. Says he has never been reported for misconduct since his confinement.

Expresses a belief that, when discharged, he shall never again run into vice. Says he was never intemperate. Believes the Bible.

Appears, on the whole better than multitudes, and still not all that sensibility which it would be pleasant to see. Nothing hard or bitter in his feelings.

JONATHAN BULLOCK—AGE 45
Born & brot up in Rehoboth till 19. Work'd at farming, then went to sea. Has been to Sea, about 7 ys off & on. Had very poor advantages for Ed[ucation]. Can barely read, cannot write. Father died when he was 15. Was poor—& his early advantages for improvements.[59] Became wild on going to seas & intemperate . . .[60]

3d Comer. First time in 1813—for 2 ys & 20 ds. Served the time out. Out about 18 mo. Then sentenced for 2 ys & 8 ds. Served it out. Then out 8 mo, & was again sentenced for 4 ys & 20 days & since here a life sentence for being a 3 comer. Been here 9½ years. Professes to be a pious man. Was baptiz'd here in prison by Mr. Collier[61] about 5 ys ago. Sentenced in Taunton. Thinks he experienced religion while he was in prison at that place before his last conviction.

Is now in the Sab[bath] School in prison. Is ignorant, and withal his intellect is not the brightest. He appears honest & sincere, & his conduct as a convict is good & I

---

[59]Thus in text.

[60]Ellipsis points appear in text.

[61]Rev. William Collier, a Baptist minister and Curtis's predecessor as the prison's chaplain. *Massachusetts Register* (1828), 162.

have no doubt his fix'd purpose is to live honestly hereafter. How he would succeed, were he at liberty, is known only to Him who knows all things. He hopes to be pardoned this spring, but as he has no friends out who can aid him, & as he is a third comer, his chance is not very fair.

He relies upon his long confinement & good conduct. I wish there were no worse convicts here than Bullock.

John Bradford—Age 22

Home in Philadelphia. Born in Scotland. Came over 10 ys ago. Father now lives in Ph[iladelphi]a. Good common Ed[ucatio]n. Weaver by profession. Was a steady boy till he came to U.S. About 5 ys ago left his father without his leave and came to N.Y. & from there to Boston. <*Since*> First conviction, Larceny. Sentenced in Boston for 3 ys. Been here 20 mo. Been punish'd slightly once & once only. Was very free in conversation, & I hardly know what to think of him. Am however inclined to believe he has been a wild young man & am fearful he does not feel exactly as he ought. Says he thinks he shall lead a different life hereafter.

John Blann—Age 30

Born in Maryland. When 9 ys old lost parents and since that time has had no home. Education very poor. Can read, not write. After he was 9, wandered about in different States till he was 19, then went to Sea & follow'd that for most of the time till he got to prison. 2d conviction. 1st time one year. Out short of month, then sentenced for 6 years. Been here 6 ys & 3 mo—the last 3 on an additional sentence. Has 3 more to stay. Says he has been a wild man, & a wicked man very profane. Not intemperate. Constitution would not bear it. Run after bad women.

From the best I can gather he has been a very, wild, thoughtless, unprincipled, & wicked fellow & I fear he is all that now. According to his own story he has been confin'd in the cell for misconduct more than 100 days. Is, I fear, a hopeless case, except the grace of God shall interpose.

May 2, 1829

THO[MA]S BARRON—AGE 33
Born, Ireland. Been in U.S. 10 ys. Not married. Read and write some, tho very poorly. Brot up a Catholic. Has lived mostly since in the U.S. in this Town—a little in Boston. Work'd as a laborer. Says he was brot up as well as most young men. Says he left Ireland in order to get better employ. Never was guilty of theft or suspected of it. Drink'd rather too freely sometimes. Convicted of forgery in Boston. Has been confin'd 5 ys & 4 mo. Sentence 7 ys. Says he has got along rather hard. Been confined in cells 4 or 5 times. Says he has always endeavored to do well. He appears mild & pleasant and well dispos'd. But an Irishman is not always to be seen through with a glance. Should, however, think him pretty well disposed. Says he believes the Bible & feels the importance of regulating his faith & life by it.

GEORGE BATES—AGE 40
Born in Hartford. Had good early advantages. Was put early into a Store. Stayed only about a year. Did not like it, & his father let him have his own way too much. Became unsteady. Went coasting, then to Sea. Work'd at carpentering some & in fact had no steady regular business. Got into intemperate habits. This was the grand cause of his difficulty. Convicted in Boston of Burglary. Has been here over 5 ys. Sentenced for life. Is a pleasant, good hearted, sensible man. Says his conduct here has been uniformly correct and this is the character which sustains him. Has work'd principally in cabinet shop. Says he believes the Bible & is

sensible of its importance. Friends respectable. 3 Sisters in Hartford. One of them married Horace Burr, former Cashier of the Hartford Bank.[62]

Bates expects a pardon when the Gov & Council meet.[63] The committee of the Council recommended him for pardon last winter. The Governor wished some recommendation from Hartford, which he has since gotten.

A pretty promising case for future good conduct.

Pardoned[64]

JASON BUMP—AGE 22

First confinement. Been here 4½ ys. Sentence 5 ys. Convicted of Store Breaking in Worster Co. Home in Wareham Plymouth Co. Early education very poor. Can read some. Learned to read here & is now in our Sab[bath] School. Parents still living and, as he says, did what they could to bring him up well. Went into a Cot[ton] Factory when 7 ys old, & followed the business till convicted. Says he does not know what induced him to commit the crime. It was his first offence. A brother who is now here was concerned with him.[65] From what I can gather I am satisfied he had no proper bringingup, & has had his own way. He is ignorant & most thoroughly corrupted & hardened. Says he has not yet made up his mind to pursue a steady honest course. Knows it would be best, but he must have satisfaction <*from*> for the wrongs done to him & others by the Gov-

---

[62]Horace Burr served as cashier of the Hartford Bank from 1814 to 1828. Accused of malfeasance, he resigned on July 26 after an investigation exonerated him. P. H. Woodward, *1792–1892: One Hundred Years of the Hartford Bank* (Hartford, Conn., 1892), 111, 131–133.

[63]Massachusetts penal law requires a pardon to come from the governor with the concurrence of the Governor's Council.

[64]This comment was probably added at a later date.

[65]Bethuel Bump. See below, p. 92.

ernment. I have no doubt he is bent on a life of infamy & crime. I remonstrated & entreated in the most affectionate manner <*with him*>, but I could not move his feelings at all. Says he has been punish'd a good deal here, & I presume from his appearance, that he deserved it.

He is a lost man, unless Divine power interpose to pluck him as a brand from the burning. Spent more than half an hour endeavoring to <*do*> make him feel.

James Brumsden—Age 33

Been here 4 ys & 3 mo. Sentence 8 ys. Crime Theft. Boston. First Conviction.

Home is in Hampton N.H. Farmer. Decent Education. Says he was steady in the early part of his life. Has liv'd in Boston & vicinity 7 years previously to his conviction. Got into bad company. Spent his money with lewd women, & this led to his crime. Never married. Mother is still living in N.H. Not much feeling. Thinks if the Government will take off a year or two of his sentence he shall be a steady regular man. If not, considers it somewhat doubtful. However, he says when the new prison is done & he can be alone he means to try as hard as he can to establish better habits of feeling & action. I fear he is a hard case. Says he gets along well here.

May 6, 1829

Edmond Bean—Age 23

Been here 3 ys. Sentence 5 ys. Sentenced in Boston for Larceny. Home in Maine. Has a mother there. Father died when he was young. Left his mother when about 11 and having no one to control him, became very wild and unsteady. Came to Boston about a year before his conviction. Drove a coach &c. Got into Bad company. Gambling &c &c

from that to theft. Can read, write, & Cypher. Before coming to Boston us'd to attend meeting some. After coming there neglected it. Had some difficulty since he came here for not doing his stint.[66] Is a smart young man. Says he is fully resolv'd on a steady virtuous life after he goes out. Never addicted to intemperance. Was formerly profane, but has quit that practice. Appears pretty well on the whole. Believes Bible.

George Atwood—Age 25

Born & brot up in Mansfield Con. Liv'd there till 18. Parents dead. Father died when he was a child. Mother when he was 8 ys old. Town then bound him out. Master died when he was 14, then livd with a son till 18, then left him. Since then has liv'd in various places. Work'd at farming mostly. Has a decent common Education. Says he was brot up to keep the Sabbath & attend meeting. Was well taught. Says he has drink'd some, tho he thinks not to excess. Convicted in Worster of stealing. Sentence 3½ ys. Been here 10 days. Says he never went astray till last fall & hope he may never do so again.

Was much affected & wept very freely. Should think he was not a very hardened offender. Hope he may continue to feel.

Seth D. Britton—Age 29

Home, Easton Bristol Co. Mother died when he was 9. Father intemperate & his grandfather took him on the death of his mother, & put him out to a farmer, where he liv'd till he was 16.

3d Comer. Came 1st when 18 for Larceny. Stay'd his time out—2½ ys—then out 18 mo. 2d offence—2 ys.

[66] That is, his work quota. See the introduction, pp. xlix, lxiv.

Stayed time out then out 18 mo & sentenced 3d time for 7 ys. Been here 3 ys. Has an additional life sentence. Always got along well here.

Is a smart active young man—pleasant & frank, very capable of doing well if he would. Education rather poor. Can read. Says he has sometimes thought considerably of religion. Thinks it important.

When he was 16, he returned to his father. Father a very drunken bad man. Two other families liv'd in the same house, one by the name of White. In this family were two young men—unprincipled & given to thieving. By them he was led astray. They are now both here.[67] It is to be fear'd, that from his long residence here, he has become very much hardened.

David Balkam—Age 40

Born in Attleboro, & brought up there & in Taunton. Good Education. Early advantages good. Till the age of 19 or 20, was as steady as any young man. Mother died about this time & his father marrying again, he left home & went to sea. Followed the sea for 9 or 10 years, off & on.

2d offence. First time sentenced for 3 ys. Out about 6 mo, then Sentenced for 12 ys for Store breaking. Been here 3 ys.

Says he fully believes the Bible to be a revelation from God. Knows that he has perverted his talents & abused his privileges & blessings. He is a man of sense but has, doubtless, in times past, given himself intensely up to vice. He is said to be a very hard case.

Still he professes more sensibility & feeling than many others. He has a wife & child in Boston & in speaking of them the tears rolled very freely down his face. Says he

[67] Charles and Josiah White, Jr. See above, p. 38.

longs to be a good man but does not know how to go to work. I gave him the best of my advice. He says he is determined if he ever is restored to freedom to live differently. Is fully sensible that a life of vice is a life of degradation & misery.

May 7, 1829

MICHAEL BUMPO (BLACK)—AGE 42

Born in this Town. Brought up in the country, & has liv'd mostly since in Boston, except when in prison. 3d Comer. 1st time 7 ys & 100 days solitary. Out 3 mo, then sentenced for 3 ys & 5 days. Out then 7 ys, then sentenced for 5 ys. Been here 4 years. Sentenced first when about 20. Had become wild by being led away by bad women, & it was this which did more to ruin him than any thing else. Had no Education. Has learned to read & write some in prison. Works in Cookery. Says he has never been called up for misconduct. Thinks he shall never go astray any more. Believes that Bible to be true. Says he swear[s] sometimes. Knows it is very wicked. Will strive to break himself. Bumpo is frank, appears mild & clever, and should think him a good convict. His 2 first crimes were committed before the Law of 1818, which subjects to an additional sentence for a previous conviction.[68]

JOHN BROWN—AGE 30

Born in Providence, and brot up there. Connexions respectable. Decent education. Wife & one child. A few years before he came here had become rather unsteady. Lov'd rude company. Says he was not intemperate. Gambled a good deal. Follow'd the sea some.

---

[68] *An Act Making Further Provision for the Punishment of Convicts* (Boston, 1818).

Convicted in Boston about 2 ys ago of being concerned in entering a Store. Sentenced for 3 ys. Has got along pretty well since his confinement. Says he is a believer in the truth of the Bible. Says the prisoners behave a great deal better than they us'd to & he thinks most of them endeavor to do as well as they can.

John Bradford—alias Cook—Age 37

Born in Scituate. From the time he was 7 was brot up in Boston. Learned Carpenters trade.

3d Convic[tio]n. First when 22 or 23. 1st Sen—1 yr. Out about 20 mo. 2d time 4 ys, then out about 20 mo. Then sentenced 4 ys & has an additional life sentence been here the last time 7 ys. Early Ed[ucation] decent.

Says he was not very wild before he committed his first crime. Committed the 3 times for Larceny. Had been in a good deal of difficulty here & punish'd a good deal. Temper very hasty & irritable, & this leads him to act often before he thinks. Is said to be a very hard & refractory fellow. In conversation, appears mild & pleasant. Says he knows he has been foolish & wicked, but is resolved to live differently. Believes the Bible to be true & knows it is all important to obey and love its precepts.

James R.W. Baggs—Age 29

Born & brot up in R.I. Early advantages tolerably good. When his father died he was 16. Soon after this went abroad to live. Got into habit of strolling about. Was married when 23. Has one child. Never has seen it. Sentenced in Dedham for Larceny. 3 Indict[ment] for 7 ys. Been here 18 mo. Has a brother here who was sentenced for same offence at same time.[69] Has been in another State prison, but not say where. First confinement here. Says he did not after

[69] See Leander Baggs, below.

his father died regard Sabbath, or attend public worship. Has not made up his mind as to the truth & inspiration of the Bible.

Has got along well here & is determined to do well hereafter. Is a smart, active, sensible man. While at Auburn Prison I was acquainted with a John Baggs, a convict brother to the 2 Baggs who are here. He was pardoned before I left there. Probably a ruin'd family.

LEANDER H. BAGGS[70]—AGE 39

Brother of the fore going J.R.W. Baggs. While he liv'd at home, work'd at farming. After this follow'd the sea some, then followed merchantile business for a time. Has also follow'd the business of ornamental painting, which he understands well. Sentenced at Dedham with his brother for 7 years on 3 Indictments. Has doubtless been in some other State Prison, though he did not say so directly. Has been wild, & his conduct very bad. Says his conscience has always reproach'd him, & he has gone directly counter to conviction. Believes the Bible, & says if he had follow'd its precepts he should never have gone astray. Is a smart sensible man and capable of doing much good. Says he has never been in any difficulty here, & is fully resolv'd never to go astray again. Is sensible that he can never be happy in sin.

ADAM BURROWS—AGE 22

Home, Halifax N.S. Is young man of good talents, good Education, & good address. Mother lives in Halifax. He has been a wild dissipated young man, & in many scenes of wickedness and folly. Is much borne down with his condition, & very unhappy.

---

[70]Manuscript index records his name as Leonard Baggs.

Says he is thoroughly sick of his past life & is determined to live very differently hereafter. Says he has almost kill'd his mother, & is resolved to do what he can in after life to make her happy. He has been in some trouble here for attempting to effect his escape twice. Declares solemnly that he will never attempt it again & that his whole conduct shall be such as it ought to be. He is very much humbled, but how far he may be reform'd or how good his resolutions may be it is difficult to tell.

Says he is sensible of the importance of the Role given of the Bible, but knows that his heart is not in accordance with its holy precepts.

He is a young man who might be an ornament to any Society. Convicted in Boston for Larceny. Is living in hopes that his mother will come on and get him pardoned.

May 9, 1829

WILLIAM BRADLEY—AGE 25
Home in Roxbury. Born & brot up there.[71] Early Ed[ucatio]n decent. Parents respectable. Father still living. Hatter by trade. Convicted Nov. 1827. Sentence 2 ys. First offence. Convicted in Cambridge of Store Breaking. Says that he was brot up to keep Sabbath & attend Meeting & was very regular in his attendance. States that in the shop where he serv'd his apprenticeship it was the practice to drink spirits daily. By drinking with the rest acquir'd the habit of drinking to excess. When of age broke off in a great measure and set up shop in Randolph. After a while, took to drinking again, neglected his business, got into bad Company & finally committed the crime for which he was sentenced.

---

[71]William Bradlee, the son of Lemuel and Mary Bradlee, was born in Roxbury, Mar. 6, 1804. *Vital Records of Roxbury*, 1:37.

Says he has got along uniformly well here. Is in the Singer's room.[72] Says there is no swearing there. They have made a law against it & have agreed to report to the Warden every violation of this law.

Is a very frank, open hearted young man & appears well. Says he now is fully satisfied of the truth of the Bible & is determin'd, when he leaves this place, never to drink another drop of spirits.

DAVID BARTLETT—[AGE 22]

Born & brot up in Penn. Age 22. Trade—paper making. Left Penn 15 mo ago. Came to Boston. Was there about 6 weeks & convicted of Larceny. Sentenced for 18 mo. Been in Prison a little more than a year. Got along in general, well. Early Ed[ucatio]n decent. His father owns a Paper Mill. Always liv'd at home till he left the State. Was brot up to respect the Sabbath & attend meeting.

Says he believes the Bible to be a Revelation from God. Says he was steady till he left home. Was led away by others. Says he intends when his time expires to go directly home & is determined never more to go astray. Is on the whole, an interesting young man. First offence.

DAVID BILLS[73]—AGE 29

Born in Manchester, Eng. Left Eng. 14 ys ago. Came into the country with Sir Ed. Packinham at the time of his attack upon N Orleans.[74] Deserted on the day of the Battle & gave himself up to Gen Jackson, who usd him well.

---

[72]Thus nicknamed because the inmates who lived there regularly sang hymns together. See introduction, p. xlix.

[73]"David Bills, 28y, prisoner in State Prison, d. there, Nov. 12, 1831." *Vital Records of Charlestown*, 2:261. See also Commitment Register, Charlestown State Prison, 1818–1840, no. 969, Massachusetts State Archives. These records indicate that Bills actually was born in Suffield, Connecticut.

After the Peace,[75] went to Canada & lived 2 ys as Clerk in a Counting House.

Then came to U.S. Enlisted into the U.S. Army. After a while deserted from the Army in Boston Harbor, was in Capt. David Perry's Company. Went into the country & was hir'd out. Livd in Suffield Con, & in West Springfield, some in N. Hampshire. Took up peddling & follow'd that for some time.

Was convicted in Northampton on 3 Indictments for forgery, & sentenced four years on each. Says he was not guilty.

While at West Springfield was put in Jail for getting a girl with child. Would not marry her. Broke out & married another girl & this, he says, ruin'd him. Says he was never intemperate & never given to gambling.

His friends in Eng respectable. Parents wealthy & his early advantages good.

Says his parents were related to Gen Packenham & he went as a ship-boy at the General's request.

Bills is a man of good address, but I hardly know what to make of him. It is thot by some here that he is, at times, partially derang'd. Professes to behave well & a determination so to do. Says he does not doubt the truth & inspirations of the Bible, but I fear there is not much to be known by him. Still, I may be mistaken. Has been confined about 1 year.

[written vertically across the page]: Whole Story Humbug. Never was in England nor with Gen. Packenham.

---

[74] British general during the War of 1812, named to replace Robert Ross after the latter's death in Baltimore. Pakenham's late arrival in the New World hampered the invasion of New Orleans, where Andrew Jackson defeated him on Jan. 8, 1815. Beirne, *War of 1812*, 350–351.

[75] The Peace of Ghent—the treaty of December 24, 1814, that ended the War of 1812 between the United States and Great Britain.

BENJAMIN BREWSTER—AGE 52
Home in Duxbury. Born & brot up there. Never married. Has follow'd the sea since he was 9 ys old. Can read & write & says he can navigate a Ship to any part of the world. Servd as a cabin-boy under his father. First conviction. Been here almost 1 year. Sentence 1 year. Is to go out this month.

Says he was sentenced for stealing a watch. Acknowledges he had it in [his] possession. Says he bought it 20 miles from where it was stolen & had not a suspicion of its being stolen property.

Then man he had it of went to Sea & he had to suffer for it.

Says he has been mate & master of a Vessel. Never very intemperate. Drink'd some. Says he is a firm believer in the truth of the Scriptures & of their importance. Has thought more of the Bible & its truths here than ever before. Says he is resolved on living a steady correct life.

Converses well and I should not think him a hardened man.

JONAS BALL—AGE 33
Born & brot up in Newtown but for the last 13 years had been most of the time employ'd in the Fur trade in the North West of N. America. Employ'd by the Am. Fur Co.[76] Decent Com[mon] Ed[ucation]. Never married. Been here 7 mo. Sentenced in Worster for Larceny for 1 year. Never in prison before. Got along well here, never punish'd. Says he was unsteady, tho not much addicted to Intemperance. Believes the Scriptures to be the word of God. Says he is glad he came here. Thinks it has taught him a les-

---

[76] John Jacob Astor's firm with which he monopolized the fur trade. *American National Biography*, 1:696–699.

son which he shall never forget. First offence as he says. Should not think him very bright, tho he appears very far from being a hardened offender.

Jesse Bradbury—Age 34
Born in N.H., but has liv'd in Boston since he was 21. Seafaring man, the few last years before coming here. Formerly kept Grocery in Boston. First offence.

Sentenced in Boston for Larceny—3 ys. Been here 15 mo. Wife & one child. Liv'd comfortably, tho not possessed of much property. Early Ed[ucatio]n Decent. Early advantages good, & his habits were good. Says he was sentenced on the charge of stealing a quarter Box of Segars which he purchas'd. A Store had been broken from which the segars were taken, & he was taken up & sentenced as above. Denies having any knowledge of the transaxtion.

Says he has drink'd some, tho not much. Says he has never been addicted to profanity at all. Has a full conviction of the truth of the Bible. Says he has been guilty of a good many follies tho he was never dishonest. Friends respectable and many of them religious people. Converses well & should hope he might yet be a useful man.

May 12, 1829

John Brown Junr. alias Rand—Age 26
Home N.Y. City. Brot up in Store with his father till 16. Got unsteady & contrary to the wishes & advice of his father left him & went a voyage to sea. Gone a year, then returned home & after a few months left home again & has been absent most of the time since. Father in pretty good circumstances. Early advantages good. Says that Gambling laid the foundation of Crime. Says that while with father he us'd to attend meeting steadily on Sabbath. Since that time has not regarded Sabbath or attended meeting.

Has run after bad woman. 2d Comer. 1st time, confined 5 ys & one month. Out 18 mo, then sentenced for 2 ys. Both times for Larceny. Been here the last time 6 months. Before his first sentence expir'd which was 6 ys, made his escape, stole some clothes in Charlestown to get away with, was apprehended & tried & sentenced for 6 ys more. Afterwards pardoned by the influence of his father. Since that, committed the crime for which he is now suffering.

Is a smart sensible young man, but I fear very far gone in Sin. Says he fully believes the Bible, and is convinced that vice must make any man miserable. Says he is determined to reform & live differently in future.

DAVID D. BARNES—AGE 28
Not married. Home in Concord. Mother alive, father died when he was 18 mo old. When quite young, mother put him out to a man. He was not a good man, but drink'd hard & his brother came & took him away. Liv'd there 3 ys. After this a guardian, who put him out to a man with whom he lived some time, afterwards to a third. Him he did not like & left him, & thus has lived in different towns & different people. Can read but not write. Education poor. Says he believes the Bible. Was convicted of Larceny on two Indictments and sentenced on both 2 & ¾ ys. Has been here about 6 mo. Acknowledges that he had become intemperate and frequently got high. Attributes his misfortunes to this cause. Is rather a simple sort of man, & should think him rather wanting in the garret.

RUEBEN BLOOD. See his case under date Apl 1, this book. Says he has thus far got along well, & is determin'd to conduct well. Says he uses no profane language. Appears softened in feeling & of good temper.[77]

---

[77] See above, p. 46.

JEREMIAH BEAN—AGE 26

Been here now about 3 weeks. Sentenced for passing C[ounterfei]t money, at Concord, for 3 ys.

Born & brot up in Bristol N.H. Parents still living. He is married, & has one child.[78] <*As*> Says that he got the money honestly & suppos'd it good. Acknowledges that he pass'd the Bills. Education decent. Says he never was accused of crime before, & his character has always stood fair. Says he was well brot up & his parents are both professors.[79] And his habits were always good. Says he fully believes the Bible. Appears very well and converses with propriety.

May 13, 1829

EBENEZER CARR—AGE 53

3d Comer. First time 3 years. Out 3 ys. 2d time 4 ys. Out 2 ys, then sentenced 3 ys and has an additional life Sentence. Been here the last time 8 years—in the whole more than 15 ys. Taken up first in 1808. Born and brot up in Bridgewater.[80] Learn'd the trade of nail-making. Says his early habits & Education were pretty good. Sentenced first for passing C[ounterfei]t Money. Says he received it in wages for a summer's work, and did not know it to be bad. Being in prison corrupted him. Has been somewhat intemperate when out. Says he has never been punished here in the whole 15 ys. Says he believes the Bible but from his conversation should think he did not value it much. Appears very stupid on religious subjects. Otherwise, appears well enough.

---

[78]Jeremiah Bean married Olivia New of Medway, Apr. 15, 1827. *Vital Records of Medway, Massachusetts, to the Year 1850* (Boston, 1905), 153.

[79]I.e., professed Christians.

[80]Ebenezer Carr, son of Thomas and Mercy Carr, was born in Bridgewater, Mar. 28, 1776. *Vital Records of Bridgewater, Massachusetts, to the Year 1850* (Boston, 1916), 1:64.

James Collins—Age 55

Born & brot up in the State of N.Y. No Education. Can not read a word. Has a wife & 8 children in Naples, Ontario Co., & a small farm of 25 acres. Says he has been a hard laboring man all his days.

Came into this State to assist a man in driving a drove of Hogs. Was arrested in Franklin County for Stealing a yoke of oxen, & confined in Jail. Broke out & went home. Was away 11 months & arrested & brot back into this State & sentenced at Greenfield for 7 years. Been here 4 ys.

Has the care of the Arches in the west wing of the Prison, and has never been call'd up for any offence.

Says he fully believes the Bible, & hopes he feels the importance of its truths in some measure, tho he knows he is not what he must be in order to inherit the Kingdom of God.

Says he was never addicted to intemperate drinking. Drink'd some whiskey tho not to excess.

Collins appears very mild, & in feeling much above most of the convicts. Is a very exemplary man here.

James Chipman[81]—Age 36

Born near Cape Ann. Father died when he was a child. When 8 ys old his mother put him out to a Sea Captain with whom he went to Sea & continu'd with him till 14. His master was a hard man and he ran away from him in Baltimore. Went to Philadelphia, & sail'd from there to West Indies, & after a while came to Boston. Never had any education at all. Says he never was given to drinking much. Would drink for fashion's sake when in Company, but not at other times.

---

[81] "James Chipman, convict in Massachusetts State Prison, d. there Feb. 6, 1837." *Vital Records of Charlestown*, 2:288.

Third comer. 1st time 2 ys. Out 4 or 5 mos, then sentenced 4 ys. Out 4 or 5 mo, then sentenced for 8 ys. Been here 7 ys. Says he has never been punish'd but once in the time.

All his sentences were for Stealing—or store breaking. Says he has always believ'd the Bible, tho he has not been guided by it. Knows he has been wicked & a great fool thus to sport with his happiness. Thinks he should never go astray again. Believes fully that the way of transgression is hard.

Chipman is a man of sense, & if he would conduct as well as he talks, he would do much better than he has done heretofore.

May 14, 1829

ISRAEL COWING—AGE 59

Born & brot up in Scituate.[82] Has been a Seafaring man most of his life. Began to go to Sea when he was 9 ys old. Education poor. Can read & write, & keep accounts. Been in prison 4 ys. Sentence 5 ys. Assault with intent to murder. Says he drink'd more than he need to, tho he did not make a beast of himself. Cowing is a rough hardy old seaman. A man of good sense, & has seen a great deal of hardship.

Says he believes the Bible to be the word of God. Knows that he is a wicked man & needs reproof & advice. Says he has never been reprimanded for misconduct since his imprisonment. Says he was in the Alms-House. Has but one Leg. Lost his leg by getting frozen at Sea. The over-

[82]Israel Cowing, son of Israel and Desire Cowing, was born in Scituate, Oct. 27, 1770. He died between Oct. 21 and Nov. 3, 1832, age 62, in Hingham. *Vital Records of Scituate, Massachusetts, to the Year 1850* (Boston, 1976), 98, 372.

seer picked a quarrel with him, & abused him. Defended himself as he could, but declares he had no intention of killing.

I should think him a man of strong passions. Says he knows it to be his duty to forgive the man, and he does forgive him, but it is a great effort. Once thought he never could but knows that he is himself a guilty creature & needs forgiveness of God, & therefore must forgive him.

THOMAS CARTER—AGE 24

Born & brot up in Brookfield. No Education. Cannot read. Is now in the Sab[bath] School in the prison. Farmer. Says he was rather a wild, unsteady youth. Never drink'd hard. Has a wife & 2 children. Says he can hardly tell what led him to do as he did. Sentenced in Worcester for burglary. Has been here 3½ ys. Has a life sentence. Has never been punished for misconduct since in this place. On being asked if he believed the Bible, He hesitated a long time, but finally said he did not know but he did. Could hardly say what he thought. Had never thought much about it. . . .[83]

He appear'd rather reserved, & was not very free to converse. It may have been diffidence or ignorance or some worse cause.

I noticed nothing, however, like obstinancy or disrespect in his language or demeanor. First offence.

APOLLOS CHASE—AGE 35

Born in this State. Had decent common Education. Ascribes his ruin to living in the neighborhood with a family by the name of Briggs—very notorious for villainy—most of whom have been once & again in this prison. Was early led away by them. 2d Comer. First time Sentenced for 5 ys.

[83]Ellipsis points appear in text.

Was here 3½ ys & pardoned. Says he went out determined to conduct well. Went to R.I., married, and for 5 years kept out of trouble. Then one of the Briggs came across him again in Boston, where he had come to work at Stone cutting for a time because he could get better wages. Was again led away by Briggs & is now suffering under a second sentence of 7 ys. Been here 3 ys. Says he thinks the Bible contains some good things & perhaps some of it may be a revelation from God.

Is very stupid & seems to have very little regard for himself. Thinks he should try to do well were he to go out, but after all considers it rather doubtful what the result would be. Rather an unpromising case on the whole.

WATSON H. CLAY—AGE 28

Home N.H. Ed[ucatio]n very poor. Wife & 1 Child. 2d Offender. First time—3 ys. Out 2 ½ ys. Second time, sen. 3 ys. Been here 2 ys. Says he was not guilty the first time, but was guilty of the crime for which he is now suffering. Is a pleasant man, and quite frank. Thinks he has come to the resolution to behave well hereafter (interview short).

May 15, 1829

EDMUND CLARK—AGE 33

Born & brot up till 20 in Prince Edwards Island in Gulph of St. Lawrence. Education decent. Brot up to farming. Followed Lumbering for a number of years, & after this, went to Sea, in which business he continued till he was apprehended, & sentenced in Boston for theft. Sentence 2 ys. Been here 20 mo.

Early habits good until he went to Lumbering. Says that those who follow this business are very apt to drink to excess, & he acquired the habit himself. This continued after he went to sea. Says he was in a drunken frolic when he committed the crime, which was stealing & selling a watch. Says he has no recollection of either stealing or selling the property, & never should have been made to believe it had not the man to whom it was sold produced his receipt for the money he paid him for it. Says he has no one to blame but himself. It is right he should be here & he hopes it will be the means of doing him good. Thinks he shall not drink any more. Believes the Bible & knows that his heart & life ought to be regulated by its precepts.

Is a man of good sense, is frank & pleasant. Says he has never been in any difficulty here. Has a wife & 3 children. Should think pretty well of him.

Moses Carroll—Age 22

Born in Beverly. Says he has never had any steady business. Has lived here and there. Is very ignorant and is hardly *compos mentis.* Has been in prison 2 years. Sentenced for 3 ys. First Conviction. Is not only a very odd looking but an odd acting fellow. Appears clever & simple & this is about the whole.

William Cooms—Age 28

Born & brot up in N.H. Ran away from home when he was 15. Says his father was pretty strict with him & workd to have him behave as he ought, but he did not like restraint & discipline & so ran away. Says he can now see his folly. Livd in various places and got very little Education. (Is now in our Sab[bath] School.) After leaving home went to tending Stable & has followd that most of the time since. Was entrusted with a horse in N.H. where he lived to bring a Gentleman to Salem, and sold him & took the money. Says he has been a wild & thoughtless man. Has not regarded the Sabbath or attended public worship much.

Does not know what to think of the Bible whether it be from God or not.

Says he was not habitually a drunkard. Drink'd some though he never got drunk until the day he sold the horse, & should not have done so had he not been in a state of intoxication. Never committed a crime of any kind before.

Since he has been here has got along well & says he intended to do well in future life. But his principles & habits are very much against him.

He appears pleasant, but very destitute of sensibility. Sentence 2 ys. Been here 18 mo.

Elijah Cole—Ag[e] 25

Born & brot up in Maine. His father went into the army during the late war & died there. Was 11 ys old when his father died. There was a large family of Children, & he had very little opportunity for schooling. Can read poorly (Is in Sab[bath] School). His mother put him out to a man who kept tavern with whom he lived several years. Has wandered about & contracted irregular & vicious habits.

2d Comer. First time 2 years. Out 7 months, then Sentenced for 6½ ys on 2 Indictments. Been here 1½ years. Says he has got along here without trouble & thinks he should do better in future life.

Says he believes the Bible, tho he manifests little feeling. Should think him a stupid man, although he manifested nothing like obstinancy, or that hardness which is manifested by some.

Charles Cooper—Age 43

No Education (Color'd man). Born in N.Y., & followed the Sea from the time he was 10 ys old. Has saild out of Boston since the Peace.[84] Says he has been a trusty & faithful hand. Drink'd some & would sometimes get high when he was ashore. Was never in any difficulty before this. Says that when in port a fellow brought him some goods & wish'd him to sell them for him & promis'd to give him half of the avails. Says he told him he was afraid he did not get them honestly, but he said he did. After all did not really believe him, & thinking he could get a little money pretty easy he undertook to sell them. Was taken up & landed here. Been here 13 mo. Sentence 2 ys. Has got along well. Says he believes the Bible and knows he has a soul to be sav'd or lost. Is frank, & mild, & appears very well.

May 18, 1829

JAMES CASH—AGE 24

Born & brot up in Yarmouth.[85] Father died about 2 ys ago. He was poor. Workd at farming until about 5 ys before he came here, then went to sea. Education poor. Can read and write poorly. Says he was brot up to observe Sabbath & go to meeting. Never in any trouble before this. Sentenced about a year ago, for life, for Burglary. Says he & some more boys had been out one night, fishing till late, when returning two of the boys, cousins, fell behind, and after a while came up with something tied up in a handkerchief, which he found to be Eggs. They had broken or took out a pane of Glass from a window in a Store & taken the Eggs, which stood in the window. Declares solemnly that he knew nothing of the matter until the boys came up with the Eggs. The Eggs being missed & inquiry made, these boys charged it

---

[84] I.e., the conclusion in 1815 of the War of 1812.

[85] James Cash, son of Elisha and Patte Cash, was born in Yarmouth, Nov. 4, 1804. *Vital Records of Yarmouth, Massachusetts, to the Year 1850*, comp. Robert M. Sherman and Ruth Wilder Sherman (n.p., 1975), 2:504.

on him & swore that they saw him coming out of the gate with something tied up in a HKF & he was convicted & sentenced as above.

Cash is a peaceable & well behaved young man, is apparently frank & well dispos'd. Says he believes the Bible, was never addicted to drinking, has never been punished here.

AUGUSTUS COLBURN[86]—AGE 24

Born in Danvers, but was brot up most of the time till 16, with an uncle in Dracut. Father died before his remembrance. His mother is living in Maine. He does not know where. At 16 left his uncle, & since that time has liv'd here & there, some in Boston & has been to sea some. Rather wild. Run after the girls some. Us'd to attend Theater considerably. Says he never drinkd to excess or gambled.

About 5 ys ago was arrested in Boston for passing Counterfeit money & sentenced to 3 months Confinement in the City prison. Sentenced now for 7 years for store breaking. Been here 16 mo. Sentenced in Boston. Says while he livd with his uncle he us'd to Attend meeting in Sabbath. Believes the Bible, & is satisfied that a life of vice is a life of misery. Appears to be an intelligent young man, & pleasant. Says he is in the habit of swearing some. Knows it to be wrong & will try to break himself.

LINSEY COFFIN—AGE 43

Born & Brot up in Nantucket.[87] Learnd the trade of Rope-making. At the Age of about 22 went to Sea & continued

---

[86] Possibly Augustus Colburn, married in Dracut to Phebe B. Ames, Aug. 2, 1834. *Vital Records of Dracut, Massachusetts, to the Year 1850* (Boston, 1907), 155.

[87] Lindsay Coffin, husband of Abigail Phinney, son of Philip and Hannah

in the business till his conviction. The last 4 ys before conviction lived in Plymouth. Married, but has no children. Decent com[mon] Ed[ucatio]n. This is his first conviction. Says it is the first offence he ever committed. Led to it by intoxication. Had become very intemperate. Says he is glad he is here. Thinks it will even cure him. Feels very sure he shall never drink any more. Was convicted of Larceny in Plymouth. Sentenced for 2 years. Been here 1 year. Has got along well so far. Says he does not allow him self to use profane Language. Some of his room mates profane. Mind not made up in regard to the truth & inspiration of the Bible. Is doubtless a thoughtless Infidel. Appears pleasant, & is a man of good common sense, on most subjects.

JONAS CADY—AGE 39

Born in Springfield, but has not lived there since young. Ed[ucatio]n poor. Can read & write. Has lived a good deal in the State of N.York.

Intemperate. 2d Comer. First time sentenced in Lenox for Larceny—7 years. Served out the whole time. Out 2½ ys then sentenced again at Lenox for Larceny for 10 ys. Been here about 1 year. Has been connected with the Jones family—famous for Stealing & villainy, though he denies much participation with them.[88] A smooth tongu'd fellow, but I suspect a pretty thorough bred rogue. Says he has always got along well here. According to his story he is a very innocent well meaning man.

(Wharton) Coffin, was born on Nantucket, Sept. 5, 1785; published his intention to marry Nabby Finney, May 23, 1807; drowned Nov. 20, 1834, age 45 [sic]. *Vital Records of Nantucket, Massachusetts, to the Year 1850* (Boston, 1925–1928), 1:294, 3:285, 5:167.

[88]See below, John W. Jones, pp. 118–119.

May 19, 1829

John Casey—Age 22
Born & brot up in Halifax N.S. Mother now living there.

Advantages for education, poor. Can read, & barely write his name. Went to sea when about 12, & has follow'd the sea most of the time since. Has been rather wild. Became intemperate. Was on his way from Providence to Boston, and committed the crime for which he was Sentenced, viz. Burglary. Says he was in Liquor, & was accus'd of Breaking into a tavern & stealing a Decanter of Liquor. Sentence—Life. Been here Since Nov. last.

Should think, from his conversation that he was not very much hardened. Appears mild, & respectful, & manifests considerable sensibility. Says he fully believes the Bible to be the word of God. Never before guilty of any crime. Has not seen his mother in 10 years. Has often sent her money. She depended much on him for support.

Otis Comey—Age 27
Been here 2 weeks. Convicted of Larceny in Worcester & sentenced for 2 ys. Born in this State. But has lived mostly of late years in Pennsylvania, for the last 18 mo in Worcester Co.

Early education good. His father died when he was about 12 ys old. His mother has been dead about 7 ys. Since the death of his father, has acted for himself. Has been in various places. No steady employ. Rather unsteady although says he worked for several years in Pennsylvania, pretty steady, & bought him a small farm. Says tho unsteady, he never was intemperate. Came in Worster Co. to realize a small property which fell to him & a younger brother, & his brother not being of age concluded to wait till he should be of age so that it might be divided. While there was led away by bad company and committed the offence which brot him here.

Manifests a pleasant temper. Says he fully believes the Scriptures. On the whole convers'd well and seem'd determined to conduct well while here. Wept very freely. Hope he may be saved from utter ruin.

Joseph Davis alias Hopkins—Age 30

Born & brot up in R.I. Father an attorney at Law. Died when he was 8 ys old. Died poor. Early Education good. Left home when he was young in 1816. Came to Boston. Had no Business. Was led away by bad associates & in 1817 was convicted of Larceny & sentenced to this prison for 2 ys. Serv'd time out. Was out 2 ys & 8 mo & sentenced again for 1 year & had 2 ys addition for being 2d comer. Served out the 3 years, and on the 2d day after discharge, was apprehended for passing C[ounterfei]t money, & convicted. Sentenced for 1 year and has an additional sentence for Life.

Says he has been a wild & dissipated young man, very easily led away by others. Says he knows what is right, but has not virtue to pursue it.

Is a sensible, smart well educated man, and very open & frank.

Sentiments on religion Deistical. Says his mind was first led to Deism by reading his father's manuscripts.

Afterwards by reading Infidel publications.

Has read a great many in prison. Paine Voltaire &c. Says they us'd to be got from the circulating Library of this Town. Had as many infidel Books as he wanted. Says his mind is often shaken on the subject & he thinks he should be glad to get at the truth.

Is probably a very hopeless case.

May 25, 1829

THO[MA]S DUNCAN—AGE 45

Born in Dublin, Ireland. Livd with his father till 18. Work'd at farming. Learned to read but cannot write. Ed[ucation] poor. Brot up a Catholic. When 18 ran away from his father & went to England & enlisted aboard of a Man of War Ship. Continued in the service 7 or 8 ys. Deserted from the Service & got aboard of an American vessel in the W. Indies & came to Boston. This was in 1810. Previous to coming to U.S. had not been intemperate. Soon after he got to Boston was enticed by others to go onto the Hill to see the women.[89] Here got into the habit of drinking & excess. Squandered the money which he had when he landed—about $500—and at last, before the year ended was led to stealing. Is here the fourth time. All, as he says, for pet[ty] Larceny occasioned by intemperance. 1 Sentence 3 ys. Out 15 mo. 2 Sentence 3 ys. Out short of a year. 3d sentence 3 ys, out short of a year. 4th Sentence 3 ys, & an additional sentence of 7 ys.

Has been imprisoned in the whole 15 ys, and all as he says from love of *rum*. Has, I believe been a remarkably good convict. Conduct invariably good. Does not appear hardened like many others, but his grand difficulty is a propensity to drink. Probably, incurably ruined.

[89]Probably the north slope of Beacon Hill, which from the eighteenth century housed the largest concentration of prostitutes in the city and also saw a good deal of heavy drinking and gambling. The term could also refer to Copp's Hill in the North End, which experienced an influx of poverty and crime after the Revolution, or to Fort Hill, though this last is the least likely since its primary decline hit in the 1830s. See Walter Muir Whitehill, *Boston: A Topographical History*, 2d ed. (Cambridge, Mass., 1968), 70–71, 112–118.

John Dunnswell—[Age] 21

Born in W. Indies. Father in good circumstances. Got discontented & ran away from him at the age of 17. Never learned any trade till he came to prison. Education decent. Brot up in the Eng. Church religion. Believes the Bible, as he says, yet the manner in which he gave his assent to its truth was rather a hesitating one.

After leaving home came to U.S. In about 3 months, was convicted in Boston of stealing & sentenced to this Prison for 2 ys, served out this time, was out 28 days & sentenced a second time for 5 ys. Been here 3 ys. Dunnswell appears pleasant, but has not much sensibility, and has been a wild Boy, & it is to be fear'd he has not yet sowed all his wild oats. Says he thinks he shall when he gets out take a different course. Is sensible that the course he has pursued is a foolish & wicked one. I hope he may do better, but it is most likely a hope against <*hope*> all probability.

Says he was not intemperate, but wild and profane. Is trying hard to cure himself of his profanity.[90]

Simion Doane (colored man)—Age 22

Born in Taunton & lived there with his mother till 12. Father died when he was quite young. At 12 mother moved to Boston & he came with her. Never brot up to any trade or any regular business. Soon after coming to Boston became unsteady & wild. No Education (is in the Sab[bath] School here). Was early led to gambling & running after bad girls. Says he never drink'd to excess. 2d Comer.

1st time 3 ys. Served out his time. Out 3 months. 2d Sentence 3 years. Has been here 2 ys & 4 mo. Says he has never been punish'd for misconduct in prison.

Doane appears to be a mild pleasant young man. Thinks

[90]This paragraph was added to the entry as an afterthought.

he shall never be so wicked & foolish again as he has been. Says he believes the bible. Is probably a good natur'd thoughtless young fellow & easily led away by others, & having never been brot up to any business, it is not strange that he should be found here, living as he has, in such a place as Boston, where there is a temptation at every corner.

June 4, 1829

JOSEPH DURFEE—AGE 62

Born & brot up in Tiverton R.I., & has most of his life resided there. For 4½ ys before coming here, resided in Freetown in this State. Sentenced a little more than two years ago for 5 ys for an assault on his wife.[91] Says he had always liv'd peaceably with her until the time of this Assault. He spoke to her & she refused to answer him, & being in Liquor & in an irritable state of mind he struck her. Was instantly dreadful sorry.

Says he was well brot up. Decent Education. Has 7 children & brought them all up well. Was a steady, industrious man until he went to sea. There contracted the habit of intemperance.

Has a decent property. Says this is the first difficulty he was ever in. Has never been censured for any thing since his confinement. Is imploy'd boiling oakam.[92] Says he has been solicited to brew Beer, but never would do it for any one. Says Prince in the kitchen us'd to brew beer. Hemphill a great hand for brewing. Does not know that he does it now. Says there is nothing so much swearing about the prison as there was a year ago. Says he believes the Bible &

[91]Joseph Durfee married Mary Hathaway, Freetown, Oct. 7, 1798. Family Archive CD-Rom #231, *Marriage Index: Massachusetts: 1633–1850* (Brøderbund Software, 1997).

[92]Treating hemp or jute fiber to soften it so that it could later be mixed with tar and used for caulking ships.

has always believ'd it. Appears to be an open hearted, clever old man.

June 9, 1829

JOHN DANBY—AGE 34
Born at Cape of Good Hope Africa. Was sent when quite young to England for his Education. Was in an Academy there 5 ys. Then went to Holland & spent some time in perfecting himself in the knowledge of the Dutch Language. Always had a strong propensity for a sea-faring life. His father was a Wine Merchant at the Cape & in good circumstances. At 16 went to sea, & for many years follow'd the business. Has been to all parts of Europe, the East Indies, & in most of the great commercial places in the world. Says he was never given to intemperate drinking. Was profane. Always believ'd the Bible & does now. Is a 2d Comer. 1st Sentence 4 ys. Serv'd it out. Was out 2 or 3 months & then sentenced for 8 ys. Has been here 2 ys. Says that the first time he was not Guilty. Owns he was in bad Company on the Hill in Boston but not guilty.[93] The second time he says he was justly sentenced. Has never been in any difficulty here. Is faithful & intends to be so. Danby is a very pleasant man, & a man of good sense. Is frank, & so far as I can judge, well dispos'd. Has doubtless been very thoughtless. Says he is not dispos'd to complain of his situation. Knows it is just.

ISRAEL DODGE—AGE 27
Born in Maine. Education decent. Brot up to farming, but has follow'd the Sea a good deal. Says he has no home—never married—and there is no place which he calls his home. Has been intemperate to a certain degree, though

---

[93] Probably the north slope of Beacon Hill. See note 89 above.

not beastly, and since going to sea has been profane. Says he knows it is a base practice & he has almost broken off & intends to break off entirely. Says he often reproves others for this vice. Believes the Bible, tho he has greatly neglectd it. Thinks this will be a good school for him & feels sure he shall never be guilty of another crime.

First offence. Sentenced in Salem for 2 ys. Been here 19 months. Says he has for the most part got along exceedingly well. Is a singular sort of a man. Laughs at every thing & one would be led to think he was very happy, tho he says he is very wretched.

June 10, 1829

JOHN DAILY—AGE 38

Born Ireland. Left Ireland when very young for England. Education poor. In 1809 was impress'd in Liverpool aboard a man of War. Was in the British service during the late War, came to Canada, was taken prisoner at Fort Erie & held a prisoner till the peace in 1815. Has been in US ever since. Drink'd some. Always spent his money as fast as he earn'd it.

2d Comer. Sentenced the first time for 4 ys. Was confin'd 88 days beyond his sentence for having been in cells that number of days for misconduct. Was a prime mover in a rebellion which took place.

Was out 2½ years then sentenced at New Bedford for 5 ys for an assault to Murder. Has been here now 6 months. Says he had no such intent. Is a very hard fellow and utterly destitute of feeling or principle.

THO[MA]S DAILY—AGE 23

Born in Ireland. Came to U.S. with parents when an infant. Has always liv'd in Boston. His mother who is now living &

is a widow gave him a good chance for schooling, but he was reluctant to attend. Abus'd his advantages & got very little Education. Is now in Prison Sab[bath] School. Was a wild, thoughtless boy & very easily led away by temptation & bad company. Was intemperate withal. 2d Comer. 1st time was in his 20th year, & sentenced for 2 ys. Was out 2 ys, then sentenced for 18 mo. Has been here 14 mo.

After going out the first time kept a grog-shop. This drew bad company around him & by this means was again led to crime. Says he has never been in any difficulty here for misconduct. Says he is sensible of his folly and thinks he shall never be drawn away again. Is very frank but I fear has no stability, & having been so much accustomed to vice & crime in early life, it is very questionable whether with his instability he will ever reform.

June 15, 1829

WILLIAM DUNBAR—AGE 44

First confinement. Sentence 7 ys. Been here 2 ys. Sentenced for shooting at & wounding his wife. Home in Bridgewater.[94]

Says he was in a state of delirium when the act was done as he has no distinct recollection of it. Had been somewhat intemperate, but does not know whether he had then been drinking or not.

Has 8 children & some property. Education decent, & was brot up to good habits.

Farmer. Believes the Bible & has generally attended meeting on Sabbath. Has got along well here. Says he does not think there is 1/16 of the profanity in the prison there

---

[94]William Dunbar, son of Dr. Simeon and Abigail Dunbar, born in Bridgewater, June 3, 1785; published intention to marry Sarah Snow, Sept. 14, 1807. *Vital Records of Bridgewater, Massachusetts, to the Year 1850* (Boston, 1916), 1:96, 2:117.

was a year ago. Is a pleasant sort of man tho not of very accute sensibility.

JOSEPH CLARK ALIAS CLASH—AGE 19
Colored man. Sentenced in Boston about 16 months ago for 4 years. Crime—Larceny. Born in Salem, but has lived most of his life in Boston. Barber by profession. Education decently good. Has attended a Sabbath School 3 or 4 seasons. Says he was never intemperate. Became rather wild & us'd to run to the Theatre a good deal. His first offence. Gets along well here & says he is determined to do well. Says he us'd to be profane but pledges himself to be guilty of profanity no more. Appears mild. Is frank & on the whole appears well.

JAMES CUMMINS—AGE 25
Born in British Dominions. Serv'd most of his life in the British Navy. Ed[ucation] decent. A Bigoted Catholic. Sentenced in Dedham for Burglary for Life. Came to prison last week & is just out of Cells. Gave him some advice &c. &c.

June 17, 1829

ERASTUS DANFORTH—AGE 37[95]
Born in Vt. Father moved early to Athol Mass. Livd there till 12. At 12 father died. Had no guardian and took care of himself. Never went to school any after he was 12. For 3 ys worked at Blacksmithing, on wages, then learned the Hatter's trade <*too*> & has follow'd this ever since. <*Is now*> Has

[95]Erastus Danforth was born in Clarendon, Vermont, the son of John and Hannah Danforth, Dec. 10, 1791. He married Hannah Newhall in Athol, Apr. 6, 1815. *Vital Records of Athol, Massachusetts, to the End of the Year 1849* (Worcester, 1910), 24, 119. Hannah died May 1, 1824, age 38. *Vital Records of Richmond, Massachusetts, to the Year 1850* (Boston, 1913), 93.

been married & has 4 Children. Wife been dead 5 ys. At Athol was burn'd out & was otherwise unfortunate. Moved to Pittsfield & burn'd out again. Mov'd from there to Lenox & from there to Richmond in Berkshire Co. Had bad luck. Lost his wife. Became discouraged and somewhat given to drinking, tho he was not what the world calls a drinking man. In May 1828 was convicted of Larceny at Lenox & sentenced for 3 years. Danforth is an Infidel in sentiment. Does not credit the Bible at all.

Otherwise he is a pleasant sensible man—mild in his temper & feelings & behaves remarkably well. Talked with him more than an hour, & have often conversed with him.

CHARLES DELANO—AGE 53

Brought up in Sunderland. A hatter by trade. Sentenced in August for Larceny for 5 ys. Been here 1 year next August. Says he is not Guilty. Says he bought some Iron of a man for Govt. tin more than two years before he was prosecuted, & the Iron proved to have been stolen, & the man who lost it got mad with him & prosecuted him. Says he has always been respected by his neighbours & acquaintances. Drink'd some a short time before he came here. Says he was not profane. Believes the Bible & has been regular in his attendance at Public worship.

Delano appears mild. Is an obedient orderly convict & has nothing like hardened depravity in his demeanor or appearance. Converses sensibly and pleasantly.

June 18, 1829

JAMES DEMPSEY—AGE 38

Born in Ireland. Education decent. Labourer. For a few years past, has liv'd in Boston. Roman Catholic in Religion. Says that until a few months previous to his conviction, he was always industrious & well esteemed wherever he lived,

& this is the first difficulty he was ever in. Has a wife and child in Boston. About 6 months ago, was convicted on 12 Indictments. Says that he bought of a bad fellow a Chest of joiner's tools. Got them cheap & thought it would be a good bargain. These tools had been taken from a great number of individuals & of consequence this number of indictments were found against him. Sentence 5 years. Says it was in consequence of his former fair character that his sentence was so light. Says that for a few months before this he had got into intemperate habits, was drawn away before he was aware by some bad companions with whom he laboured. Says his wife often warned him of what would be the end. Dempsey is a man of good sense, of perfect frankness & openness of heart. Appears very sincere in declaring that he feels grateful to God for plucking him as a brand out of fire & placing him out of the reach of *Spirits*, & his former associates. Says he now looks back with astonishment & horror at the course he was going. Few prisoners conduct as well as he, or appear on the whole better.

ERASTUS EATON—AGE 22

Born in Kennebunkport in the State of Maine. Parents live there now. Lived with them till 16, then ran away & it was 2 years before he let them know where he was. Lived in Salem for 2 years, & some in other places.

Came to Boston. Lived a considerable time with Gen Dearborn[96]—some with Mrs. Holmes &c. Finally opened a cellar[97] for himself. Did not succeed well. Says that his early

[96]Henry Dearborn (1751–1829), physician and soldier, member of George Washington's staff, and secretary of war, 1801-1812. Dearborn commanded the northeast section during the War of 1812, but with his increasing age he showed less good judgment. He was removed in 1813 after Hull's defeat at Detroit and other failures along the Canadian frontier. *American National Biography*, 6:299–301.

[97]I.e., a bar.

education was decently good. Was well brot up. Always attended meeting on the Sabbath till he left home & while he lived at Salem. Habits continu'd good till some time after he went to Boston. Got into bad habits after opening cellar. Gambled a good deal, <*and*> drink'd some tho never to intoxication, went after bad women some, & these practices led to theft & theft to this place. Sentence 3 ys. Been here 2 ys & 5 months. Has never been punish'd for any misconduct here.

Says he was formerly very profane, but has in a great measure broken off, & is resolved never more to indulge in it. Eaton appears very well. Say he has resolved to go directly home when he shall be discharged & pursue a correct course the remainder of his life.

Charles J. Evans—Age 24
Born & brot up in Boston. Education not very good. Can read & write. Constitution has always been very feeble, & for this reason was never brot up to any regular business. Father a seafaring man. Supposes he is dead as he has not been heard of for 20 ys. Mother lives in Boston. Says he was a wild, wayward youth. Has been in prison 4 ys & 3 mo. Sentence 5 years.

Says he is determined hereafter to be steady & to live as he ought. Does not manifest very much feeling. Formerly, he says was punish'd considerably, but for 15 months past has not been punish'd. Says Mr. Bowman, a former Keeper, was an unprincipalled man, & abused him often without reason.

Daniel McFall—Age 44
Born Ireland. Came to this country in 1818. Labourer. Until a short time before his conviction, was temperate, industrious, & honest, & sustained a very fair character. Wife

became very intemperate and conducted very bad. In consequence of her conduct parted with her several times. Could not live with her, but loving her very much & she making fair promises, would receive her again.

Finally got disheartened & began to drink himself to get rid of trouble. Became quite intemperate, & at last was led away by a couple of old villains to commit crime. Was tried on two indictments & convicted. On one he was sentenced for 6 ys with 2 others who led him astray. The other charge, on which he was sentenced for 2 ys he says he was not guilty of—viz stealing a coat.

The first sentence has served out & 6 months on the Second. Says that one of the villains who was the instrument of his ruin, stole the coat & could have clear'd him, but would not.

McFall converses with much apparent frankness & appears humble and dispos'd to behave well here and after he gets out.

Joseph Foster—Age 35

<*Second*> Third offender. First time 6 mo. Out 1 year. 2d Sentence 5 ys. Out 3 ys. 3d Sentence 5 ys. Been here 4 ys & 8 mo. Has an additional Sentence as 2d Comer of 6 mo. The first offence having been committed before the law in regard to additional Sentences was passed, he was sentenced only as a 2d comer.

Says he was sentenced wrongfully the first time. Has follow'd the Sea since he was 11 ys old. Can read & write. Ed[ucatio]n poor. Came into Boston from a voyage & met a man on the wharf who had a piece of Linen & offered it for sale very cheap, bot it & carried it to a shop to have it made up. Was apprehended by Reed,[98] & not being able

[98] Constable George Reed of Boston. *Massachusetts Register* (1826), 223.

to find the man of whom he bought it, he was convicted & sentenced to this prison for 6 months. After coming here, learned mischief very fast and by the time was out thought he understood villainy well enough to set up for himself, & since that time, whenever out of prison has followed it. Says he is now sick of it & shall never follow it any more. Intends to go to sea immediately after his time expires. Says he was like other sailors, thoughtless and rude, tho never a rogue till he was placed here. Drink'd his allowance while at sea tho never a drunkard. Us'd when in port, to run after bad women. After leaving prison the first time got married to a loose woman. She is now married again. No children. On being asked whether he believed the bible to be a revelation from God he said he thought it a "good History." A pleasant, but thoughtless man & probably very destitute of morals or religious principle. Says he has never been punished here but once & has got along well.

HENRY FRINK—AGE 43

Has a wife & family in Stonington Con, where he has himself usually lived. Early Education decent. Followd the Sea some when young. Afterward learnd the trade of a Machinist & has follow'd that mostly ever since except when in prison. Liv'd awhile in Canaan Con. While there went with another man, Abbot, to Sheffield in this State, adjoining & robbed a Store, concealed the booty under the pulpit in the Meeting-house. Were detected, & sentenced to this Prison. He made his escape & went into Connecticut, where he committed a crime for which he was sentenced to Newgate.[99] This was known where he was first convicted &

[99]Newgate, opened in Greenwich Village in 1796, was the first New York state prison. It was named after London's chief prison, where con-

when he had serv'd out his time there he was demanded & brot on here where he is now serving his sentence which will expire in a few months. A good convict, but no religious principle. Infidel.[100]

June 22, 1829

JOHN FICK—AGE 39

Born in Nova Scotia, but came when 6 or 7 ys old into the U.S. Has liv'd mostly in the State of N.Y. Education decent. Has generally work'd in the Factories. Is a dyer, weaver &c & is a thorough workman in almost every branch of manufacturing.

Has been in this prison 3 ys & 9 mo. Has three months more to stay. Sentenced in Springfield for Larceny. Has been married, wife dead, has a son 12 yrs old in Utica with his grand parents. Is said to have been a very good convict here & to have work'd well. While I was at Auburn I found that he had been in that prison & serv'd out his time there. He was out some what more than a year as I think before committing the crime which brot him here. He is a man utterly destitute of principles usually entertained by men in regard to right & wrong. Does not believe the Bible. Believes there is a God. Is a fatalist, & does not believe that men are accountable beings, or can help doing what they do, & therefore are to blame for nothing. No wonder he is in prison, & it would be a wonder if he kept long out. Says he intends to do well when discharg'd. Is pleasant enough in manner but a strange being.

---

demned criminals were held before execution. David J. Rothman, *The Discovery of the Asylum: Social Order and Disorder in the New Republic* (Boston, 1971), 61.

[100]Curtis dated this entry June 18.

W[illia]m Foster—[Age 42]

Born in England. Age 42. Came into U.S. in 1808. No Education. Is in our Sabbath School & has learn'd some. Has been a sailor all his days until he came to this Country, & has follow'd it some since. Was a soldier in U.S. Army during the late war. Has been very intemperate, which, he Says has brot all his troubles upon him.

3d Comer. 1st time 3 ys. 2d time 2 ys & 6 mo. & an additional sentence for being a second comer of 3 ys. 3d time 3 ys—& for being 3d comer, has a life sentence. Has been imprisoned on the whole 13½ ys.

Is a singular old man. Weeps like a child, frankly acknowledges his sins & follies. Says he believes the Scriptures. Thinks if he could only have one trial more he should never do wrong again.

Seems to be a man of tender good feelings & is said to be a quiet, good convict. Drink has ruin'd him, & probably he is better off here than he would be out.

June 23, 1829

W[illia]m Fowler[101]—Colord man—Age 20

Born & brot up in Boston. Can read but not write. Brought up to no regular business. Once put out to a trade but soon run away. Been a very wild vicious boy. Drink'd considerably. Gambling led him to stealing & stealing to this place. 2d Comer, first when he was about 14—3 ys. Out 62 days & then sentenced for 10 years. Been here 2 ys & 4 months. Says he has been in considerable difficulty here. Attempted last week to escape. Got outside the wall but was soon brought back. A hard case.

[101] "William Fowler, 25y, convict in State Prison, Charlestown, d. there, Oct. 13, 1834." *Vital Records of Charlestown*, 2:287.

June 24, 1829

EMERY DELANO—AGE 23

Has liv'd mostly in Braintree & Randolph. His mother lives in Salem. Learnd the trade of a Shoemaker. Can read & write. Ed[ucation] poor. Says he has been rather wild, was intemperate & kept bad company. Is married. Convicted of an assault on a man & wounding him. Been here 4 mo. Sentenced 1 year. Is frank & appears very well. Says he thinks this confinement, by leading him to reflection will be the means of saving him from ruin.

Says that his habits would certainly have destroyed him. Is resolv'd now to live a different life. Has got along well here. Was often warn'd before he got into this trouble but did not regard it.

Now is made to feel that the way of transgression is hard.

JOSEPH FISHER—AGE 19

Home in Salem. Parents live there. First offence. Been here 1½ ys. Sentence 4 ys. Larceny. An interesting young man in his appearance. His demeanor modest & respectful.

Says he became early rather wild. Did not like the restraints laid on him by his parents, & when about 16 ran away with 2 other lads of the Town. Went to Portland where he stayed 6 mo. His father then went & brought him home. Continued wild, run after bad women and gambled, was profane & finally committed a Larceny, which sent him here. Says he can now clearly see & can feel his folly. Has got along well here & intends to conduct himself as he ought. Says he was very profane when he came here, but has almost broke himself of it. Knows it is wrong & intends entirely to reform.

Zachariah Fineman[102]—Age 55
First offence of any kind as he says. Been here 13 months. Sentence 2 ys. Has lived mostly in Shutesbury. Family now live in Amherst. Farmer.

No education. Wife & nine children. Convicted of receiving stolen goods. Says all his children have been well schooled & brought up, & taught to go to meeting. Appears very sober minded & by his conversation should think that his mind was a good deal on religious subjects. Says he never uses profane language & has by his persuasions broken several of his room-mates off from the habit. Never intemperate.

A good convict, I should think, and a much better man, to appearance than most men who are here.

June 25, 1829

S.I. Frink—44 ys of Age
Born in Haverhill, but has not lived there for 20 ys.[103] Has follow'd the sea. Saild out of Boston some, for a number of ys out of Philadelphia, & has been in the English service many years. Sentenc'd for attempting a Rape & has been here 7 mo. Sentence 4 ys. Says he was crazy when he attempted the Act. Was doubtless partly intoxicated. From his conversation should think him a hard case. Feels cross. Has a complaining disposition, & nothing is right with him. Says he has got along well here thus far. Is quite deaf, & it being hard conversing with him, did not say a great deal to him.

---

[102] "Zachariah Finneman, 55y, convict in State Prison, Charlestown, d. there, Oct. 9, 1829." *Vital Records of Charlestown*, 2:303.

[103] Samuel, son of Samuel and Betsy (Roff) Frink, was born in Haverhill, Mar. 30, 1786. *Vital Records of Haverhill, Massachusetts, to the End of the Year 1849* (Topsfield, 1910–1911), 1:131.

William M. Freeman—Age 45

Born & brot up in Wrentham. Never married. Was an illegitimate child, and brot up with his grandfather who made an idol of him. Would never suffer him to be restraind or punish'd. In this way grew up without restraint, & full of self will. Education decent. By trade a Machinist. Has been to sea some. Became intemperate & this led to the crime which brought him here which he says was stealing 4 lbs of Cheese. Has been here 4 mo. Sentence 1 year.

Is a man of good sense & appears pleasant.

Is a free-thinker. Does not receive the Bible as the Word of God. This with his habit of intemperance will account for his being here.

Should think him a quiet peaceable prisoner.

June 27, 1829

Gardner Fox—Age 33

Born & Brot up in R.I. Has been married. Wife dead, no children. Says he has been a hard labouring man. No property. Has been intemperate, & has a plenty of rum blossoms now on his face. Sentenced in Berkshire Co. in May last for 1 year. Convicted of Stealing, as he says, a silver Tea spoon from a Mr. Laflin[104] of Lee. Says he is not guilty. He doubtless lies about it as his own story would go far to convict him.

Can read, not write. Has been a sort of wandering man & this with his intemperance would ruin any man.

Says he does not swear. His room-mates, one of whom is Salsbury,[105] are very profane.

---

[104] Probably Walter, Winthrop, or Cutler Laflin, owners of the local paper mill. *Lee: The Centennial Celebration and Centennial History of the Town of Lee, Mass.*, comp. C. M. Hyde and Alexander Hyde (Springfield, 1878), 290.

[105] Inmate Joseph O. Salisbury. See above, p. 14.

June 29, 1829

BETHUEL BUMP—AGE 24

Born & brot up in Wareham. Says he never had much bringing up. Education very poor. Work'd at farming some and some in a Factory. Has been rude & thoughtless. Not intemperate. First time he was ever convicted. He & his brother[106] were convicted & sentenced together for Larceny, for 5 ys. Time will expire in October next. Says he gets along well in prison & intends to behave well when he goes out. From the manner in which these brothers were brot up & their careless & profane habits here it is greatly to be fear'd what will be the result. Says he is now & then profane, but will try to break off. Knows it is wrong. Converses pleasantly and is very respectful. Urg'd him very hard & closely as to his future course and did what I could to make him feel what belongs to his peace.

Bump was engaged when I sent for him in his turn & for this reason his name is out of place.

JESSE B. GOULD—AGE 28

Born & brot up in Vermont. Can read & write. Father died when he was a child. Mother married again. When he was old enough his Step-father put him out to a trade. When in his 14th year ran away & has ever since, when at large, liv'd a roving unsteady life, became intemperate & this led him to crime. 2d conviction. Been here on the second, 5 years. Sentence 7. Hopes he has become a better man since he has been here, & thinks that by Divine help he shall here after live a good life. Has no confidence in himself. All his confidence is in God. Appears humble &

---

[106] Inmate Jason Bump. See above, pp. 50–51.

frank, & seems to feel to a considerable degree his folly & his guilt.

Is said to be a quiet, industrious convict. Is in some respects a rather singular man.

Should, on the whole, think him a well disposed convict.

CYRUS GRAY—AGE 27

Born in Vermont. Left home when quite young & wandered about. Was not as he says, vicious—rather wild & thoughtless. Is a second comer. Convicted first when between 18 & 19 & sentenced to this prison for 3 ys. Served time out. Was out 3 months & then sentenced for 5 ys. Been here 4 ys & 8 months. Says his conduct since his present confinement has been good. The first time, says he behaved bad & was a hard case. Education poor. Can read & write. Is a confirm'd Infidel & does not believe in the truth of the scriptures. Is a man of pretty good mind. Says he shall behave well when he goes out. Perhaps he will, but I fear he is a real hard case, & a lost man.

LEWIS GRAY[107]—AGE 40

Born in Boston & has for most of his life, except when in prison, liv'd there.

3d Comer. Was first convicted when about 26 ys of age. First Sentence 2 ys. Out 6 mo. 2d Sentence 2 ys & an additional Sentence for being a second comer of 4 ys. Out 3 mo, & sentenced 3d time 2 ys & has an additional sentence for life. Been here the last time 4 ys. Been in prison, in the whole 13 ys. Is now in miserable health & will probably not live long. His father died when he was a child. Had not

---

[107] "Lewis Gray, 41y, prisoner in State Prison, d. there, May 6, 1831." *Vital Records of Charlestown*, 2:274.

much care exercis'd over him. Wandered about the streets. Liv'd 4 or 5 ys with an uncle in the country who sent him to school some. Ed[ucatio]n not good. After leaving his uncle, returnd to Boston, tended stable, Drove stage, &c &c. Sav'd up some money to the amount of $700 Dollars. Became unsteady, drinkd some tho not very much. Went after bad women. Spent his money & then went to stealing, & from that to prison. Is a confirm'd Infidel in sentiment. Will probably die so. Appears mild & respectful, & should not think him the worst of *convicts*, but is a ruined man.

June 30, 1829

JOHN GETCHEL—AGE 31

Born & brot up in Maine. Ed[ucatio]n good. Well brot up. By trade, Tanner, currier, & Shoe-maker. Sustained a fair character & was not addicted to vicious habits. Never intemperate. Has a wife & 1 Child who are now in Boston.[108] Sentenced 2 ys ago for forgery for 5 ys. Forged a Check on one of the NY Banks, & sold it in Boston. Says Avarice led him to the commission of the act. Could not make money fast enough in the usual way. Says he is fully sensible that the act was not only foolish but wicked, & he is astonish'd at himself. Believes the Bible to be from God, & knows that he ought to shape his life by its precepts. Since here, has got along well. A painful place but he knows it to be his duty to submit. No expectation of being releas'd till his sentence expires. Says he has been profane & is occasionally so now. Is sensible it is a horrible practice, & will break himself. G. is a sensible man, has seen good society, converses well, & if disposed may yet do well.

[108] Possibly John Getchell, who published his intention to marry Elizabeth Duntlin, Charlestown, Jan. 5, 1828. *Vital Records of Charlestown*, 1:592.

Says he would never endure to live where his disgrace has been known, thinks he shall leave this part of the country when he goes out, & go where he never was heard of.

George Gordon—Age 37

Born & brot up in Scotland. Father a Clergyman of the establish'd church. Was well brot up & had respectable & influential friends. Has born a commission in the British army. In 1818 came to Canada. In 1820 came to the U.S. Kept School 2 Seasons in Westford, near Portland in Maine. Became intemperate and at Ipswich in this State was Convicted & sentenced to this prison for 3 ys. Servd out his time, & after 18 months was again convicted of Larceny in Worcester & sentenced for 2 ys. Has been here 14 months. Says he has never been reprimanded for misconduct while in prison.

Gordon is a sensible, open hearted Scotchman, has a fine pleasant countenance, & his case shows what intemperance will do, even with the most promising.

Left Scotland very much against the wishes of his friends, & for that reason has never let them know his situation. His father has died since he left S.

Says he has a full conviction of the truth of the Bible.

John Gibson[109]—Age—he does not know—thinks about 38 or 39

<*Black Man*> Born in Schodack N.Y. Born a Slave. When a boy his master sold him to a Gent. in N.Y. From N.Y. his master sent him to N Haven Con, where he was put aboard

[109] "John Gibson, 44y, prisoner in State Prison, d. there, Nov. 2, 1833." *Vital Records of Charlestown,* 2:274. See also Commitment Register, Charlestown State Prison, 1818–1840, nos. 173 and 774, Massachusetts State Archives. According to these records, Gibson was born in New Haven, Connecticut.

a Schooner & taken to New Orleans & sold for $800. Lived there 10 ys & then run away. Came to Charleston S.C. & shipped as a Sailor for Liverpool. Made several voyages. Afterwards came to Boston & shipped for Canton. On his return says he was worth $700, which he had sav'd. Spent his money freely, & soon it was gone. Lent some & could never get it again. Took to stealing, & was convicted and sentenced for 4 ys. After his time was out, work'd, as he says, steadily & honestly for near 3 ys, & had determined never to steal any more. About this time Riley,[110] a very wicked black fellow now in this prison, found him & by over-persuasion led him away again. They broke open a Store. Were detected & he was again sentenced for 14 ys. Been here 3 ys. Says he never drink'd to excess. Appears mild, frank, & sincere. Says he has always behaved well here. Never swears & always reproved prisoners when he hears them swear. Says he believes the Bible. Can read tho his Education is poor. Reads the Bible everyday.

BENJ[AMI]N GOODRICH—AGE 48

Sentence 1 year. Been here 10 months & over. Has followed the Sea since he was 11 ys old. Can read & write. Sentenced in [111] for Larceny. Born in Beverly.[112] Says that of late years he has been intemperate whenever he has been on shore. At sea was regular. Ran away with a Boat lying at a wharf in broad day light. Says his vessel was setting sail & his things were all aboard. He was away & was too late. The vessel was under way in the Harbour & he took the Boat to catch the vessel. He was soon seen, was chased & overhauld

[110] Inmate Robert Riley, 2d. See above, pp. 14–15.

[111] Blank in manuscript.

[112] Benjamin Goodridge, son of Robert and Hannah Goodridge, was born in Beverly, Mar. 21, 1780. He died of consumption, Nov. 30, 1848, "age 68 y., 8 mo., 9 d." *Vital Records of Beverly*, 1:152, 2:452.

and convicted for the theft. Seems to be a very honest frank, whole-sould Sailor. Conduct uniformly good as a prisoner. Says he believes & reads the Bible a good deal.

Says he never intends to drink any more spirits, and then he knows he shall keep out of trouble.

THO[MA]S GOFFS—AGE 27

Born in Ireland & brot up there till about 20. Can read & write. Educated a Catholic. Took a notion to come to this Country. Has lived mostly in Boston as a servant. Intemperate. This led to the commission of crime. 2d Comer. 1st time 1 yr. 2d time Sentence 3 ys. Been here 8 months. Been punish'd once by being shut up in cell for one night. Otherwise got along well. Appears frank & clever, like many Irish men, but is, most likely, like many Irish men, better outwardly, than at heart. Drink, drink, drink, is the ruin.

NATH[ANIE]L GILES—AGE 27

Born & brot up in Providence, R.I. Of late years has liv'd in Tiverton. Has a wife & 3 children. Brot up in Ignorance. Cannot read. Has followd the sea since he was a Boy. Became intemperate to a great degree. Came home from a voyage, & before he was paid off, purchased 25 Dollars worth of clothes & was to pay for them when he was paid off. Went to drinking & got into bad Company, & when he got his pay squandered it away, & getting out of money sold the clothes for 5 dollars & was prosecuted for swindling & sentenced for 18 mo. Has been here 7 months. Says he rejoices he came here. He was a ruin'd man & now he thinks his eyes are open & he sees the awful gulph. Considers this punishment better than thousands of Dollars. Talks very well & frankly & seems to feel what he says. Says he has behaved well here & has never been reproved for a fault.

July 1, 1829

PRINCE W[ILLIA]M HENRY[113]—AGE 40
Born in Island of Barbados. A slave. Learnd coopering business. At 16 ran away & came to State of Maine in the year 1805. For a year or two was steady & did well. Took a fancy to a Black girl & intended to marry her, but was disappointed, became unsteady, got into bad company, & became vicious. Is a 3d Comer.

1st Sentence in 1807 3½ ys
2d do 5½ ys
3d Sen 2 ys

& has an additional life sentence. Been here the last time 8 ys. Been in prison 17 ys in the whole. Is considered a tough fellow & has made a good deal of trouble. Appears pleasant in conversation, but has a violent temper. Says the state of things here now is so much better than formerly that he gets along much better of late & intends now to do well. Can read & write a little. Is very ignorant. Will most likely stay all his life.

PHILIP HASKINS—AGE 36
Belongs to Freetown. Livd with his father till he married which was before he was of age. Early education very poor. Had a good chance, but neglected it. Cannot write but can read poorly.

---

113 "Prince W. Henry, 44y, prisoner in State Prison, Charlestown, d. there, Apr. 13, 1832." *Vital Records of Charlestown*, 2:277. See also Entries of Convicts in the State Prison, Charlestown, Mass., 1805–1818, unnumbered entry and nos. 73 and 36; Commitment Register, Charlestown State Prison, 1818–1840, no. 333, Massachusetts State Archives.

Says he was steady when young & till after he was married. Has 3 children. Has not liv'd with his wife for more than 12 ys. Says she was false to him and has to do with other men & has had two children by other men, & now lives in Adultery with another man. His domestic troubles made him unsteady. Says he was not intemperate. 2d Comer. First time for Assault & Battery 4 ys. Out 1½ ys then Sentenced for Larceny for 8 ys. Been here Seven & more. Does not seem to have much feeling, tho he says he believes the Bible & us'd to attend public worship on the Sabbath. 11 years imprisonment have doubtless done much to harden his heart.

Converses well enough & says he intends to do well. Has been in the Cells 7 days since he came here. Gets along well.

ANDREW HACKER—AGE 21

Born & brot up in Providence R.I. No learning. Is now in the Prison Sab[bath] School. Father a Seaman, & gone most of the time, & his mother died when he was very young & he was thrown upon the world without protector or guide. Became early wayward & vicious. Is a Second comer. 1st time 1 year. Out 2 months then Sentenced for Life for Highway robbery. Has been here now 6 ys on the last sentence.

Says he gets along well & behaves much better than he us'd to do, & is determined that his conduct shall be uniformly good. Hopes he shall yet get out & then he will never go astray any more.

Seems to have considerable feeling, is frank & manifests a very good temper. Hope he may yet be a reformed man.

July 2, 1829

Melzar Hatch—Age 57

Born & brot up in Scituate.[114] Education decent. Livd with his father till he went to a trade. Serv'd his time with a Ship Carpenter & Joiner in Charlestown. When his time was out went to sea in the capacity of the Carpenter of a Ship & has follow'd the Sea ever since till he came to prison. Was once taken by the Algerines & sold into Slavery & continu'd the Slave of a Wealthy Algerine for 4 ys. Was well us'd, but kept closely watch'd. The man had 2 daughters. When the father was on a certain time absent, one of the daughters pitying his condition unlock'd the place of his confinement & bid him flee. He did so, & went to the Harbour, where he saw a British vessel, swam aboard & thus gain'd his freedom. Went to Gibraltar & from there to England. In England was impress'd aboard a British Man of War and was detaind in their service for 15 ys. Was 3 or 4 times wounded. Was in the Battle of Trafalgar, where Lord Nelson was kill'd. At the Peace which followd, was discharg'd & came home. Sentenced 6 ys ago for an attempt to commit a rape on a child. Says it is all false. Seems to be a clever old fellow. A strange sort of a man. Behaves well here.

_______[115]

Hatch again. The old man is strangely ignorant of himself. Says he never did anything wrong or wicked in his life. Has always lov'd God with all his heart &c & does so now. Does

[114]Melzer Hatch, son of John and Deborah Hatch, was born in Scituate, Oct. 22, 1773. *Vital Records of Scituate, Massachusetts, to the Year 1850* (Boston, 1976), 176. See also Commitment Register, Charlestown State Prison, 1818–1840, no. 529, Massachusetts State Archives.

[115]Four lines illegible.

not know why he is not prepared to die. Believes the Bible & reads it. Knows he must be saved by Gods mercy, & yet has done nothing wrong.

Silas Holden—Age 31

Born & brot up in Leicester, Worcester Co. Mass.[116] Can read, write, & cypher. Father & mother have both died since he came here. Was steady till 22, then left home & work'd at farming here & there. Finally came to Boston. Kept a Grocery. Got into bad company & bad habits, gambling &c. Says he was not intemperate. Says he was brot up to attend meeting, & believes the Bible to be the word of God. Sentenced in Boston between 5 & 6 ys ago for Store breaking for 15 ys. Says he has never been in any trouble here. Has always behav'd well & has got along well. Is a sensible man, appears very well and says he is determind to live differently if he lives to get out of prison.

John Howard—Age 20

Born in Maine. When he was quite young his parents moved to Ohio. Can read and write. When about 9 ys old left his parents & went down the Ohio River to N. Orleans, & went to Sea, follow'd the Sea for some time & for most of time till he got to this prison. Was once taken prisoner by the Spaniards in South America, confin'd & treated very cruelly, his constitution broken by disease, & has never been well since. After being releas'd came on to Boston & having some money he went to the haunts of bad women where he got into the company of bad men also. Followed stealing considerably, & finally was convicted and Sentenced for 5 ys & 10 days. Has been here four years next

[116] Silas, son of John and Zipporah Holden, was born in Leicester, June 2, 1798. *Vital Records of Leicester, Massachusetts, to the End of the Year 1849* (Worcester, 1903), 50.

November. Says he has been a wild, wicked boy & can now see what it has brought him to. Thinks he shall never live wickedly any more. Has some feeling. Is quite frank, & appears very well. Says the convicts are very wicked men & do all they can to injure & ruin each other.

Never punish'd but once since he has been here and then Perry[117] propos'd to use him for the commission of an abominable crime & he knock'd him down with a hammer. Says he would do it again.

Believes the Bible.

JOHN HATHAWAY
A non compos as I should think. New Bedford. Sentenced for 3 ys. Been here between 2 & 3 ys. Says he was sent for shooting.

July 3, 1829

NEHEMIAH HAYFORD—AGE 25
Born in Halifax Plymouth Co. Moved from there when young. Has work'd in a Cot[ton]Factory since he was 8 ys old. Been here 3 ys in Nov next. Sentence 4 ys. Convicted in Dedham. Assault to Rape. Education poor. Can read but not write. Father liv'd in Walpole Norfolk Co. when he came here, & has of late years liv'd there himself. Stutters badly & it is quite difficult for him to talk. Has been rather thoughtless & rude, & never had much instruction given him. Says he never was intemperate. Believes the Bible, & intends never to do any thing wrong again. Has been confined 8 days for misconduct here. Does not appear bad, but from his impediment of speech, cannot judge perhaps as well as I might otherwise.

---

[117] Inmate Charles Perry. See below, pp. 149–150.

ENOCH HURLBUT—AGE 22

Born in Thompson Con. but has liv'd mostly in Boston. Can read & write.

2d Offence. First time 3 years. Out about 3 <*months*> weeks. 2d time sentenced for 7 ys for Store-breaking. Been here near 2 ys. No regular employment. Drove a team some in Boston. Was led away as he says by old villains to crime the first time, when he was about 17. Says he was not guilty of the last offence & had nothing to do with it. 3 or 4 fellows who boarded in the house where he did broke the store, & one of them accus'd him of being an accomplise. Is with the others now here & they know perfectly & acknowledge that he was innocent.

Is very destitute of feeling, a low, ignorant infidel. Says he knows nothing about the subject, but does not believe the Bible. Unless he changes his sentiments & views, he is forever a ruin'd man. Warn'd him most solemnly on the subject. Says he gets along well here.

JOSEPH HANSON—AGE 33

Born in Boston. Education very poor. Can read. Has lived in various places. Tended store some, tended Bar, Stable, &c. Drove a Hack in Boston. Also kept a cellar there.

Parents died when he was young & he had no one to bring him up. Always has had his own head & done what he saw best.

Says he was not guilty of the crime for which he was sentenced. Sentenced for Larceny in Boston for 2 ys. Time expires in Septr next. Is an Infidel. Says he believes some of the Bible & some he does not.

Appears pleasant enough but has little or no sensibility. Says he intends to be honest & industrious when he gets out, if he can find employ. If not, he does not know what he shall do. Has got along well here, and says he studies to do well. Not much hope of him, if I divine rightly.

JOSEPH HATCH—SAYS HIS NAME IS STEWART—[AGE 31]
Born in Pensacola. Follow'd the Sea since 11 ys old. Good common Education. Age 31. 2d Conviction. First 2 ys. Away 4 ys. Second Sentence 18 mo, & has an additional sentence of 6 mo. Been here about 20 months. Says he was sent for nothing. Is a hardened Infidel & full of complaining & bitterness. Says he has been greatly injured & he does not know what he shall do when he gets out. Cant tell yet. Seems to feel that somebody ought to pay for it. Will most likely end his days in Prison. Is hardened & profane. Drink'd some—probably a good deal.

July 6, 1829

JOHN HAMILTON—AGE 20
Home in Maine—Topsham. Mother still lives there. His father died not long ago. Education decent. Learn'd the Trade of a painter & glazier.

Became discontented, and left home. Liv'd in various places, and went to sea. Became intemperate and vicious. Sentenced in Salem for larceny in Nov. 1827 for 4 ys.

Says he has been punish'd some here for misconduct. The fault has been his own. Has not been misus'd. Says he us'd to swear some when he first came here, but has left it off. Thinks he shall live a different life when he gets out. Says he believes the Bible.

Should not think him to profess much feeling, although he converses sensibly. Many speculate well who cannot practice.

John Hewit—Age 27

Born & brot up in Penn. Farmer. Lived with parents till 21, about which time his father died. The property was sold to pay the debts & he then left home & work'd in various places. Was steady till he left home. Went into Virginia & finally went to sea. Follow'd the coasting business. Got into the habit of drinking rather freely. Came onto Boston where he work'd about the Wharves a spell, got into bad Company, gambled some, & finally was led to Larceny. Sentenced in Boston for 2 ys. Has been here about 15 mo. Has got along well here. Never punish'd at all. Has some feeling, and appears pretty well. Should rank him among the better half of convicts.

Josiah Harris—Age 29

Born in this Town, but has liv'd most of his life in Maine.

Father died when he was 5 ys old. His mother put him out to a man who follow'd the sea. Liv'd with him 2 ys & then he took him to sea with him & has follow'd the sea ever since. His mother now lives in Boston. Can read decently & write poorly. Advantages poor. Is in our Sab[bath] School. Says he has always been steady, industrious, & honest, and was always esteem'd where ever known. Sentenced for Larceny, taking some silver money from a vessel. Sentence 3 ys. Been here about a year & a half. Says that the charge against him was malicious & false he never had any knowledge of or concern in any such act. Says that he was to have had the command of a certain vessel—that the man who saild her, with a Brother, to prevent his getting the Birth charged this theft upon him and swore to what was absolutely false, so true as he has a Saviour.

How this is, the Saviour knows. Says he never was given to drink & was never in his life the worse for Liquor.

Harris appears like a sincere man—frank, ingenious & humble. Conduct good. Still he may be very deceitful though he is far from having that appearance.

William Hagar—Age 49

Born & brot up in Boston. Serv'd a regular apprenticeship at the Coopering business. Says he was as steady as young men in general & had no vicious habits. Education decent. After he was of age went to sea in the capacity of Cooper & followed that business ever since. Has made 42 voyages to the West Indies. Says he was never addicted to drinking. Has always believed the Bible to be the word of God. Wife died a year ago last March.[118]

Sentenced in Boston for stealing a piece of Copper for 1 year. Been here 10½ months. Says he was guilty & that it was the first act of the kind he ever committed. Has never been in any difficulty here. Has 2 daughters in Boston. Says he thinks he shall never get into any more trouble.

It is very questionable, whether he has told the whole truth in regard to himself. Appears very well.

Henry Harvey—

(Sketches of his history given me in writing by himself)[119]

Rev Sir,

As you are the only person, (prisoners excepted)[120], since my estrangement from home, who has spoken kindly, or seemed to have the least sympathy for my misfortunes and as you seem desirous of knowing our histories, I hope

[118]William Hagar married Sally Hildreth in Boston, Nov. 17, 1808. *Report of the Record Commissioners of the City of Boston* (Boston, 1876–1909), 30:387.

[119]This entry written in ink. Commitment Register, Charleston State Prison, 1818–1840, no. 691, Massachusetts State Archives.

[120]Close parenthesis supplied.

you will not deem me impertinent in thus giving you a short sketch of mine.

I was born in New London in the year 1807—remov'd to N. York in 1817. My parents were both members of the Baptist <*Church*> Society & taught, both by precept & example, the excellence of the Christian religion. Would to God I had attended to their admonitions. In July, 1822, I was bound an apprentice to a cabinet-maker with whom I lived but 4 months, when, in consequence of ill treatment, I ran away. It was no imaginary ill usage—it was precisely this.

He gave me, as is customary for masters to do with their apprentices, a task. I did it, but refused to do any more, unless he allowed me the customary perquisites. This he refus'd to do. I being stubborn, he beat me, not as he ought to have done, but knocked me down 3 times with a piece of a board. On my remonstrating, & telling him I should leave him & go to New London, where my parents were, & inform my father of his conduct, he threatened to put me in Bridewell—or if I did get away from him, he should write to my father that I had been caught stealing, for which he had corrected me.

As he was a man of respectability, I fear'd his assertions would have more weight than mine & that I should be sent back.

I therefore determined to make the best of my way to Boston. There I tried to ship on board of some vessel, but could not—and getting acquainted with some profligate characters, I soon squandered away what little money I had.

I then redoubled my exertions to get into employment, but in vain, some calling me a run-away, & advising me to return to my master—others telling me I had stolen something at home & dared not return.

Conceive for a moment, my situation, at this juncture. A mere child, being little more than 15, in a distant & strange part of the country, destitute & friendless, known to & knowing none but the most worthless of the community, unable to get employment & laughed at for trying, witnessing the commission of crime daily & even hourly, & judge whether any thing short of a divine interposition could save me.

Such, precisely, was my situation. I flew to my companions for consolation. They advis'd me & helped me to commit a theft, for which I was sentenced to the house of correction for one year. From this place, I made my escape, after serving 10 months.

It was early in the evening when I left the prison. I travelled all night & the next day; but being enfeebled by so long and close confinement, I found myself the next evening, but a few miles from Boston, so sore & exhausted that I considered it hopeless to try to gain a greater distance. I therefore gave up and laid myself down, by the roadside, where I lay all night, expecting every moment to be taken.

The next morning, I made shift although very stiff & sore, to get on a mile or two, when I espied a horse, which I took. In this I know I was very culpable, but it was not with a felonious intention that I took him. It was to further my escape. I intended to leave him, as soon as I could get a few miles further from Boston.

But it was otherwise ordered, for I was caught in three hours after I had taken him & committed to Cambridge Jail, where I remained until the sitting of the Court, when I was sentenced to Concord Jail for one year.

There I was put into a room with a young man, who was the most unprincipled person I have ever met with.

Being very fluent, & having a specious way of reasoning;

& arguing often that none but fools & children were hones[t] and that men of the greatest responsibility were knaves, that he wrought me up to such a pitch (I blush to own it) that I longed for nothing more than for an opportunity to signalize myself in such a manner, as to be called a *Game one*, a term he us'd for a bravado.

One day as we were sitting at the window, we saw the Jailer put a small roll of money into an outer pocket. This we agreed to get if possible.

This we did get & were using it very freely, when having a dispute, he sent for the Jailer & inform'd him that it was I who had got his money & gave him such a train of circumstances as fully convinced him.

For this crime, I was sentenced for 7 years to this place & I think it was the most fortunate occurrence of my life; for had I been liberated then, it is quite probable I should have continued in a course of crime.

But thanks be to an all-wise being who has removed me for a time from temptation, that I might see the heinousness of crime & prepare myself for a life of usefulness; & by habits of temperance & industry, try to regain that station in Society, from which my folly has precipitated me.

I have now been confin'd 6 years & 6 months, & have never heard from home but once, & then, not directly. It was then that I heard of the death of my father.

If you recollect, you asked me if my mother was in prosperous circumstances (but owing to my surprise, at being questioned in such a sympathizing manner, by one who could have no interest in my welfare, I believe I gave you an indefinite answer). I know not how she is situated, but I should think not very prosperously.

My father, I believe was involved in debt, debt contracted for his vessel, & must have left his property considerably embarrassed. Whatever may be her situation, she has a family of six small children with no one to assist her to support them. My greatest regret arises from not being able to render her those services, which none can do so well as a son. But I have transgressed the Laws of my country, & must wait, without repining for the day of emancipation.

Your obedt. & humble Servt.

Henry Harvey

N.B.—The confinement of 6 ys & 6 mo, mention'd in the foregoing, includes the whole of his imprisonment, both before & since coming to this prison.

His sentence to this prison was in Apl. 1825, & he has serv'd somewhat over 4 years.

J. Curtis

July 8, 1829

George W. Harvey[121]—Age 32

Born & brought up in Penn. Educated at Princeton College until Junior year. Left College & commenced the Study of Law & pursu'd it for 18 mo. Then quit & went to Sea and continu'd several years in the merchant service. Was 2½ years in the Columbian Navy in S. America.

Has spent 1½ year travelling in Europe. His father is dead. Left him a handsome patrimony. Says he has an income of 1000 Dollars a year.

About 9 months ago was convicted in Boston of a forgery & sentenced for 5 years. Says he was not guilty & had no knowledge of the transaction.

Says he was not an intemperate man. His greatest failing, he says, was his devotion to loose women.

Harvey is a man of sense, of good acquirements, & ad-

[121] "George W. Harvey, 34y, prisoner in State Prison, Charlestown, d. there, Oct. 10, 1831." *Vital Records of Charlestown,* 2:277.

dress. Says he believes the bible to be the word of God, but from his devotion to the world & to pleasure, has not studied or regarded it as he ought. From what I have heard of his case, there can be no doubt of his guilt, & most likely he has been a very dissipated man & this has led him to crime. His conduct, as a convict, I believe, very good.

Charles Howard[122]—Age 22

Born & brot up in Boston. Father dead. Has a Step-father. Friends respectable & in good circumstances. Education good. When about 17 went out into the country and work'd at farming 3 years & more. Says he was not unsteady or vicious in early life. Has been to sea some. Has been here about 9 months. Sentenced in Boston for Larceny for 2 years. Acknowledges that he has been in the house of correction 1 year before he was sentenced to this place. Does not seem to have much feeling, tho his appearance is not bad.

Says he behaves well here & is resolved to do well when he gets out. Does not swear. Believes the bible, & knows that the course he has pursued is foolish & wicked.

John P. Harvey—Age 20

Born & brot up in Watertown. Father died when he was 10. Was in low circumstances. Mother now lives in Watertown. Is poor. Education not good, though he can read & write. When he was 8 ys old was attacked with a white swelling which confin'd him for 2 ys. Lost the use of his left leg, and is now obliged to walk with a crutch. Partly learned the trade of a shoemaker by himself. His ill health prevented him in a great measure from active life. Lived in a bad

[122]Text gives his name as Howard Charles, but the manuscript index records him as Charles Howard.

neighborhood, where there was a great deal of Butchering & drinking & he got into intemperate habits & finally committed Larceny & was sentenced for 2½ ys. Been here about 8 months. Punished once. Says he gets along pretty well. Not much feeling. Says he believes the Bible & if he had read it more & observed its precepts he should never have come here.

Joseph Haskell—alias Mitchell—(cook in the Hospital) did not see him in his turn))[123]

Tho[ma]s S. Haywood[124]—Age 23

Been here 2 months. Sentence 2 ys—at Taunton—Stealing. Born & brot up in England. Been in U.S. 3 ys next Sept. His father has been disabled by palsy for 16 ys. His mother died when he was a child. Serv'd his time as a manufacturer of woolen goods. Says he sustained a fair character in England & was not intemperate. Has a wife & 1 Child.

Says he is master of his business, & had the oversight & management of one half of a Factory at Fall River & his imployer had great confidence in him & paid him good wages. Sometimes earned $50 a week.

In the same establishment was another Englishman whom he found there, who was a shrewd fellow and very intemperate. Was persuaded by him to defraud his employer & was detected. Appears very frank & humble, & mourns very much his folly & wickedness. Says his conduct here has been & shall be such as it ought to be. Says he believes the Bible. Appears, on the whole, very well.

---

[123] Two close parentheses in text.

[124] Possibly died in Saugus, October 1832, age 27 years. *Vital Records of Saugus, Massachusetts, to the End of the Year 1849* (Salem, 1907), 73.

Calvin Ingersoll—Age 28
Born & brot up in Cambridge. Parents died when he was young. Went to live with an old gentleman, a farmer & work'd while young with him. Went to school some. Can read & write. Got a notion that farming was rather a low business. Left the old man & went to sea some, off & on, but could not settle his mind to be a farmer. Wish'd to be something in the world. Was self will'd & rather impatient of restraint.

Thought if he had his own way he should be *something* and he says, that in following his own way, he has become something with a witness & cuts a fine figure.

2d Comer. Sentenced first for 6 ys. Pardoned after 3 ys & 5 months. Out 9 months, then sentenced again for 6 ys. Been here almost 5 ys.

Says he has always conducted himself well here. Believes the Bible & thinks he shall yet live a good life. Has given up the idea of cutting much of a figure & thinks he shall be contented to work as a farmer or mechanic.

Is a sensible fellow & converses well.

July 10, 1829

David Jonah—Age 30
(Blk). Born & brot up in Natick. Education poor. Can barely read. Put out to a farmer when he was 9 ys old. Lived with him till 14. Then went & liv'd with another man. When about 15 became unsteady. Gambled. Frequented bad company and drink'd. 2d offence. First time 18 months. Out about 3 or 4 mo, then sentenced for store breaking & sentenced for 7 ys, & has since receiv'd an additional sentence of 3 years. Has been here now about 9 ys & 3 mo. Says he has always behav'd well in prison. Had very

little trouble. Believes the Bible. Says he knows he has been very foolish and wicked. Has learn'd to his sorrow that sin will makes a man miserable. Thinks he shall never go astray again. Jonah appears frank and clever. Says he does not swear, nor is there any swearing allow'd in his room. They have a law against it. 10 in the room with him.

ANTOINE JOHNSON—AGE 32

Now says he was born & brot up in Baltimore. When convers'd with on a former occasion said he was born in the Canary Islands, & came to US 25 ys ago. No Education. Is now learning in our Sab[bath] School.

Has follow'd the sea the greater part of his life is a yellow man, about as dark as a common Indian. Says he has been a very wicked & abandoned man.

Drink'd hard, & this led him to almost every thing else that was bad. Very profane. Says he is mending, & means to break himself. Has been a hard fellow here some part of his time. Latterly has done much better than formerly, & says he is getting sick of such a course. Sees that it makes him very miserable. Has a very irritable temper & says it plagues him to govern it, but is trying. 2d Comer. First time 2½ years. Out 2 months, then sentenced for 5 ys. Time almost out. Expects an additional sentence.

Johnson says he believes the Bible. Is a man of natural good sense, is frank, but has been very wicked, & it is feard that he will never be what he ought to be—a truly honest man.

JOHN JOURDAN[125]—AGE 25

Born & brot up in Medford. Early in life, was kept at school. When <*about*> young, got uneasy, ran away, & went

[125] Entries of Convicts in the State Prison, Charlestown, Mass., 1805–1818, no. 461; 1805–1824, no. 456; Commitment Register, Charlestown

to sea. After following the sea for a time, came home, & his father, finding he had a taste for a seafaring life told him if he would improve his time, he would send him to an Academy for two years, that he might fit himself to command a vessel. He accordingly went, and after 5 months, the preceptor died. He then went away from home again & enlisted on board a privateer & continued in this business till the war closed. In 1817 his father died. At sea had become very wild & vicious. Says he was never given to Drink & that this is almost the only vice to which he was not addicted.

2d Comer. First sentence 2 ys. Was here two years & about 7 mo, for misconduct. Was out about 3 months, then sentenced for one year for stealing a horse. Says he hired the horse on pretence of going to a particular town, but in reality to come to Boston, to exchange about two Hundred Dollars of good money for counterfeit. Calculated to go largely into the business. Had no intention of stealing the horse, although he says he richly deserved his sentence.

While here, wrote a very wicked & threatening Letter to Mr. Going the Keeper[126] for which he was sentenced 7 additional years. Has been here between 4 & 5 years. Says that during the fore part of the time of his confinement his conduct was as bad it could well be. He was up to any thing & his glory was to be disobedient & to be the bully of the prison. His mind was made up to be a finish'd villain. Was confind'd to the cells a considerable portion of his time for misconduct.

Something like 2 ys ago, turned his thoughts to painting, & practiced some in rough sketches, finding that he

---

State Prison, 1818–1840, nos. 531, 1481, Massachusetts State Archives. In these records, where his name is spelled "Jordan," his birthplace is given as Port Elizabeth, Maine.

[126]William Going, the keeper of the prison. *Massachusetts Register* (1826), 161.

had some talent at it, was led to think whether he might not yet be something in the world & get respectable & honest living by pursuing it. Resolved to try, & to give up a life of degradation & crime. Since that time says his conduct & resolutions have been good. He has been led to reflection & consideration, is ashamed of himself, & resolved that he will live an entire different life.

Jordan is frank, and appears now determined to make something. Is a man of good sense & decent attainments, & I hope is not absolutely beyond the reach of redemption from a life of crime. Has been permitted to devote some of his time for several months back, to painting. Is much attached to it, & has doubtless had a very happy effect upon his mind & conduct. Is profane. Says he disapproves of it wholly. Has reform'd very much and intends to leave it off wholly. Sometimes speaks before he is aware of it.

July 14, 1829

WILLIAM JONES—AGE 22
Born & brot up in Roxbury. Parents now living in R. Island. Early advantages pretty good. Went to school till about 15. Father then put him out to a cabinet maker. Work'd with him till he died, then return'd home & went into a factory, where he work'd some time. Had an Uncle who was a mason, who wish'd him to work with him. Accordingly went & workd at mason work. Says his early habits were good. Us'd to attend meeting on Sabbath. Has always & now does believe the Bible. About 6 months before coming he got rather unsteady. Left his uncle, got into bad company & bad habits, drink'd & run after bad women & finally got into crime.

Has been here a little over 3 ys. Sentence 5 ys for Larceny in Boston. First Offence.

Says has never been punish'd since here for any offence. Aims to do right & perform his duty.

Jones appears very well, mind soft, and I should think much better of him than of most.

Says no swearings allow'd in the room he occupies. Has 7 or 8 room-mates. Says he us'd to swear but has entirely left it off. Has not sworn any for some months past.

Andrew Jackson[127] (Col[ore]d man)—Age 22

Born on Long Island but came to Boston when quite a child. Parents died when he was young & at the age of 9 was thrown upon the world. Was bound out but being ill treated ran away. Liv'd some at service but became very unsteady & having no friend to guide him soon run into crime. Says he attended Sabbath school some. Learn'd his Alphabet there & that was about all he knew when he first came to prison. 3d Comer. Convicted first when about 11. Was in prison 2 ys & 9 mo. Out about 2 ys, & then convicted again & was in prison 2 ys. Out about 2 ys & convicted a third time. All for stealing. Has now been here almost 3 years, & has life sentence. Says he behaves well & gets along well.

Converses frankly & sensibly. Says there are 8 in his room & no swearing is allow'd. They have a Law against it, with a penalty, Whipping, for violation.

Can now read & write. Not a great deal of sensibility.

Tho[ma]s Jennings—Age 23

Born & brot up mostly in Philadelphia. Early education poor. Parents died when he was quite young. Says he has no friends. Being life early without friends as a protector, liv'd rather a wild unsteady life. Work'd some at Tayloring, but

[127] "Andrew Jackson, 24y, convict in State Prison, d. there, Aug. 17, 1829." *Vital Records of Charlestown*, 2:303.

got no trade fully. Became vicious & run into crime. Says this is his first conviction. Sentence 3½ ys. Has been here some over 2½. Says he has got along well without much trouble. Not very frank & communicative. Should think him a shrew'd crafty fellow. Not much feeling, & cut out for a rogue. Perhaps, however, I judge him too hard. Do not like his appearance. Says he believes the Bible.

William Jackson[128] (Blk. Man)—Age 27

Home, Worcester. Mother & Step-father live there. Some education, tho not very good. Liv'd for 17 ys in a good family in Worcester. Was industrious and steady. About 4 <*ys ago*> before he got into this trouble, came to Boston & set up the business of hair dressing. Did very well. Married and has one child. Wife and child now in Boston. After a while, got into bad company, who led him away. Says he never drink'd to excess. Says this is his first offence & he is fully resolved it shall be his last. Sees his folly, & knows that this will be a good school to him.

Jackson appears open and frank, & should think from his appearance, that he is a good convict, & has his mind set upon doing well. Believes the Bible. The man he lived with in Worcester was Sheriff Ward.[129]

John W. Jones—Age 32

Born in Hancock (Mass). Has of late years liv'd mostly in Madison Co. N.Y. Has a wife there.

2d Comer. First time 2½ ys. 2d time Sentenced in Lenox for 1 year in May 1828 & has an additional sentence of 6 mo, as 2d comer. Education very poor. Says he gets along well here. Believes the Bible &c. The Jones family to which

[128] "William Jackson, 31y, prisoner in State Prison, d. there June 2, 1832." *Vital Records of Charlestown*, 2:281.

[129] Thomas W. Ward, sheriff of Worcester County, 1805-1824. *History of Worcester County, Massachusetts* (Boston, 1879), 1:42.

he belongs, is very famous for all manner of villainy, particularly for stealing in all its branches. Women as well as men. Being myself a Berkshire man I have often heard of their depredations & most of them male & female have been often in prison.

July 15, 1829

James Johnson—Age 20

Born & brot up in Virginia. Parentage respectable. Advantages & education good. His father a merchant, died when he was about 15. Was with his father some in Store & after his death, went into the store of Mercht in Petersburg Va, where he continued near 2 ys, then came on to N.Y. city, where he spent a season in a Store, then came on to Boston & through the agency of a pretended friend got into the difficulty which confines him here. Sentenced in Boston for swindling for 3 ys. Been here somewhat over a year. Says his habits were always good & his character unstain'd till this transaction. Friends do not know where he is. Has one young sister in N.Y. True name not Johnson.

He is a very interesting, intelligent, pleasant young man. Converse with frankness & propriety. Judging from appearances, I should think him far above most of his fellows.

Isaac Jackson—(Color'd man)—[Age 27]

Born in State of N.Y. Age 27. Parents are dead. Has 3 brothers in State of N.Y. For the last 9 years has lived in Mass., mostly in Stockbridge, where he has a wife. Brot up without education. Has been in our Sabbath School about 3 months & begins to read some.

Has been rather a wild young man, & fond of scrapes. Has been here about 11 months. Sentenced in Berkshire Co. for Larceny for 1 year. Has got along well here and says he has sown wild oats enough & intends now to be steady & honest.

Is a pleasant fellow but I fear very thoughtless.

Being from Stockbridge myself, I have been acquainted with him. He was always very thievish, and wo to any poultry that came in his way. Forever stealing little things.

James Johnson—(Black man)—[Age 18]

Born & brot up in New Bedford. Age 18. Parents now living at New Bedford. Says they brot him up well. Has a decent education. Says he was never given to drink or gambling. Was led by bad company to steal. Sentenced in Taunton for Larceny for 20 months. Has been here a little over a year. Is a waiter in the yard & his conduct invariably good.

I have found but very few persons if any, who appear to profess as much sensibility & tenderness as Johnson. He weeps like a child, & thinks he shall never again be led astray.

Henry C. Jaques—Age 43

Born, brot up, & has always liv'd in Newbury.[130]

Is a man of sense and converses with much propriety & a good degree of sensibility & feeling. Has been here 2 months. Sentence 22 months. Says he had not the most distant idea of stealing the Articles for which he was prosecuted. Had offended the man who prosecuted him & he did it for revenge.

Lost his parents when a child. At the time his mother died she entrusted him to a female friend, with whom he liv'd till 11, then went to sea with her brother or some relative & continu'd with him till 21. Has follow'd the Sea for

[130]Henry Cromwell Jaques, son of Henry and Hannah Jaques, was born in Newbury, Mar. 23, 1783. He married Polly Follansbee of Newburyport, May 9, 1807. *Vital Records of Newbury, Massachusetts, to the End of the Year 1849* (Salem, 1911), 1:247, 2:257.

a livelihood ever since. Says his habits & character were good untill about 4 ys ago. He had amass'd about 6000 Dollars, which he had let to a merchant or merchants who faild & he lost his all. This preyed upon him & he began to drink & became quite *intemperate.* Has a wife & 7 children. Says almost all his connections are pious. Says he firmly believes the Bible. Is very much cast down.

July 16, 1829

JOSEPH JOHNSON—AGE 26

Born in Boston. Parents both dead the same year within 4 months of each other. He was then about 6 ys old. Could then read in the Testament.

Was now thrown upon the world. Had no relatives to take him home, & no guardian to take charge of him. Lived wherever people would take him in. When he was about 9, went into the country & livd. Workd mostly at farming. Went to school one winter. When about 14 came back to Boston and work'd at shoemaking. The hands in the shop were in the constant & regular habit of having their drams & he usually went after the liquor, & for his trouble they usually gave him some. Was prone to be steady before this, but did not drink, but here got into the habit of loving his drams, & became more unsteady. The man he liv'd with was a universalist, tho a moral man, & he us'd to attend the Universalist meeting. This he thinks did not do him much good.

When 16 was convicted & sent to this prison for 3 ys. A part of this time behaved very bad. Was confin'd in cells 87 days for misconduct.

Is now here a second time. Sentence 18 months. Been here 9 months.

While here the first time thought he experienced Religion. Was baptized by Mr. Collier the Chaplain, a Baptist minister. When he went out, determined to live a christian life, joined a Baptist Church & for 3 ys, sustained a fair christian character. Was once sent as a delegate of the church with the minister. By & by before he thought of it, his thirst for liquor got hold of him. This led to bad associates & bad practices & finally to prison again.

Has a wife & 1 child. Johnson is a man of good mind. Converses well. Appears humbled very much, but after all that has past, we cannot but look upon him with suspicion & trembling. Conduct good. Feels very certain that he shall never drink again or go astray. "Let him that think he standeth take heed lest he fall."

JOHN JOHNSON—AGE 28

Born in Norfolk, Virginia. Mother lives there now. Has been to sea almost constantly since he was eight years old. Education very poor. Can read but not write. Says this is the first difficulty he ever had, & if God spares his life to get out, it shall be his last of this sort. Says he never was intemperate and was always a faithful sailor. Gave to his mother most of his earnings, she being poor, not married. Came into Boston some thing like a year ago, & got into a bad scrape, as he calls it, & was sentenced to this prison for 1 year. Been here 8 months.

Has been in no trouble for misconduct. Converses very well. Believes the Bible, tho not much feeling.

July 17, 1829

JETHRO KENNY—AGE 56

Born in Middleton, Essex Co.[131] Both parents died when he was but a child. After their death was put out in Reading.

[131] Jethro Kenny, son of Archelaus and Phebe Kenny, was born in Middleton, Jan. 21, 1773. He married Mehitable Eaton of Reading, Mar. 7,

Learned the trade of a Shoemaker. Brot up in that town & livd there untill he was more than 40, then mov'd to Billerica where he lived till within 2 or 3 years before coming to prison, then moved to Dunstable. Early education rather poor. Can read & write. Says that with the exception of the transaction for which he was sent here, his character for industry and honesty has been unimpeach'd. Not intemperate. Has work'd hard & minded his own business.

Has some property. Has always regarded the Sabbath & been steady in his attendance on public worship.

Wife & 8 children. Sentenced for Adultery for 3 ys. Has been here 2 ys & 3 months.

Conduct unexceptionable. Is mild, & seems to have considerable feeling. Indulges a hope that he is a Christian, but I am fearful he deceives himself.

So far as I can learn tho not from himself altogether, his wife was for a long time sick and his wife's sister liv'd in the family to assist. They became intimate & she became pregnant. In this predicament, the plan was adopted by himself, wife & wife's sister that she should live with them both as his wives, & so it went on, by general consent & in concord & he had children by both & for this he was prosecuted.

In reproving him for such conduct, he seem'd dispos'd rather to palliate his crime, & cited David & others to justify himself, which I much disapproved & gave him my mind very plainly. Says he shall never continue this connection, & had broken it off before he was prosecuted.

James Kidder—Age 36

Born & brot up in Lexington. Has wife & 4 children. Never learn'd any trade. Work'd at farming. Decent common ed-

---

1799. *Vital Records of Middleton, Massachusetts, to the End of the Year 1849* (Topsfield, 1904), 32; *Vital Records of Reading, Massachusetts, to the Year 1850* (Boston, 1912), 378.

ucation, & parents did what they could to bring him up well. Became intemperate, & this was his ruin. 3d Comer. Sentenc'd first when about 24, for 2 ys. Out 16 mo. 2d time 18 months. Out 3 mo. 3d time 2 years & additional for life. Been here almost 5 years.

Says his conduct is orderly & good. Feels that he has conducted very foolishly & wickedly & knows that a life of sin will make its votary miserable.

Says he believes the bible & reads it a great deal.

Wishes the new prison to be done that he may be alone. Not much feeling, tho he converses sensibly. Says he never had any propensity to steal except when he had drinkd too much.

John Kinder—Age 35

Born in England & brought at by his father to the Hatting business. Education decent. Brought up in the faith of the Church of Eng. Believes the Bible &c. Was rather of a roving disposition and about 6 ys ago came to this Country. Work'd in various places at his trade. The last place was Springfield, where he was convicted & sentenced for 2 ys. Been here 10 months. Says he never was in any similar difficulty before. Did not drink to excess, tho he occasionally took his glass. Has got along well. Says he thinks this will be a good school & that he shall hereafter be content to be steady. Is a pleasant sensible man, and appears very well.

July 20, 1829

James Loomis—Age 51

Born in Connecticut. Left that State when about 18. Brot up to farming. Early education decent. Parents both pious. Well brot up, & habits good. When he left Connecticut went in to the County of Otsego, N.Y. Married at 24. 2 Children. When 21 made a profession of Religion. Joined a

Presbyterian Church, and for a number of years maintained a respectable standing in the Church. Was a steady industrious man & his character above suspicion. Wife not a professor of Religion. His marriage was unfortunate. His wife prov'd untrue to his bed & he parted from her. This conduct of hers & its results preyed in his mind till he became partially deranged. Withdrew from Society & wandered about in the woods desolate & in despair. Was watch'd for a season by his friends who tried to keep him under their care, but he went off, & finally for a theft committed in this state of mind, was sentenced to the N.Y. State Prison. His friends, learning what had happened, made a representation of his case to the Governor & he was pardoned after having been there 30 days.

He continued after his discharge, much in the same state of mind—in almost complete despair, & reckless as to what he did or what should become of him. In about 2 ys was again sentenced to the same prison for a similar offence. His friends, after a time again, interfered & procur'd his pardon on the same ground as before viz Insanity. He was confined 18 months this time. For 8 or 9 years after this he continu'd to live here & there—sometimes with his brothers & sometimes elsewhere. Work'd some on the Erie Canal, and there contracted a habit of drinking too much. This was about 8 ys ago. After a while, wandered off into this State in a restless, despairing state of mind without object or aim, & in the County of Franklin was apprehended for a felony & put into the Gaol at Greenfield. While there, he and another prisoner set fire to the Gaol in order to get away. The fire was discovered before it had advanced much & they were both tried for this offence and sentenced here for life. This was 6 ys ago in June last.

Loomis had been in some trouble here, tho not much for 2 or 3 ys past. His mind is generally lucid, tho at times there is a sort of restlessness about him. Seems honestly dispos'd & I think is determined, if ever restored to liberty, to do well. He still cherishes his hope of piety. How well grounded this hope is, is best known to Him who searcheth the heart.

JOSEPH LEVICK—AGE 53

Born in Canada. Extraction French. When quite young his father mov'd to Vermont. Was educated in French, and a Catholic. Learn'd the trade of a Carpenter & when 18 or 19 came to Boston & has for many years past, work'd in Boston & vicinity. Has spent some time working at his trade in Philadelphia & Baltimore. Went to the Island of Cuba & work'd at Havana about 3 years. Has now some property. Was a soldier during the whole of the late war. Says he was never an intemperate man.

Spirits did not agree with him & when he was in the army, us'd always to sell or give away his ration of spirits.

Says he has work'd hard always. Married. Has one child. His wife proved a loose, bad woman, & very intemperate. Could not live with her. Left her several times, & she kept following him about the country. Has been here 6 ys next Oct. Life, for Burglary. Says he did not commit the crime. He bought the goods and they were found with him & the man of whom he had them had gone off.

Never in any trouble before.

Is, I believe a very good convict. Health feeble, bleeds at the Lungs. Says his friends in Vt. are wealthy & respectable. They live in Montpelier.

HENRY H. LEE—AGE 18

Born in State of N.Y., but his parents moved into Vt when he was a Child. Was brot up in Vt. No education till he came here. Is now in our Sab[bath] School. Has been a very wild, thoughtless boy.

When about 15, left Vt & came to Boston. Had no regular business. Very soon got into bad company and to Stealing. Sentenced for theft, for 5 ys. Has been here 2 ys & 2 mo.

Is a hard boy. Very little feeling & has been in considerable trouble here.

Says he has been a hard character & knows he has acted foolishly & wickedly, & from his appearance, I should think he cared very little as to what he did or as to the future. Possibly he may yet be brought to his senses. Very ignorant, & no elevation of feeling.

George Lamb—Age 41

Born in England & lived there till 28. Education decent. Follow'd the Sea in Early life for a number of years. Came to State of N.Y., & has liv'd there mostly since he came to U.S. Was a Labourer. Work'd where he could find employ. Laboured on the Erie Canal considerably. Says he was intemperate & very profane. For a good many years past, has neglected the Bible, Sabbath, Public Worship, &c, although he says he believes the Bible. Before coming here, lived for two or three years in Hampden & Hampshire Counties in this State. Sentenced in Springfield about 2 ys ago for an attempt to rape, for 10 ys. Says he has been in no difficulty here. Has behav'd well & got along well.

Is a very thoughtless man, I should think, & possessed of very little feeling.

July 21, 1829

Patrick Lynch—Age 31

Born in Ireland. Education quite good. Bred to the business of an Apothecary.

Left Ireland for U.S. 11 ys ago & follow'd the business to

which he was bred about 9 ys in Boston. Has 3 children. Wife is dead. Says he did well in Boston, was respected, & his habits were correct until some few months before his commitment.

On account of misfortune & affliction, took to the Bottle, & in a short time plung'd himself so deep that he was quite given up.

Says his friends & relatives are respectable. Convicted of Larceny in Salem, & sentenced for 4 ys. Been here 21 months. Says he fully believes the Bible & is deeply sensible of his folly & wickedness in thus giving way to the beastly vice of intemperance. Is a man of good sense, mildness of feeling, & in conversation is affected to tears. Is a good & orderly convict & far above most of his fellows, as I should think. I have always been pleas'd with his appearance.[132]

David Lansdale or Lazedale—Age 30

2d comer. 1st time 18 mo. 2d time, been here over 3 ys. Has 9 months more. Ignorant and a strange being. Should think him either partly insane or non compos.

[132]Date of entry originally read July 22; corrected in ink to read July 21.

VOLUME II[1]

July 22, 1829

[Henry H. Livingston][2]
for 4 ys. Has now one years & 11 months to stay. Has been in Cells twice for attempting to escape but says he has seen the folly of such a course, & is determined now & for some time past has resolvd to behave undeviatingly well. Acknowledges that he has lived a very wicked and foolish life, & till of late has not elevated his mind to a different course.

Says his mind is now fully made up to a life of honesty & usefulness. Knows he can do it if he but wills it & is resolute & says if he lives I shall yet see him redeem his pledge. Is a smart, sensible young man. Has of late conducted very well, & may possibly yet rise above this degradation of vice & crime. Says he believes the Bible though he has greatly neglected it.

William Lyons—or Lines—Age 36
Born in Dutchess Co. N.Y. Father a Slave. Had no education. When a small boy, a gentleman moving to Vermont took him with him & he liv'd with him till he was 15. Work'd at Farming. The man was an Infidel and never went to meeting, nor taught his family to go. He was therefore brought up without religious instruction. During the

[1]Two pages have been torn out of volume 2, which now begins on page 3. The manuscript index at the end of volume 2 indicates that an entry for Timothy B. Loker began on page 1.

[2]Name of subject determined from the manuscript index at the end of volume 2.

late war enlisted into the Army and serv'd through the war. Until this war, his habits were good & he never drink'd. While in the Army, contracted the habit of intemperance, & this habit grew upon him in after life. Says he was always honest & never addicted to stealing at all. Since leaving the Army has lived mostly in Albany, N.Y., but some in other places. Last residence before coming here was WmsTown, Mass. Has a wife & 3 children in WmsTown.

Convicted in Lenox for an assault with intent to kill, & sentenced for 10 ys. Been here near 4 ys. Says he never had the most distant idea of killing. Went to a Turkey shoot, stayed in the evening and gambled, drink'd pretty freely, set out to go home. A fellow from whom he had won some money, said he should not go, but should play longer. A quarrel ensued, & he was prosecuted &c.

Lyons is naturally of kind, good feelings. Drink has been his grand difficulty. Is very much humbled & weeps very freely over his follies & sufferings. Says he has never been call'd to an account for any thing since he came here. Has not us'd a profane word in several years, though he was formerly profane. Is certain he should never drink any more & could not be so base as to abuse God's goodness by resuming into Sin. Few prisoners appear as humble as Lyon.

John Lavis—Age 31

Born & brot up in South Carolina. Bred a Tailor. Education decent. Is a man of a good mind, but I fear without any principle. Third comer. First time sentence 3½ ys. Out but few months. Second, 5 ys & 3 mo. Third 5 ys. Been here now somewhat more than a year, & is liable to a life sentence. Has made a number of attempts to escape & break out, for which he has been in cells a good deal & in chains. Aside from this, he says he has had no difficulty, & is determind hereafter to submit quietly to his situation. Has been somewhat intemperate. Says when he went out the last time he was fully determind on conducting himself well, but one morning was led to drinking, took too much & was lost.

Suspect he does not believe the Bible, although he did not say directly. Thinks it a good Book.

Probably a very hard case.

William Lloyd—Age 33

Born in Manchester Eng. Can read & write. Went to the Woollen manufacturing business, but pretty early in life went into the naval service. Was aboard of a man of War about 8 ys, where he imbibed all the habits of Sailors. Was thoughtless & wicked. Parents religious, good people.

In 1815, deserted at Quebec & came to U.S. & has liv'd in various parts of the country. Was quite intemperate, & attributes his misfortunes to this cause. 2d Comer. 1st time 2 ys. Out about 4½ ys, then Sentenced for Burglary for life. Been here almost seven ys. Appears a good deal humbled. Weeps, & feels positive he should never drink or go astray again were he to go out. Says he came to a firm resolution 3 ys ago. Has often had opportunity to drink, but would not, & has conducted himself well in all respects. Lloyd has a very good name as a prisoner.

David Lampson[3]—Age 42

Born in Ipswich, now Hamilton. Mother still living there. Can read & write. Thrown early on the world by the death

[3]David Lampson, son of Matthew Lampson, was baptized in Ipswich, Feb. 3, 1788. *Vital Records of Ipswich, Massachusetts, to the End of the Year 1849* (Salem, 1910–1919), 1:233.

of his father. Went to sea a number of years, then quit & learned the Joiner's & carpenters trade and workd at it most of the time till he got into Prison. Livd about 12 ys in Salem. During the war, went one cruise with Com. Rogers,[4] & one on a privateering expedition. Became Intemperate. 2d Comer. First time 2½ ys. Out last September and return'd again about 2 months ago for 2 ys. Is out of all concert of his fellow man. They are all dishonest, & scrupple not to wrong & abuse all who come in their way. Is doubtless a bitter & malicious minded man—hardened—and no proper feeling. Every thing is wrong, and every body but himself.

James Lawrence—Age 32

Born & brot up in Connecticut. Education good. Family & friends very respectable. Was formerly a Cadet at the Military Academy at West Point. Afterwards a Lieutenant in the U.S. Army.

Has for the most part of the time since the war, lived in the State of N.Y., in the Western District. Has a family there & some property. Was a contractor to a considerable amount on the Erie Canal &c &c.

Is well acquainted with Mr Van Buren, present Secretary of State.[5] Says he has been in good standing in society, & has been actively employ'd in business. Came on to the East with a Cargo of flour, and after selling it, being on his return home, fell among gamblers. Says he has been

---

[4] Probably John Rodgers (1773–1838), the U.S. Navy's senior captain during the War of 1812. *American National Biography,* 18:724–725.

[5] Martin Van Buren (1782–1862), Democratic politician from New York who was elected to the Senate in 1821. He headed the influential "Albany Regency." Van Buren served as Andrew Jackson's secretary of state and was elected president in 1836. *American National Biography,* 22:159–162.

adicted to gambling, & withal was in the habit of drinking too much.

Lost his money & committed the crime for which he was sentenced. Sentence 5 ys. Been here about one year.

This is his story. Does not incline to be very communicative, & probably keeps back most of what it would be most desirable to know.

Says he was never in any difficulty before. This, I think is doubtful.

Is a sensible man and converses well, & behaves himself well. Acknowledges that his true name is not Lawrence.

July 23, 1829

JOHN LOWELL[6]—AL[IAS] COLSON—AGE 34
Born & brot up in Maine. Father now lives there. Education very poor, can scarcely read at all. Brot up to farming. Mother died when he was quite young & his father soon married again & had other children. His first children were greatly neglected & over looked. Early became wild & vicious & when 18 was convicted of Larceny & sentenced to this Prison for 7 years. This was before Maine was a State. Serv'd out his time, and was out about 8 years, when a little more than 3 months ago, he was convicted of Larceny in Boston & sentenced for 18 months.

During the time he was out, livd in various places. Was 3 ys in the Naval service in South America. Became intemperate, & this, he says was the cause of his second offence. Is quite feeble in health. Gets along well, & says he has no one to blame but himself.

[6] "John Lowell, 40 y, convict in State Prison, Charlestown, d. there, May 18, 1830." *Vital Records of Charlestown, Massachusetts, to the Year 1850*, comp. Roger D. Joslyn (Boston, 1984–1995), 2:303.

SAMUEL LOMBARD—AGE 23
Born & brot up in Goram, Maine.[7] Father died when he was 18 months old. His mother married again. His Stepfather was always kind & good to him. Lived with him & work'd on farm till 17. His health became feeble so that he could not work on the farm & he went & learn'd that business of Chaise making. Work'd at this Trade with his Brother & continu'd with him till 21. After wards work'd out as a journeyman. Education good & says that his character was fair, & his habits correct. Never drink'd, and was esteemed by his acquaintance. This Spring came down to Boston on business, to stay only a short time. While there, a man by the name of Smith, as he said, introduced himself to him. Was entire stranger, but put up at the same house & got some bad money into his hands.

Pass'd a five Dollar Bill, was arrested & sentenced for 3 ys. Has been here 2 months.

Lombard appears very humble & sincere. Is deeply affected with his condition, weeps freely, & seems a good deal concerned in regard to his everlasting peace.

I am satisfied he cannot be a hardened offender. Says this is the first departure from duty of which he was ever guilty so far as his fellow men are concerned, & it shall be the last.

WILLIAM LOVEJOY—AGE 24
Born & brot up in Andover.[8] Parents live there now. Can read & write. Liv'd with them till he was about 20. Partly

---

[7]Samuel Lombard, son of James and Bethiah, was born in Gorham, Maine, May 11, 1807. Hugh D. McLellan, *History of Gorham, Me.* (Portland, 1903), 635.

[8]William Lovejoy, son of Orlando and Abiah Lovejoy, was born in Andover, Feb. 28, 1805. *Vital Records of Andover, Massachusetts, to the End of the Year 1849* (Topsfield, 1912), 1:255.

learn'd the trade of a shoemaker. Says he has been a pretty steady *fellow* & never drink'd too much. Convicted in Ipswich on two Indictments for stealing & sentenced for 3 ys & 4 mo. Been here 4 days.

Should think him greatly lacking in intellect. Appears perfectly frank. Tells without reserve, all his feelings, & weeps very copiously. His mind is evidently under a religious excitement of some cast, but from his singularity of appearance, it is difficult telling how far he may be affected by genuine conviction.

JOHN INGALLS, AL[IAS] DEARBORN—AGE 24

Discharged in March last after confinement of more than 6 ys, and came back to Prison in June last, sentenced in Boston for passing a Counterfeit Bill. Is very innocent of the crime, and his sentence oppressive and unjust. Is a ruin'd young man—hard, revengeful, & unfeeling. His present sentence 2 years. His return was not at all unlook'd for. Gave him some advice, but not with much hope. God is above him, & can subdue him & this affords all the hope in his case.[9]

July 24, 1829

W[ILLIA]M MERRILL—AGE 38

Born & brot up in Salisbury Essex Co. Has a wife & 3 children in Haverhill. Early Education pretty good & was well brot up by his parents. When 16 his father died. Went then to learn the Trade of a cabinet maker, & after getting the trade, set up for himself in Haverhill. Did not meet with very good encouragement. During the last war, was a member of an independent Company & his company, among others, was ordered on duty at Boston. While ab-

[9] Entry mistakenly dated June 23.

sent, his creditors struck upon him & attached his property. This troubled him very much, & he ran into excess in drinking & finally after a while was guilty of crime. Sentenced to this prison for 2 ys in 1818. Serv'd his time out. Was out 3 ys. In 1823 was again sentenced for Store Breaking in Boston, for 7 years. Is now on his seventh year, & is liable to an additional sentence. Says he has had no trouble the last 4 years, has conducted himself well. The fore part of the time, did not conduct as he ought. Made some attempts to get away. Believes the Bible & is very sensible he has lived a bad life. Thinks he shall be wise enough if he lives to get out, to behave himself as he ought. Appears mild & agreeable.

W[illia]m Moran[10]—Age 46

Colored man. Home in Charleston, S.C. Born free. Learn'd the trade of a Cabinet maker. Says he was steady when a boy & a steady young man. No Education when young. Learn'd to read a little after he was of age. Came to this State 19 years ago. Lived in Boston & there fell into bad company & was led astray. Says he never drink'd to excess. Is a third comer & sentenced for life. First time 1 year. Out 4 or 5 ys. 2d time 2 ys. Out 3 ys. Been here the last time near 9 years. Says he has never been punish'd for misconduct since he came to prison.

Works in the wash room, & when he has done his days work is permitted to read. Is in the Sabbath School, & studies his Bible a great deal. Is pleasant, has some feeling, ignorant, seems well dispos'd and thinks he could never be led astray again.

---

[10] "William Moran, prisoner in the State Prison, d. there July 28, 1830." *Vital Records of Charlestown*, 2:287.

Francis Mitchell[11]—Age 29

Born in the Island of Cuba. When 7 ys old came to Charlestown S.C. Born free. Is a Mulatto. No early education. Since in prison has learned to read well, write, & cypher. Left his parents without their knowledge & has never heard from them since. Went into a gentleman's family in Charleston. Could understand no English. They knock'd him about pretty hard & being a child he knew not what to do. Stay'd there 2 ys, & finally went away & came across an Italian Gentleman who could speak Spanish, who took him & befriended him. Liv'd with him till he died. His partner then took him to Wilmington N.C., and put him with a Barber where he learned the Trade. After getting the trade came on to Boston & opened Shop. Did well. Had as much business as he could do. Says he had always been steady & industrious & was addicted to no bad habits. After a while took a partner, who prov'd a bad man. Lost his customers, & finally was led to commit a crime. Sentenced to this prison for 2 ys. Was about 20 ys old, serv'd sentence & was out about 15 mo & then was led away by an old rogue to engage in a Burglary for which he was sentenced for Life.

Mitchell is very frank & intelligent, pleasant, appears very well, and behaves well. Is the principal Barber here.

William Millard—Age 56

Born in England. Moved with his parents to Canada when young. Education tolerably good. By trade a Tailor. Has wife & 2 children in the State of N. York. Says he was steady & regular until after he was 20.

---

[11]Commitment Register, Charlestown State Prison, 1818–1840, nos. 242 and 527, Massachusetts State Archives. According to this record, he was born in "Port-au-Prince, West Indies."

Never intemperate, but ran into vice & got into State Prison. Has been in State Prison first & last more than 20 years.

1st time	3ys & 6 mo
2 do	5 ys & 2 mo
3 - do -	4 ys
4 - "	3 ys
5 - "	2 ys
6 "	4 ys, 9 mo & is now sentenced for life

Says he has always got along well. Thinks he is a man of pretty good feeling. Has no disposition to wrong any body. Says the government never show'd him any clemency, and always turned him out destitute & somehow or other he would get into trouble. Thinks if he was only pardoned, he should never forfeit any confidence placed in him & should not abuse the clemency of the government.

Most likely, he never will. Talks freely & with mildness. Believes the Bible as he says, and after all calls himself a pretty good man. How little do we know of our own hearts!!

July 27, 1829

HENRY MARSTON—AGE 28

Born & brot up in N. Hampshire. Parents were poor, & his education very poor. Can barely read. Is now in our Sabbath school. When a boy, went to live with a man who married his cousin. A farmer, & respectable. Lived with him till 15. Some difficulty then arose & he ran away. Now sees his folly in so doing. Work'd in various places. Was steady. Got good wages & did very well.

Finally came to Boston & there found bad associates. Run into bad habits, though he was not intemperate except he would have a *high* now & then as other young men do. After a while began to Steal & got into State prison.

Is a second comer. First time 3 years. Out 4 months. Second time sentenced for 7 years. Been here somewhat more than 3½ years. Has got along for the most part well. Sees his folly & is determined no more to follow the ways of vice. Feels very sure he shall keep his resolutions.

On the subject of religion is very ignorant. Believes the Bible "What there is of it" to use his own words. Is frank, & I should think not a very bad convict, & that he belonged to the better half.

HENRY MOULTON—AGE 28

Home, Newburyport. Good common Education and brought up to good habits. His mother still living & one of the best of women. Learn'd the trade of a Shoe maker. When out of his time, set up for himself. Did very well. After a while met with some severe losses which resulted in a failure. Previously to this had married. Has 2 children.[12]

After his failure, left home & visited various parts of the country. In his absence his wife died. This affected him very much, & with his losses disheartened him, & he became unsteady. Drinkd some & at last committed crime & sentenced to this prison for 3½ years.

Has now 10 months to stay. He is a man of good sense, & very good personal appearance. Converses with much propriety & apparent sincerity. Says he believes this trial will be of essential service to him & he is confident he shall play the fool no more. Has got along well here & intends his conduct here shall be correct. Says he believes

[12]Possibly the Henry Moulton who married Eliza Buswell, July 15, 1821, in Newburyport. *Vital Records of Newburyport, Massachusetts, to the End of the Year 1849* (Salem, 1911), 2:328.

the Bible. Shall leave this part of the country as soon as his sentence expires.

John P. Marlow—Age 27

Born in Ireland. Has been in America 9 ys. Home in Montreal, Canada. Has a wife there. Has lived as a servant in various families as he could find employ. Says he was rather a wild, unsteady boy. Education decent. Left Montreal because wages were low, & came to Boston. Was addicted to drinking too much. Stole a coat & was sentenced for 3 ys to this prison. Has been here now 18 mo. Says it is the first crime he ever committed and was never before arraigned before a court.

Has had no difficulty here & means to behave well. Thinks he shall do better when he goes out than he us'd to do. Shall never drink any more.

Make a fish live out of water, & then an Irish man may stop drinking when once given to it.

James Marvel—Age 42

Home in Bristol Co. Town of Freetown. Wife & 8 children, 7 sons & 1 daughter. Decent common Education. Married at the age of 20. Wife of a respectable good family & a pious woman. When young, work'd at farming, & occasionally at the business of a Ship Carpenter. When about 18 follow'd this altogether & became master of the business. For many years, spent his winters at the South, at work at his trade.

Says he was always strictly honest, & never had but one failing & that was *drinking too much.* Was convicted of passing a Counterfeit Bill. Declares most solemnly that he did not know of its being bad.

Sentenced at Taunton for 2 years. Been here about 15 months. Has never been in any trouble & is resolved to do well. Believes the Bible to be the Word of God.

Is a sensible man and converses well.

MICHAEL MANSFIELD—AGE 28

Born in Ireland. Lived in the U.S. 14 ys. Labourer. Can read & write. Says this is his first imprisonment. Convicted of Larceny in Northampton. Says positively that he is entirely innocent. Been here now 15 months. Sentenced for 18 months. Seems to be a very clever fellow, frank & professing a good degree of feeling. Roman Catholic. Says he was never given to drinking—does not think he has drink'd a half gallon in 14 years. Has livd mostly in Boston—has a wife & 4 children there.

HARVEY MOREY—AGE 23

Born & brot up in Montgomery Hampden Co.[13] Has a mother living. Father dead. Education decent. Was born with what was considered a mark on his left hand or arm. When about 6 ys old it became sore & prov'd a cancer, & after about a year, his arm was amputated near the shoulder. Being unable to attend to any ordinary business, when he was old enough he follow'd peddling goods & has follow'd this ever since till coming to prison. Sentenced in Springfield for forgery for 2 ys. Been here about 3 months. Says he has been rather a wild, giddy young man tho not vicious. Never intemperate, though he drink'd occasionally as Others do. Convicted of forgery. Says he believes the Bible. Thinks peddling a life not very favorable to virtue as men in that business are apt to be sharpers. Has got along well so far. Should not think he has much feeling, though nothing improper was manifest in his conversation. Have never convers'd with him before.

[13]Harvey Morey, son of Abner and Nancy Morey, was born in Montgomery, Mar. 2, 1806. *Vital Records of Montgomery, Massachusetts, to the Year 1850* (Boston, 1902), 26.

July 29, 1829

Samuel Merrill—alias Hemphill—Age 43
Home in New Hampshire. Good common Education, and well brought up. Is one of 18 children by the same mother. Says he has seen the whole family, father, mother, & the 18 children seated at the same table. His father & mother & all the children, excepting himself, hopefully pious, and this fact he says adds doubly to his shame & guilt, in that he has abus'd such light and advantages. His family respectable.

First began to go astray by gambling, then got to drinking, & from that to stealing. 3d Comer. Has now a life sentence. Has been here the last time about 3 years. In the whole not far from 11 years.

Says he has got along well. Believes the Bible & is sensible of the supreme importance of Religion.

Prison a painful place, but he knows it is better for him to be here than to be out and live as he has. Condemns himself fully. Thinks if he has one more trial of his liberty he should never run into intemperance & crime. How sincere he may be in his declarations & professions I know not. By the officers, he is considered a hard case & probably is so. Is a smart sensible man.

Justin Morse—[Age 35]
Born and brot up in Cambridge says he was never 50 miles from home in his life.[14] Has been an industrious, hard laboring man, but the latter part of his life was very intemperate, which led him to his present conditions. Convicted

[14]Justin Morse, son of Josiah and Hannah Morse, was baptized in Cambridge, Sept. 22, 1793. *Vital Records of Cambridge, Massachusetts, to the Year 1850* (Boston, 1914–1915), 1:501.

of Larceny about 2 ys ago. Sentence 3 ys. Education decent. Says he lived about 4 ys with Doct Chaplain of Cambridgeport,[15] & served him faithfully & is very sorry he left him. The Doctor wish'd him to stay & told him he would get into difficulty if he left him.

Was offered higher wages & was fool enough to quit. Says that Doct C. owed him at one time for work $700. Has not spent it all. Some of it still remains on Interest. This was his first trouble, & this was the result of going to Independence one 4th of July & getting high.

Morse is remarkably pleasant & frank, and a really good hearted fellow. Works in the front yard a part of the time & takes care of garden. Gets into no difficulty. Believes the Bible, says he reads it a great deal. Knows for certain, that he shall never drink any more. I wish he were as sure as he thinks he is.

THOMAS MARR[16]—AGE 32

Born & brot up in Scotland. Early education decent. Was always a wild wayward boy, & that led him to leave home & country. Wish'd to be roving about. Came to American in 1818 or 19. Lived first in Canada. Came to the US and soon after got into State Prison. Says he was never given to drinking or gambling. Running after bad women, he says was his ruin. 3d Comer.

1st time 3 ys—out 1 month
2d time 3 ys—out 14 months
3d time 3 ys been here 2 weeks, & is liable to a life Sentence.

---

[15] James Prescott Chaplin (1782–1828), Harvard M.B. 1805, M.D. 1811. *Sibley's Harvard Graduates* (Cambridge and Boston, 1873–), 18:28n., 33.

[16] "Thomas Marr, convict in State Prison, Charlestown, d. there May 23, 1834." *Vital Records of Charlestown*, 2:287.

Says he was never in any difficulty when here before & is determined to conduct well now. Believes the Bible, and know that he has lived a foolish, wicked life.

JONATHAN MOREY—AL[IAS] MORRIS—
COLORED MAN—AGE 29

Home in Portland, Maine. Has wife & child there. Moved there from N. York last spring. Born in Virginia. Born free. Went to school when young & can read & write. Has follow'd the sea for a living since he was 11 ys old. Father is dead. His mother is still living in N. Jersey. She has had 21 children—6 pair of twins. He is a twin with a sister. Has now nine brothers & nine sisters living. One Brother & 2 Sisters married in Boston. Says he was made prisoner during the late war & was in Dartmor prison England.[17] Says he had gotten into intemperate habits. Acknowledges that he was guilty & deserves his Sentence. Sentenced in Boston for Theft for one year. Been here 2 weeks. Says he should have been sentenced longer but for a recommendation which he had.

Appears humble. Is a man of good sense and converses very well.

Says he believes the Bible, tho he has greatly neglected it & has not regarded its truths as he ought.

July 31, 1829

DANIEL NEWELL—AGE 30

Born in Wilbraham. Liv'd there till 10. Father then moved to Munson,[18] where he liv'd about 10 ys more. Has lived

---

[17]Dartmoor Prison, Devonshire, was built to confine French prisoners in 1809. *Encyclopaedia Britannica*, 14th ed. (London, 1929), 7:63.

[18]I.e., Monson, Massachusetts.

since then, the greater portion of his time in Boston, say 7 years. A large part of this time drove carriage for different Gentlemen. Liv'd one year at the Subscription or Club house, where gentlemen meet to play billiards, read news, drink &c. Thinks this rather unhing'd his mind, tho he says he was never intemperate. Kept a Cellar in Cambridge Street part of year. Early education as good as common & his habits as regular as most young men. Believes the Bible to be true. Convicted of Larceny in Boston and sentenced for 3 ys. Been here 20 months. Has never been in any trouble here.

Appears mild & pleasant. Thinks he shall keep away from Boston hereafter—a bad place to live. Intends to conduct well when he goes from this place.

Elias Nash—Age 19

Born & brought up in Boston. Education pretty good. Father & mother live in Boston. His father a Mason & rather intemperate. His mother he says is an excellent woman. (His mother I have seen several times at the prison and should think her one of the tenderest & best of mothers & a truly pious woman.) Brought up to believe the Bible, & does believe it. Has tended store some. Was rather dispos'd to be wild & thoughtless. When 18 was led to crime by some unprincipl'd fellow. Before this drink'd, gambled, & run after bad women and was in the way to ruin. Sentenced about 16 months ago for 5 years. Has got along well. Says he can see that the course he was running was ruinous & is resolv'd to live very differently hereafter.

Is sensible & frank, but does not seem to profess much sensibility of feeling, though he manifests nothing like hardness.

CHARLES NICHOLS—AGE 22
(Colored man). Born & brot up in Boston. Education quite good. Had good parents, who while they liv'd brot him up well & gave him good advice.

Was taught to believe and revere the Bible.

After their death, was left in a great measure, without advice & salutary discipline. Learn'd the trade of a Barber. Had a shop of his own & did very well and might have done well, had he continu'd steady & attentive to business. 2d Offender. First time 1 year. Out 5½ ys. 2d time been here 7 months. Sentence 5 ys. The last time, did not steal the goods, but harboured them knowing them to have been stolen.

Says he has never been call'd to an account here for any misconduct. Is a pleasant, sensible young man. But probably the atmosphere of Boston has poison'd him pretty deeply. Says he shall never attempt living in Boston again. Has an uncle in the West Indies in good circumstances & he intends to go to him.

JOHN ORMSBY—AGE 23
Born & brot up in Baltimore. Education decently good. Parents now live in Baltimore. Says he has a very fine mother. Brot up to the Business of a Baker. Was a wild, wayward boy. Has been on board U.S. Vessel of war 2 ys, & of merchant vessel 11 months. His father bought him off. Has given his parents a great deal of trouble. Says he was never in a State Prison before. Has been in jail. Has a brother in the Baltimore S. Prison. Came into Boston only 9 days before he was apprehended. Sentenced on 2 Indictments 5½ ys. Been here 21 months. Says he was not really an intemperate man, but when in U.S. Service, contracted somewhat of a love for spirits, & got merry occasionally.

Says he believes the Bible to be the word of God.

Knows he has liv'd a sorry life, and one calculated to make him miserable. Thinks he shall live differently if ever gets out. Has been punish'd some since he came here. O. is sensible man, but I fear has been very much hardened. I should think him a shrewd, calculating fellow, & yet he may be better than my fears. He converses very well.

August 3, 1829

SIMEON NORTON—AGE 27
Born & brot up in N. Hampshire. Parents now living there. Early Education good. Lived with his father till he was 11 ys old. The reason of his leaving his father was that he had a Stepmother who was very cruel to him, & his father, being a mechanic, was call'd abroad a good deal & was away several months at a time and when he was not at home his Stepmother usd to treat him very cruelly. His uncle who lived near by, finding how he was treated took him away from home when his father was absent. He lived with him some time & went to school. Learn'd the business of Stone cutting, & has follow'd it for a livelihood. Work'd in a great many places in almost every part of the country. Work'd a good deal in Boston. Sentenced in Boston for Larceny—for 1 year. Been here about 6½ months. Gets along well here & says he is resolved to conduct well when he gets out. This is his first difficulty. Never married. Says that he and another man agreed with a gentleman in Boston to take up a Well which did not afford water permanently, & sink it till there should be a constant supply, and were to have 50 Dollars for the Job. The second day they were so fortunate as to strike a fine, copious spring, and the Man refused to fulfill the contract.

As it was only verbal & could not be proved they could not help themselves, & he turn'd them off with two Dollars per day.

They were mad and resolved to be revenged & in getting revenge, got into the State Prison.

Is a man of pretty good sense, but of not much sensibility.

DAVID PETERS—AGE 34
Born & brot up in R. Island. Farmer. Early Education very poor. Can read, but not write. Is now in our Sab[bath] School. For the last 10 or 12 ys has livd most of the time in Douglass, Worcester Co. Has been married. Wife is dead. Has one child. Has been rather thoughtless, & giddy. Lov'd rum pretty well, though not a drunkard. Sentenced for an attempt to rape for 15 ys. Been here about 4½ ys. Not guilty. Was a little rude, but us'd no violence.

Prosecuted once before for a similar offence & acquitted.

Says he believes the Bible & studies it a good deal. Thinks he should alter his course very much were he again to enjoy his liberty. For a few months back, says he has thought much on his past life & the importance of living like a rational creature.

Should not think he had much feeling, but perhaps his ignorance has led me to this conclusion. Is respectable, and pleasant.

August 7, 1829

WILLIAM PAINE—AGE 39—COLOR'D MAN—(for a sketch of his case see Vol 1)[19]

[19]See above, p. 4. The previous entry gives Paine's age as 36.

Alexander Palmer—Age 40

Brot up in State of N. York in Hebron, Washington Co. His father died when he was 5 ys old. Says he was a wild boy, was put out, but that the man did not use him very well & ran away. Learned no trade. Work'd here & there. Can read, write, & cypher. During the late war, learnd to weave & follow'd weaving for some time. Says he never was addicted to drinking or gambling, but was thoughtless & rude. Believes the Bible to be the word of God.

Is a second comer. Was sentenced the first time for Life—for burglary. Was here 5 ys & 5 months & was pardoned. Went to the State of N.Y. where his wife & family were. Found that his wife had been false, could not live there, & returned to Boston to get business as an upholsterer, which he had learn'd in prison. Was feeble & could not work on a farm. At Boston got into company with an old villain & was persuaded to engage in breaking a Store. Was sentenced in Concord for 7 years. Has been here 5 ys & 5 months. Was out about 7 months. Since here the last time, made his escape by concealing himself in the Box or seat of a Sofa, which he had made & prepared, & when it was sent for he slyly got into it, & his fellow convicts took it up & put it on the cart & he was carried out without suspicion of the cartman. After a while, slyly crept out & was not discovered. Went to Philadelphia where he stayed 7 mo, then was betray'd by an old convict who saw him & was brought back here.

Says he has generally got along well & feels certain that he shall never run into crime again. Time will show.

Charles Perry—Age 30

Born in Milton, but has liv'd mostly in Boston. Was put out there, lived as a servant in different families, & finally learned the trade of a Copperplate printer.

For a season lived in a Boardinghouse, where a number of Stage players belonging to the Theatre boarded. This brought him into contact with the Theatre a good deal. Says he was pretty thoughtless though not particularly vicious. Drink'd what he call'd occasionally and moderately, except on high days, when he indulged more freely. Education decent. Married in 1817, Jany. And in April was sentenced to this prison for a small forgery for 2 ys. After going out got into trouble again & sentenced for 4 years. Served out his time and went from the prison to Boston, & being out of money, he borrowed five Dollars of an old convict whom he came across.

Had no suspicion of its being bad. Offered it for some article he had purchas'd. Was apprehended for passing bad money, & in 4 or 5 hours from the time he left this prison, was in Boston Jail & immediately was sent back to this place. Sentenced 3½ ys & has an additional life sentence.

Says not guilty of the last offence. Gets along well here & feel very sure of behaving well if he ever gets out.

Has a wife & 3 children. I fear he has not much feeling or principle, tho he talks very fair and behaves very well.

Mial Parker—Age 33

Born & brot up in Groton.[20] Father & mother live there now. Education tolerably good. Says he was as steady as young men in general. Brot up to farming. When 18 came to Boston, & lived there 1½ year. Tended stable. Then went home & lived till he was 22, when he came back to Boston & drove a coach for some time. Often drove com-

[20] Mial Parker, son of William and Susanna Parker, was born in Groton, Aug. 18, 1796. *Vital Records of Groton, Massachusetts, to the End of the Year 1849* (Salem, 1926–1927), 1:175.

pany to houses of ill fame, & in that way became acquainted with the principal woman who kept a particular house. She proposed to him to come & keep the House, assuring him that he might make a great deal of money, and he being poor consented & went. As she said, he did make money very fast, but it was his ruin. Says he now looks back upon his conduct with astonishment and horror. In an affray which took place one night *on the Hill*,[21] a man was kill'd and he & his brother were charged with the murder. They were on a second trial, convicted & sentenced to be hung, but their Sentence as commuted to State Prison for life. Lay in jail 2 years before coming here, and have now been here about 4½ years.

Declares most solemnly that he had no agency in the death of the man & it was the fact that it was not quite doubtful whether he was guilty that led to the change of his Sentence. Still he says he ought to suffer much for the life he lived & he thinks it will do him good, & make him sick of vice.

Is a mild, pleasant man, some feeling & converses very well. Says he is confident if he ever gets out that he shall live an honest life.

The question of his pardon & that of his brother is now pending before the Gov & Council.

They hope to prove that they were not guilty. Parker is the head cook, & conducts very well. Says he us'd occasionally drink, when in company, but never had a thirst for ardent spirits. Believes the Bible, reads it a good deal, & thinks he finds some support & consolation in so doing.

[21] Probably the north slope of Beacon Hill. See note 89 in volume 1 above.

August 10, 1829

WARREN PARKER—AGE 30

Born & brot up in Groton.[22] Is brother to Mial Parker & was sentenced with him, as concerned in the same transaction. Education decent. Lived with Mial at the time, & was convicted in the same kind of business viz—keeping a bad house. Lived a very wicked life. Has been in no difficulty here. Never call'd up for an offence.

Seems to be mild. Some feeling. Weeps when conversing & feels great assurance that he shall never run into vice, should he be restor'd to his liberty. Declares that he knew nothing of the transactions for which he was convicted. Hopes to get pardoned on the ground of innocence.

Came to Boston when he was 22. Till that time was always steady & regular in his conduct. Says he was never addicted to drinking. Was led away by bad company & finally brought to the situation in which he now finds himself.

JAMES PRICE—AGE 25

Colored man. Born & brot up in Baltimore. Parents free & are living now. Learn'd the trade of shoemaking. Education very decent. Was brought up religiously, believes the Bible &c &c. For the last 5 or 6 years, has follow'd the sea. Says he us'd to drink like other sailors, sometimes get high but did not call himself an intemperate man. Thinks he shall now try to live without Spirits altogether. Was convicted in Boston in Feby. 1828 of receiving stolen goods of a black girl, & sentenced for 18 months. Time will expire in

---

[22]Warren Parker, son of William and Susanna Parker, was born in Groton, May 17, 1798. *Vital Records of Groton,* 1:179.

2 weeks. Was never before convicted of crime & thinks he never shall be again. Has in general, got along very well here. Punishd slightly twice. Talks like a man of sense & appears pretty well. Sail'd out of Boston the 3 or 4 last years before coming to prison.

VARNUM POWERS—AGE 28

Born & brot up in Pepperell. Education as good as common and his early habits steady & correct. Brot up to farming, but when about 20, learn'd the Coopers trade & afterwards work'd at it. Had become somewhat intemperate previously to his conviction though he does not ascribe the commission of his crime to this cause. Had got into a very wicked transaction previously to this with a number of others, viz the forging of the *Will.* The villainy was finally detected, & unravelled. Says that in 2 courts he took a false oath, swearing to the truth of the will as one of the subscribing witnesses, but his conscience troubled him so that he had no rest day nor night. He felt worse than being in St. Prison & he finally disclosed the whole affair. In this business lost all he had & was tempted to pass some small counterfeit coin. Had a dye for stamping. Was prosecuted & sentenced for 4 ys. Has been here 2 ys & 4 mo.

Has got along well. Appears humble, frank, & sincere. Weeps when he converses, & says he knows he has conducted in a manner very wicked, but feels his mind relieved when he confesses his sins to God. Before the affair of the Will usd always to pray, night & morning & ask God's blessing, but after engaging in that transaction, dare not pray, as he knew he could not ask God to bless him. Has wife & 2 children.

William C. Parker—Age 43
Brother to Mial & Warren Parker whom names & cases will be found a few pages back.[23] Born & brot up in Groton.[24] Is a man of good talents—naturally pleasant, & might have been a good deal of a man. Is a cabinet maker & Turner. Has been married but his wife has been dead 10 ys & more. No children.

Says he has acted like a madman, & no man has played the fool worse than himself. Was once in N.Y. State prison 3 ys. Is a second comer here. 1st time 3 ys. Out 6 mo, then sentenced on 2 Indictments—on one for 2 ys on the other 15 ys. Has been here now over four years. Expresses his full belief of the Bible and converses with great frankness & with some feeling in regard to his folly & wickedness, and says his conduct here shall be good & good should he ever get out. Says he was not guilty of the crime for which he was sentenced for 15 ys. Says Balkham,[25] another old convict here, was the villain, & has been the cause of a larger share of his troubles. Appears pretty well, but is, most likely a ruined man.

August 11, 1829

Barney Phillips—Age 25
Born & brot up in Ireland. Has parents there now. No relations in this country. Came first to Canada. Did not find business as he wish'd & came to the U.S. and went to

[23]See above, pp. 150–152.
[24]William Parker, son of William and Susanna Parker, was born in Groton, Feb. 28, 1786. He published his intention to marry Elizabeth Hudson of Cranston, R.I., in October 1809. *Vital Records of Groton*, 1:179, 2:131.
[25]Inmate David Balkam. See above, pp. 53–54.

work on the Canal near Springfield.[26] Been in U.S. short of 2 ys. Sentenced for an attempt to Rape for 2 years. Been here almost one year. Says he did not know what he was about when he committed the crime. Had been drinking to excess. Shall never be caught with drink again, he is very sure. No Education. Is now in the Sab[bath] School. Says he has not been spoken to for an offence since he has been here. Intends to behave well & as soon as he gets out & can earn money enough, to go back to Ireland. It is wish'd that he may.

Seems to be a harmless, clever sort of fellow.

BENJAMIN PATTERSON—AGE 34

Born & brot up in Portland, Maine. Has a mother & other friends there. Education good. Mother a pious, good woman and took great pains to bring him up well, but he has greatly neglected her counsels and abused his privileges. Believes the Bible to be a revelation from God. Brot up to the trade of a printer, & has work'd in various offices in Maine, N.H., & Mass. Was pretty steady till 18 or 19, & did not go much out of the way till he was out of his time. After that got into bad company, gambled, ran after bad women, & drink'd too freely, & on the whole has lived a very sorry life. Never guilty of crime until of late. This is his first offence. Sentenced in Boston for Larceny, for 2 ys. Been here 18½ months. Says he has not been punish'd at all since here, & is resolved that his conduct shall be good. This <*this*>confinement has opened his eyes & he shall quit a life of dissipation & folly. Appears very well. How far he will do when he is discharged, is another question.

[26] Presumably the Hampshire and Hampden Canal. Work on the canal lasted from 1823 to 1835. *"Our Country and Its People": A History of Hampden County, Massachusetts*, ed. Alfred Minot Copeland (n.p., 1902), 1:174–175.

John Phillips—Age 38
Born & brot up in N. Hampshire. Partly learn'd the Shoemaking business with his father. After leaving home learn'd Blacksmithing. Early Education tolerably good. Parents now dead. Has a sister married in Boston & has one brother there, others in the country. Says he has lived a dreadful life, a life of dissipation, & shame and crime. This ascribes originally to leaving his parents & coming to Boston where he fell into bad company, & every evil work. Does not call himself an intemperate man, but us'd occasionally to get high. Dashing & pleasure were his ruling passion. Wanted to dress well, live high, appear smart, &c. & kept the company of Lewd women a great deal.

This is the third time of his coming to this prison.

1st time 4 ys—out 1 year
2d time 6 ys out 1 year
3d time sentence 5 ys—been here over 4 years.

Besides this has been 3 ys in the N.H. State Prison—in the whole about 18 years.

Says that he has never been called to an account for misconduct since his last confinement. Phillips is a man of good sense & converses with much propriety & apparent frankness. Says that in all his round of folly & wickedness, he has never given up his belief in the truth of the Bible, tho he has shut his eyes to the light of it. Thinks he now looks at life, & vice & folly, very differently from what he once did, & is a wonder to himself. Says he cannot tell how he should feel were he to go out, but thinks he should never run into crime again. Most likely he will be permitted to spend his days here, & very likely to die here.

August 12, 1829

THOMAS PRATT JUNR.—AGE 24[27]
Born in Malden, but his father moved when he was a child to Boston where he has since liv'd. When 8 ys old was put out to live in a family. Never went to school any, but is able to read, write, & cypher some. Acquired what learning he has at odd spells. When 14 went to sea, and has follow'd that business mostly ever since. Has a wife & 4 children.

Says he was a steady boy & has never been wild or vicious. Sentenced in Boston 2 months ago for 3 ys for an attempt to commit a rape. Says he is perfectly innocent. Never drink'd to excess. Was brought up to believe the Bible & does believe it. Has got along well so far & intends to conduct well. His father is now living. His mother is dead. She had been twice married. And by both marriages has 22 children—3 pr of twins. 16 are now living and he says all are members of some Church except himself. 14 are his own fathers children, 2 by the first marriage.

Pratt appears pleasant and converses sensibly, although he does not exhibit much feeling.

ERASTUS PLUMBLEY—AGE 18
Brot up in Wilbraham. Parents are now living there. Advantages for education very poor. Can scarcely read at all. Brot up to farming & tending ferry. Says he never was guilty of any offence till he committed the one for which he came here. Stole a pocket book & sentenced for 1 year. Been here some 3 months. Says he did not drink to excess,

---

[27] Curtis may have made an error in recording Pratt's age. A Capt. Thomas Pratt, the son of Thomas and Anna Pratt, was born in Malden, Nov. 25, 1794. *Births, Marriages and Deaths in the Town of Malden, 1649–1850*, comp. Deloraine P. Corey (Cambridge, Mass., 1903), 69.

tho he says he drank some every day. Has made up his mind never to drink any more, or commit any more crime. Thinks this a good school, & will be of great service to him.

Says he us'd to go to meeting in the Sabbath and believes the Bible.

Has got along well here & intends so to do.[28]

August 17, 1829

WILLIAM READY—AGE 46

Born in Ireland & liv'd there till 17. Decent common Education. Has follow'd the sea a great portion of his time. In religion a Catholic. Has made Boston his home since 1816. Work'd some at Rope making. Has been intemperate. Wife & 8 children. This his first offence. Convicted in Boston of larceny & sentenced for 2 ys. Been here one month.

Carries a pretty bold face, is prompt, tho respectful, & I should think, does not feel very deeply affected with his condition. Is a man of pretty good sense & says he shall behave well.[29]

August 25, 1829

HENRY WILLIAMS—AGE 40

Born in Canada, but has livd in the U.S. for more than 30 years. Parents liv'd in Albany N.Y. more than 20 ys. Education poor, reads poorly, but cannot write. Work'd as a Tobacconist for a number of years, then went to sea for

[28]Following the entry for Plumbley, Curtis inserted cross references dated Aug. 12, 13, and 17 to entries in volume 1 for Joseph Purchase, John Quiner, Dick Richards, David Remick, Robert Riley, Jacob Russell, Robert Riley 2d, John C. Russell, John Reed 1st, George Rossiter, Solomon Russell, John Reed, Henry Reed, George E. Roulstone, John Rogers, and Charles Rivers.

[29]Following the entry for Ready, Curtis inserted cross references dated Aug. 19 to entries in volume 1 for Joel Severance and J. O. Salisbury.

8 or 9 ys, from N.Y. & Philadelphia. Says he was never intemperate. Was profane. Was convicted of Burglary in Taunton in June 1820 & sentenced for life. Says he has not been call'd to an account for a misdemeanor for 7 ys. Thinks he should shape his course right, were he to be restored to his liberty. Seems to be a clever, good hearted sort of a fellow. For the last years has been employ'd in the hospital.

Always work'd for a living although he says he is sorry to say he was not always as honest as he should be.[30]

August 28, 1829

ENOCH STEVENS—AGE 30
Brot up in Andover. Was an illegitimate child, & his aunt took him from his mother when he was four months old. Was brought up in his younger years by his aunt. Says he had his head very much after he was 12 or 13 ys old. Education rather poor. Can read & write. Learned the trade of a Shoemaker. Us'd to attend meeting with his aunt sometimes, but did pretty much as he had a mind to. Always believ'd the Bible & does so now. Married when he was between 17 & 18. Has a wife & 6 children. Was poor, & his family are now in the Almshouse at Newburyport. Drink'd Some, tho he says he was not a sot. Convicted on two Indictments for Stealing. And sentenced for 4 years. Been here 3 months. Says he has got along very well thus far and intends to do well. Thinks this will be a good school for him and learn him to live as he ought. Appears frank & pleasant.[31]

---

[30] Following the entry for Williams, Curtis inserted a cross reference dated Aug. 28 to an entry in volume 1 for David Sawyer.

[31] Following the entry for Enoch Stevens, Curtis inserted cross references dated Aug. 28 to entries in volume 1 for Aaron Shepardson and William Stevens.

JOHN C. SMITH—AGE 23
Born & brot up in St. Albans Vt. Lived there till about 17. Education decent. Learned the trade of a Joiner. Health failed & came down to Cape Cod where he had a brother, for the purpose of regaining his health, where he has liv'd ever since. Is married & has 2 children. Has been here not far from three months. Sentenced for <*passing or*> having counterfeit money found in his house—or store. Kept a small Store and was engaged in the fishery business, and was succeeding well & had accumulated some property. Says he was always steady & industrious & never addicted to any vice—was temperate & prudent. Says he is perfectly innocent, & that some individuals must have deposited, in a secret manner, this money & then given information against him to throw suspicion off from themselves.

In confirmation of his statement, one of the Selectmen of the Town, was at the prison yesterday with a petition for his pardon sign'd by most of the respectable people of this place. He stated that it was satisfactorily ascertained that Smith was innocent, & that a game had been play'd off upon him by some Scoundrels who had been concern'd in the business of counterfeiting. If so he will most likely be pardoned.

(Afterwards, facts show'd that he was an old rogue & was not pardoned.)[32]

August 31, 1829

DANIEL SMITH—AGE 22
Came here in May last. Sentenced in Boston for Larceny—for 2 years. Born in Ireland. Been in the U.S. near 4 ys.

[32]Following the entry, Curtis inserted cross references dated Aug. 31 to entries in volume 1 for William Smith and Stephen Symms.

Has follow'd the Sea mostly since he same to U.S. Has liv'd in Boston. No Education. Is learning to read in our Sabbath School.

Says he had a falling out with his officer, while in port, & he went away and got pretty drunk. Found a cellar open & went in to get out of sight & out of the way, fell asleep, and was lock'd up at night in the Cellar & continued to sleep till next day, & was found in that state in the cellar. Appears like a simple sort of an Irishman.[33]

September 4, 1829

CHRISTOPHER SUTCLIFF—[AGE 25]
Been in prison now between 4 & 5 mo. Sentenced at Concord for 18 mo—for Theft. Age 25. Born & brot up in Eng. Left there 2 ys ago. By trade a Shoemaker. Education pretty good. Parents respectable & in good circumstances. Had for some time cherish'd a desire to come to this country, but his parents were unwilling. Finally had a good chance to come over with the family of a manufacturer engaged at Lowel and came. Married last Christmas.[34] Says his habits were always regular & good, not intemperate. Received a religious education. His wife is of a respectable family & a professor of religion.

Prosecuted for theft. Declaims most solemnly that he is intirely innocent. Says he was never at the house where the theft was committed, and knew nothing of it. A note

[33]Following the entry for Daniel Smith, Curtis inserted cross references dated Aug. 31, Sept. 1, and Sept. 3 to entries in volume 1 for Ebenezer Shannon, Calvin Spelman, Alpheus Spring, Charles W. Spaulding, Jonas Spaulding, John Snow, William Seymour, Thomas Snyder, Reuben Shaw, Joseph Severns, and William Starkweather.

[34]Christopher Sutcleffe married Rhoda Richardson in Dracut, Dec. 25, 1828. *Vital Records of Dracut, Massachusetts, to the Year 1850* (Boston, 1907), 242.

of hand which was stolen among other property, was presented to the drawer in another town & the man identified that he was the man who presented it. Says it is not true.

Appears remarkably well, frank, mild, tender in his feelings, but after all may be guilty. Conduct here exceedingly good. Says he has a legacy due him in England of $800, left by an uncle. Has had fifty dollars of it.

ORREN SMITH—AGE 33

Belongs in West Springfield.[35] Is nephew to the Smith who was a representative from that town for many years who died in Boston while attend[36]

________[37]

first time three years. Out almost 8 ys. Has been here now near 4 months. Sentence one year.

Says he conducts himself with propriety & has no difficulty. Appears pleasant. When conversing with such a man, it is overwhelming to think what Rum will make of them. <*Sept 17*> Wife, child son, house, friends, property, reputation—body, soul, time, family, all sacrific'd for rum.

EPAPHRAS SQUARE—AGE 24

Born in Mansfield, Con. Has wife & one child there. Ed[ucatio]n poor. Can read & write.

---

[35]Oren Smith, son of Leonard and Lucinda Smith, was born in West Springfield, June 26, 1796. He published his intention to marry Keziah Brooks of West Springfield, Nov. 13, 1822. *Vital Records of West Springfield, Massachusetts, to the Year 1850* (Boston, 1944–1945), 1:202, 2:152.

[36]Jonathan Smith of West Springfield served in the State Senate, 1794–1806, and in the House of Representatives, 1807–1819. Card Index, Massachusetts State Library, Boston.

[37]Approximately half page illegible. The manuscript index to volume 2 indicates that the obscured text pertains entirely to Smith.

_______[38]

Has been here 4 months. Sentence 2 ys.

Says he never drink'd to excess, was quite temperate. Work'd some on farm and some at coopering. Does not seem to have a great deal of feeling, although his conduct and conversation were very proper. Has has been punish'd once, since he has been here. Says he means to conduct well & do well.[39]

September 10, 1829

THEODORE TIFFANY—AGE 23

Brought up in Westfield, Hampden Co. A farmer. Father dead—his mother still lives there. Says although he has not been as steady as some yet he has never been addicted to vice & was never intemperate, in the common acceptance of the word & never gambled. Us'd to drink occasionally as other people do. His father always kept Spirits in the house.

Was in the habit of attending meeting on the Sabbath. Has been here about 4 mo. Sentenced in Springfield for forgery for 2 ys. Says he had lent his brother in Law 20 Dollars. Carried the Note in his pocket-book. Lost his pocket-book and with it the Note. Instead of going to his brother in Law to get it renewed, he wrote another Note for the same sum & signed his brother in Law's name. Afterwards sold the note & when presented for payment, his brother in Law, declar'd it a forgery & would not pay it, & that led to his arrest & conviction.

---

[38] Approximately half page illegible. The manuscript index to volume 2 indicates that the obscured text pertains entirely to Square.

[39] Following the entry for Square, Curtis inserted cross references dated Sept. 7 and 10 to entries in volume 1 for Benjamin Thompson, Job Thayer, Mose Thompkins, William E. Todd, and Samuel Thayer.

He appears very well & I should think was a good convict, and would conduct well.[40]

March 1, 1830

GEORGE BALL—AGE 34
Wife & 5 children in Glastonbury Con. Born & brot up in Springfield Mass, & has liv'd there most of his life. Is a Gun Smith by trade & has work'd a good deal in the U.S. Army there. Education pretty good. Has usually been pretty industrious. In the habit of attending meeting on the Sabbath, until within 2 or 3 years past, since which time has been most unsteady & wild. Tried hard to be a Universalist, but could not. Convicted of Burglary in Spring[fiel]d in Sept last & sentenced for life. Us'd to drink some, but not as much as some men. Says he has got along well here & is resolved to do well. Is frank, & pleasant.

JOHN BAYD (COLORED MAN)—AGE 21
Born & brot up in N. Jersey. Born a slave, but his father bought his freedom about 2 ys ago. Father is now dead. Always work'd on a farm until he got his freedom. Went to N.Y., & engaged for a time in the coasting business. Came to New Bedford & there in consequence of visiting bad women, got into a quarrel & was sentenced there for an assault for 3 ys. Has been here only a few months. Cannot read at all.

Says he never was in the habit of drinking, and never much profane. Says bad women brought him here. Been punish'd once since he has been here for whistling in his cell—says he was not guilty.

---

[40]Following the entry for Tiffany, Curtis inserted cross references dated Sept. 24 to entries in volume 1 for Dyer Vespasian and John Van Vaught.

Says he should be glad to learn to read.

Appears frank and pleasant.

March 2, 1830

EZRA BAILEY—AGE 49

Born in Providence & brot up there mostly. Learnd trade of Housewright. Early education—good—has some knowledge of Greek & Latin. Father died when he was 9. Was then put out by his mother. Early habits good, excepting the love of spirits. Says he always lovd spirits too well. Married when 26. Wife been dead 13 ys. Has 3 children. Never had much property. Has always followd his trade, with ornamental painting for a living. Might, if he had been temperate, been wealthy. Convicted at Cambridge of Larceny & sentenced for 5 ys. Has been here 3 ys 4 months. Previously in Boston Jail twice for petty Larcenies.

Is a man of sense—frank & pleasant—ruined by rum. Constitution ruined by the same source. Says he is better off here than he should be out. Is fearful if he should go out he should drink & be destroy'd.

JOHN W. BOWERS[41]—AGE 27

Born and brought up in Taunton. Colored man. Read but not write. Brot up to work in house, waiter & tender. Says he was never in any trouble before. Was pretty steady about a year ago. Got to drinking & from that to crime. Convicted of Burglary at New Bedford, and Sentenced in Nov. last for life. Says he was never profane. Drink led him to ruin. Says he has got along well & intends to do well. Should not think him a hardened convict.

---

[41] "John W. Bowers, 31 y, prisoner in State Prison, d. there, Dec. 21, 1833." *Vital Records of Charlestown*, 2:261.

MOSES BLIGH—AGE 59
Born at Salem Mass. Lived there till 10 or 12, then mov'd to Maine. Education rather poor. Had but few advantages. Has workd at farming some, but in the summer has generally work'd at Brick making. Saco is his home. Has liv'd there 5 ys. Wife & 3 children. Sentenced in Salem in Nov. last, for Stealing a yoke of oxen. Says he bought them in Maine, of a man, & could not prove of whom. The man was a stranger, & the cattle prov'd to be Stolen. Says that a certificate from many people of Law, with the names of the Selectmen, certifying to his good character & habits, was the means of his getting a short sentence—only one year. Says he was always industrious, sober, & steady. Believes the Bible &c &c &c. Appears to possess considerable feeling and converses very well.

March 4, 1830

JAMES BROWN—AGE 52
Born in Ireland. Parents poor & gave him no learning. Cannot read. Says he was brot up to farming. His father was drafted into the army & he took his place. Went to Spain. Was one of Lord Wellington's men.[42] Continued in the army 14 years. Has been in this country 13 years. In the army became intemperate, & has continued so since. Stole a watch, when he was drunk. Sentenced in this County for one year. Has been here 4 months. Has got along well so far & intends to do as well as he can. Says he hopes this affair will do him good & break him of his bad habits.

Never before convicted of crime as he says.

---

[42] Arthur Wellesley, first duke of Wellington (1769–1852). *Dictionary of National Biography* (Oxford, 1885-1890), 20:1081–1115.

DANIEL BOUKER—AGE, ABOUT 39
(col[ore]d man). Born in Virginia. Has been to Sea a good deal. Wife & 3 children in Boston. Came there from Salem last August. Had lived at Salem 7 or 8 years. Convicted about 2 months ago in Boston of Larceny. Sentence 4 ys. Cannot read. Is a man of sense. Very fluent. Has a smooth tongue. Says he never was in prison before.

JOSEPH B. BOSSUET—AGE 20
Born & brot up in Boston. Has livd some in the West Indies. Had the care of a plantation. Returnd when about 17. Got among an unprincipled set of Boys, & was led astray. Has been once in the house of correction in Boston. Came here in Jany last. Sentenced on 2 Indictments for 4 years. Says he was not Intemperate. Run after bad women some. Gambling brought him here. Education decent. Talks sensibly & pleasantly.

March 5, 1830

ISAAC CHURCHILL—AGE 22
Born & brot up in Plympton, Plymouth Co.[43] Parents now living there. Advantages for Education pretty good. Brought up to farming. Has been to sea some. Has been a wild young man, & became intemperate. This led him to commit the Theft for which he was sentenced to this prison. Sentence 1 year. Been here about 9½ mo. Says that when sober, he never wrong'd a man. He is sensible that his course was ruinous & is fully resolvd to avoid drinking alto-

[43] Isaac Churchill, son of Isaac, Jr., and Polly Churchill, was born in Plympton, Oct. 14, 1807. *Vital Records of Plympton, Massachusetts, to the Year 1850* (Boston, 1923), 66.

gether when he gets out. Believes the Bible & has read it a good deal since he came here. Is a pleasant young man and I hope may take warning from the past. Has got along well since he came here.

ALONZO CHASE—AGE 23

Born & brot up in Walpole Mass. Has a mother living there. Father dead. Had but poor advantages for Education. Can read & write poorly. Has workd at taverns, tended Stable, drove stage, and workd at blacksmithing some. Says he has livd rather a sorry life. Been unsteady. Got rather high now & then. Says getting high led to his present trouble. Sentenced in Worster for Larceny 5 months ago. Sentenced 2 ys. Has got along well thus far, & intends to do well. Says he thinks this will be a good school for him. Is frank & I hope he may do well.

JOHN CRAFTS—AGE 30

Born & brot up in Manchester.[44] Has livd in Boston 8 ys past. Early Education good. Has follow'd the Sea most of his life. Can navigate a vessel to any part of the world. Says he never was intemperate & never gambled. Had been in the habit of Smuggling a good deal. Some goods were entrusted to him, which proved to have been Stolen. Did not know the fact when he received them. Was prosecuted for the theft & convicted. The real owner absconded & could not be found. Sentence 2 ys. Been here 6 mo.

Is a man of sense, should think him a good convict, & determined to behave well. Says he peruses the Bible what leisure time he can get. Has a wife & 1 child in Boston. Never had much property.

---

[44]John Craft, the son of Eleazar and Anna Craft, was born in Manchester, May 14, 1799. *Vital Records of Manchester, Massachusetts, to the End of the Year 1849* (Salem, 1933), 35.

March 12, 1830

William Crossman—Age 25

Belongs in Dorchester. Wife & 2 children.[45] Education Decent. Brought up to farming. Says he us'd to get *pretty drunk* on special occasions, when others did, such as husking &c &c, but did not make it a practice to get drunk.

<*Say*> Convicted last Novr in Dedham of Larceny & sentenced for 2 ys. Says that a man by the name of Adams was tried with him for taking money from a drawer. Adams was acquitted. Says that Adams took the money out of the draw. Acknowledges that he cut Gen. Capens[46] Carriage out of revenge. Knows it was wrong. Has got along well so far, & intends to get along well, to be obedient & orderly. Says he knows it to be ruinous to drink & will never drink any more.

Should think from his appearance, that he has been thoughtless, & had reflected very little on his duty or the consequences of sin. He has, I should think, been the creature of impulse & passion.

William Brown—goes in prison by name of James Brown—colored man—Age 18

Says his true name is Ebee Brown. Home is Montpelier Vt. Been absent from home about 3 ys, & has followed the Sea. Can read pretty well & write poorly. Says he was never intemperate. Convicted in Boston in Nov last of Larceny & sentenced for 3 ys. Appears to be a pleasant boy & intelligent. Gets along well, and intends to behave well.

---

[45] William Crossman married Sarah Delano in Dorchester, Apr. 29, 1827. *Report of the Record Commissioners of the City of Boston* (Boston, 1876–1909), 36:116.

[46] Brig. Gen. Aaron Capen of Dorchester. *Massachusetts Register* (1828), 93.

DAN[IE]L CHAPLIN—AGE 25

Born & brot up in Rowley Essex Co.[47] Mother living. Not married himself. Decent Com[mon] Education. Farmer. Work'd some at Shoemaking. Well brot up. Was esteemed & loved. Father a man of education & standing in Society, <*became*> but he became Intemperate, wasted his property, got into debt. Says he was bound for his father & had to pay a good deal of money. Got discouraged & left home. Work'd in various places, some in this town. Says he was never intemperate. Took a pair of [illeg.]yards & a coat from a man & threw them into the river out of revenge & got into the State prison in consequence. Sentenced in Cambridge in Nov last for 3 ys.

Has got along well here & intends to behave himself. Appears pleasant and is intelligent.

March 15, 1830

ROBERT EVANS—AGE 34

Born & brot up in Ireland. Can read. Ropemaker by trade. Came to this Country in 1819. Has a wife & child in the City of N.Y. For the last 7 ys has follow'd the sea most of the time. Became intemperate. Was convicted of Burglary in Boston in July last & sentenced for life. Says he has no knowledge of the crime of which he was convicted. Was in a state of intoxication, & so much so that he had no recollection of any thing that passed.

Appears mild & pleasant. Is frank & manifests a good deal of feeling. Weeps. Says he is determined to conduct

[47] Daniel Bishop Chaplin, the son of Joseph, Jr., and Polly Chaplin, was born in Rowley, Aug. 9, 1804. *Vital Records of Rowley, Massachusetts, to the End of the Year 1849* (Salem, 1928), 42.

well in every respect, & to give no occasion for his officers to find fault.

William Egglestone—Age 35
Born in Ireland. Can read & write. When young learnd to weave. During the late war came in the British Army to this country. When the war clos'd he returnd to Ireland & spent a few months with his father. Then, as he lik'd this country well, concluded to return and has been in the U.S. most of the time since. Has liv'd in Vt. & N.Y. Has work'd mostly at farming. Follow'd boating some in the Champlain Canal. Came to this State with a man who had a drove of Horses to help him drive them. Stop'd at Springfield and work'd there some. Then came to Brookfield & there got into trouble.

Says he work'd for a man who would not pay him, & he attempted, in a state of partial Intoxication, to get his pay. Has been here 4 mo. Sentenced at Worcester for 3 ys. Says he has got along well & intends to do well. Should think him a shrewd sort of an Irishman.

Lewis Fazey—Age 35
Born in Paris, France, but left France early in life. Education pretty good. Has follow'd the Sea a good deal. Has own'd a vessel & traded from Cuba to New Orleans. Lived in N. Orleans a number of Years. Has also been a number of years in the Patriot Service in South America. Came on to Boston about 2 ys ago, where he was convicted of Larceny & Sentenced for 6 years.

(Did not get through with him before he was calld off.)

(Fazey palmed himself off as Gen Jackson before he came here)

Saw him Again March 16th. Says he was sentenced on 3 Indictments. Acknowledges that he was guilty in part. Says

Dunlap the Lawyer[48] swindled him out of a Gold watch & establishment worth 60 Dollars—paid him the money for pleading his case, & the watch was committed to him for safe keeping only. He will not give it up. Wept some. Is a singular sort of a man.

March 16, 1830

James Fox—Age 34
Born & brot up in R.I.

Read but not write. Sentenced in Berkshire Co. in May 1829 for one year. Drinkd too much as he says. Has got along pretty well here. A man of very little feeling.

(See No 1 G. Fox)[49]

March 18, 1830

Obadiah Gorton—Age 50
Born in R.I. but has livd most of his life in Con. Good parents, who brought him up well. Education decent. Has been twice married. First wife dead had 9 children by her—7 are now living, as he supposes, in R.I. Second wife is now living had no children by her. Has not livd with her lately, & does not know where she is. Says they never had any difficulty or quarrel & yet he has not livd with her of late. Brot up to farming. Says he was steady and industrious until after his first wife died. Since that time has not done as well. Denies that he has been what is call'd a drinking man. Has taken a little now & then, but not to excess. Says he has gambled some & run after bad women some. For

[48] Probably Andrew Dunlap of Boston, district attorney. *Boston Directory* (1829), 94.
[49] Inmate Gardner Fox. See above, p. 91.

the last 7 ys has follow'd peddling. Convicted of Larceny in Boston in Nov last and sentenced for 3 ys. Says he has got along very well & intends to do as well as he possibly can. Appears clever enough.

JOHN GILBERT AL[IAS] SCROGGINS[50]
2d Comer. Went from here in June last, & returnd about 3 months ago. Born in England. Is a Sailor. Been in U.S. about 9 years. No Education. Can't read. Intemperate. Sentenced in New Bedford. Was here 4 ys the first time. Present sentence 2 ys. Says he never gets into any difficulty here. Behaves well. I should think him a very stupid man.

March 22, 1830

DAVID GRIFFIN—AGE 28
Home in Haverhill Mass. Parents died when he was quite young. Was brought up by an uncle. Learnd the trade of a Tinman & has generally work'd at his trade. Education decently good. Says he was brought up to good habits. Never married. Convicted & sentenced about 4 months ago, as he says, for an assault on a Constable for one yr. Intemperance was the cause. Says he will drink no more if ever lives to get out. Should think him rather thoughtless, and without much feeling.

ALEXANDER HAVEN—AGE 20
Born and brot up in Sherburn in this State.[51] His father lives there. Mother dead. Has not livd at home since he was 9 ys old. Education decent. Says that he was not brought up

[50]This entry is written upside down. Probably same as John Scroggins, p. 14.

[51]Alexander Marsh Haven, the son of Jesse and Sally Haven, was born in Sherborn, June 1, 1809. *Vital Records of Sherborn, Massachusetts, to the Year 1850* (Boston, 1911), 43.

as he ought to have been. But little pains were taken to bring him up in good habits.

Drove team some, & has driven Stage.

For two years past has been very unsteady & in almost all sorts of bad Company. Says he was not in the habit of drinking to excess. Got into debt & committed a forgery, & sentenced for 2 ys. Been here about 3 months.

Says his father is respectable, & has respectable relatives. Had not heard a Sermon for 2 years before he came here. Says he is glad he came here. Thinks it will be the means of saving him from ruin. Is a frank young man. Shed some tears. Appears amiable & interesting.

March 30, 1830

MICHAEL GRANT—AGE 23

Born & brot up in Boston. Father died when he was 7. Went to sea at 12 & has follow'd the Sea ever since. Mother still lives in Boston. Can read & write. Has been very unsteady. Intemperate. This led to his imprisonment. Has once been in County prison. Says he stole a pair of Boots when he was *high.* Sentenced 1 year; been here 1 month. Says he is resolv'd never to drink any more. Knows it will ruin him. Gets along well here.

WILLIAM HAGGITT—AGE 23

Home in Dracut in this State.[52] Father dead. Mother still lives in Dracut.

Education pretty good. Work'd at farming till he was 16 or 17, then workd at Masoning, & has follow'd this business, mostly ever since. Says he was steady & industrious till within a year or two.

---

[52]William Haggot, the son of Thomas and Parmelay Haggot, was born in Dracut, July 7, 1806. *Vital Records of Dracut,* 59.

Workd a good deal at Lowell. Got into difficulty there, & was imprison'd for 4 mo for thieving.

Says he thought that would cure him, but it did not. Sentenced about 2 mo ago for Stealing for 3 ys. Ascribes his troubles to *Intemperance.*

Should think him a man of pretty good sense. Feels pretty sensibly. Weeps freely, & I hope he may be cured of his folly. Says his aim is to do his duty faithfully. Appears very well.

April 1, 1830

AB[RAHA]M JOHNSON—AGE 30
Born & brot up in New Hampshire. Education decent. Early habits good. About the time he became of age left N.H. and came on to Boston. At that time character & habits were good. Soon got led away by bad Company. Engaged in counterfeit money. Convicted & sentenced for 2 ys. Served out his time. Was out about 2½ ys, then sentenced to this prison again for 3½ ys. Servd out this time & was discharged in the Spring of 1829. Not long after committed a crime of which he was convicted & is now here on a sentence of 8 ys, & liable to a life Sentence.

Says he was not what is usually call'd an intemperate man, tho he us'd, sometimes, to drink more than was for his good.

His friends know nothing of his condition. His true name is not Johnson. Manifested some sensibility. Probably a ruin'd man. Conduct in prison orderly & good.

WILLIAM JOHNSON, COL[ORE]D MAN—AGE 23
Born & brot up in Boston. His father is living & follows chimney sweeping. Mother is dead. He used when young to sweep chimneys. For the last 7 ys has been a Sailor for most of the time. Can read. Usd to attend Sunday school some.

Has been very wild & thoughtless. Did not drink but was rude. Has been in the house of correction 3 time for noisy riotous conduct in the night time. Sentenced for 2 ys for Stealing about a month ago, in Boston. Says he means to try to be an honest man when he gets out.

Does not appear to have much feeling. Is probably about as happy here as any where, & is much better off I doubt not.

April 2, 1830

JOHN LORING—AGE 30

Born & brot up in Boston. Education Good. Parents respectable. Learnd the trade of a Harness maker & has always followd that business. Not married. Ever since of age has been wild & unsteady. Work'd in various places—some at New Orleans. Intemperance has destroy'd him. Owes his fall & all his misfortunes to this. Says he never was a gambler. Lovd rude drinking company. Been here 7 mo. Sentenced 3 ys. Says he has got along well here—better than he expected. Thinks he shall alter his hand when he gets out. Is now obliged to think. This thinking is a painful business. Week days, can work it off. The Sabbath is a painful day to him. Hopes this will be a good school.

Is frank & a man of good sense.

PATRICK LARKIN—AGE 19

Born & brought up in Ireland. Can read & write poorly. Parents living. Ran away from them & went to sea.

Says he became unsteady & got his mind unsettled by other boys. His parents talk'd to him & advis'd him but he was a fool & would not hear them. Drink'd too freely, and to get rid of constraints of home he ran away. Came to this country. Continued to go to sea. Came on to Boston, &

about 6 months ago was convicted of crime and Sent to this Prison for 2 years. Works at coopering here. His father was a cooper. Says it was *Drink* that got him here. Knows that drinking is a horrid practice & will ruin him if not discontinued. Is determind never to drink any more. Seems to be a frank open-hearted-boy, and is very sensible that he has been playing the fool.

GEORGE LINCOLN—A COLOR'D MAN—AGE 16

Home in Taunton.[53] Father & mother living there. No Education. Can not read at all. Says he does not wish to learn to read. Says he was mowing last summer, with another man & he beat him mowing, which vexed the man, and the man having drinkd too freely, under took to flog him. At this time had finish'd mowing & was raking. Had a knife in his hand, mending a rake tooth. And as the man assaulted him, he, in defending himself, hit the man with his knife & cut him. Says he had no idea of cutting the man. Was not in the habit of drinking him self. Says he behaves well here & is determined to do so.

Has been brought up in ignorance, & has not much sensibility.

JAMES LEE—AGE 34

Born & brot up in England. Has follow'd the Sea. Has been in U.S. about 3 ys. Can read poorly. Was in the U.S. service. Deserted & came on with a shipmate to Boston. Intemperate and while in a scrape with his shipmate, an officer of the peace attempted to arrest them when they assaulted

[53] George Crane Lincoln, the son of Aaron and Hannah Lincoln, was born in Taunton, Dec. 8, 1813. He married Mary H. Wilbur of Taunton, Mar. 1, 1837. *Vital Records of Taunton, Massachusetts, to the Year 1850* (Boston, 1929), 1:264, 2:304.

the officer, & were sentenced by the court either to pay a heavy fine or be confined for 1 year in State prison. They could not pay the fine & are now suffering the time of imprisonment. Been here 3 mo.

Says *drink* did it all. Hopes this will cure him of drinking. Intends to be faithful here, & behave well.

April 5, 1830

JOS[EPH] BRADFORD—AGE 28

Home in Philadelphia. Born in N. York. Parents died when he was about 6 ys old. Was left with some property. Connections of the first respectability. After death of his father livd with an uncle, who early put him to a boarding school in N. Jersey, at which he continued for 9 or 10 years. Education very good. Has been in a Store some, but for the last 7 or 8 ys has follow'd the sea. The reason of his first leaving home & of his subsequent misfortunes, was running after bad women. Says he was never addicted to intemperance. Bad Company was his ruin.

Is a young man of good appearance & address. Is tender in his feelings. Weeps bitterly over his past follies. Hopes & trusts that this will be a school to recal him from his wanderings from virtue & from duty. Sentenced in March last in Boston for 18 mo. Appears well.

HUTCHINSON[54]

2d Comer—See No 1.[55]

Has been discharged within a year & returnd a few days ago. Is a very intemperate man, & owes all his misfortunes to this cause.

---

[54] First name unknown.

[55] Volume 1 does not include an entry for an inmate named Hutchinson.

But for this, would be a respectable man. When he was discharg'd, he would not promise not to drink at all, only that he would not drink to excess. I fear'd then he would return soon.

He thinks now that he shall have resolution to give up drink forever.

John S. Jones—Age 23

2d Comer. Convicted in Dedham. Been here four or five months. Sentenced for Larceny for 2 ys. First time here 18 mo. Was out 2 ys.

Education decent. Brot up principally to farming, but has work'd at Ship Carpentering some.

Ruined by Rum. Says he has resolvd a great many times never to drink any more, but some temptation has drawn him away. Has wife.

Thinks he shall never sell himself so cheap as a glass of rum again.

Should think him a very good natured & a very thoughtless man.

David Marrill—Age 25

Home in N. Hampshire. Education decent. Has been rather intemperate & unsteady a few years past. Blacksmith by trade. Has been to sea some. Convicted in Boston about 6 months ago of theft & sentenced for 18 mo. Says he was not Guilty. Fell in company with a bad fellow, & received of him a cloak, which prov'd to be stolen. Had no suspicion of such a thing till he was arrested. Father respectable. Says he has never been in any such trouble before, & though he has drink'd too much, yet he has been industrious & honest.

April 9, 1830

NURSE[56]—AGE 29
Born & brot up in Boston. Father died when he was very young. Mother died when he was 8. After that, lived with his Grandmother 3 ys till she died. Education decent. Learnd the trade of a printer. Says he was rather a wild young man. Did not regard the Sabbath very faithfully. Attended Church only occasionally.

Drinkd some, though he says he was not a drunkard. Gambling & going to the Theatre ruined him. Does not know whether he believes the Bible or not. Says if he had obey'd its precepts he should never have gone astray.

2d Comer. First time here 2 ys. Went out in May last. Came here the Last time in March for 1 year.

Has not much feeling although he freely acknowledges the folly of his course.

SETH ROBBINS—COLORD MAN—AGE 18
Been here about 5 mo. Sentence 2 ys. Home Dedham. Parents live there. Education tolerably good. Can read and write. Brot up to farming. Sentenced for Larceny. Says he bought some cloth of a fellow, for a suit of clothes. Suspected that he did not come honestly by it, but as he offered it cheap, thought he would take it. The fellow of whom he bought it was sentenced only 3 months in County jail. They put it on to him because the cloth was found on him.

Says he has been pretty steady. Not intemperate & before this, has never been in any difficulty. Should think him a decent kind of a young black.

---

[56]First name unknown.

John Jones—Age 41
Born in Charleston S.C. A very short man. Speaks like a foreigner. Ignorant. Cannot read nor write. Can spell a little. Never married. Has follow'd the sea all his days. Has sail'd with Com. Rogers, Capt Jones &c &c. Lovd Rum, was in the habit of getting high, came on to Boston, got into bad Company, got high, stole, & was sentenced in Boston in Feby last for 2 years. Works in the y[ar]d team. A Stupid, careless sort of a Sailor.

April 12, 1830

Henry Himleer—Age 32 or 33
Born & brot up in England, Town of Windsor & County of Berkshire.

Father died when he was a child. Mother was poor. Sent him to school about 3 months, & this was all the school he ever had. Can spell a little in the spelling book.

Has follow'd the Sea from a Child. Has been many years in the English naval service. Came to this country about 8 ys ago. Has work'd in various places. His grand failing is *intemperance.* Says he us'd to have *Sprees.* Would work steadily for several months without taking a drop, then would have a high, & would keep high till he has spent all his wages, & would then go to work again. Came on from the State of N.Y. last fall, & in the County of Worcester, committed a theft while in a State of partial intoxication & was sentenced in October for 1 year. Has been here 6 months. His nose is still very red.

Is frank. Says he has a good deal of a thought never to drink anymore as it is a very bad thing.

Works in team.

Jos[eph] Ramsdell—Age 39
Came here Nov 28, 1829. Sentenced for 2 ys.

Born & brot up in Lynn.[57] Education poor. Shoemaker by trade. Has been married. Wife died last summer. Has 3 children living.

Says he was never an intemperate man, although he us'd to drink something every day. Says he got into trouble by a man who livd in the house, leaving his pocket Book in his chamber, where he found it, & the owner swore that there was some money missing. Says he never took it. Appears to have some feeling. Weeps. Says he thinks he shall live more circumspectly hereafter, if he lives to get out. Says he has better health since he came here than he has before, which he ascribes to not drinking his daily allowance of grog. Says he will drink no more. Is satisfied it is hurtful.

April 14, 1830

Charles B. Reed—Age 24
Born & brought up in West Bridgewater.[58] Parents are now living, but do not know where he is.

Education rather poor. Lived with parents till he was about 18. When quite young drove a baggage waggon from Braintree to Boston for some time. During that period got

[57]Joseph Ramsdal, the son of Joseph and Janey Ramsdal, was born in Lynn, May 21, 1791. He married Sally Larrabe on July 20, 1815. She died July 6, 1829. *Vital Records of Lynn, Massachusetts, to the End of the Year 1849* (Salem, 1905–1906), 1:337, 2:318, 574.

[58]Charles B. Reed, the son of Ezekiel and Rebecca Reed, was born in West Bridgewater, May 21, 1806. He published his intention to marry Eunice B. Harden Aug. 28, 1831, and died on May 3, 1836. *Vital Records of West Bridgewater, Massachusetts, to the Year 1850* (Boston, 1911), 91, 165, 214.

into habit of drinking moderately which afterward became a *habit* & produced his fall. When 18 went to work in a Nail factory and followd it for 2 ys. Since that has workd at nailing mostly, & became quite intemperate. Set out to go to Malden to work in a Nail factory. Got as far as Boston, where in a drinking scrape with some bad fellows got into difficulty. Sentenced in Jany last for 1 year.

Says he has been rather unsteady & wild. Never before in any difficulty. Hopes this may cure him of his follies and his intemperance. Converses well. Is frank. Manifests a good degree of humility. Weeps & seems determin'd to do better.

James Riley[59]—Age 29

2d Comer. First time 3 ys. Out 10 months. Came back in November last for 6 ys. Says he has not been an intemperate man. Only drink'd his grog when he work'd, as other people do. Says that *Gambling* has been his besetting sin, & the sin which has ruin'd him.

Born & brot up in Scotland. Education decent. Follow'd the Sea when young, After that workd at Tailoring.

Been in U.S. 12 ys. Does not seem to have a great deal of feeling. Says if he ever lives to get out he thinks he shall behave very differently from what he has heretofore. Has a wife in Boston, no children.

Ephraim Henderson—Age 47

2d Comer. Been here the last time about 2 months—both times for Larceny. Has a wife & 5 Children. Is a man of Good Education. Has studied Medicine. Parents & friends very respectable. They know nothing of his condition. His father has been a Clergyman & is now a Physician.

[59] "James Riley, prisoner in State Prison, d. there, Apr. 21, 1833." *Vital Records of Charlestown*, 2:300.

Says he has labourd under partial derangement for many years to which he attributes his troubles. Says he never was intemperate or given to vice, and has both times been unjustly accus'd & condemned.

Should think him a singular sort of a man.

Weeps very freely and manifests a good deal of feeling, but all his feeling is probably "like the morning cloud."

Says he believes the Bible, & reads it every opportunity he can get.

April 15, 1830

George Smith—Age 18

Born & brot up in Liverpool Eng. Parents died when he was quite young. Education decent. Has followd the sea most of his days. Been in U.S. 2 years. Says he has been a wild boy. Not intemperate. Once in the House of correction in Boston for breaking windows. Sentenced about a week ago in Boston for 3 ys & 2 months for Larceny. 3 Indictments. Looks like a very hard character for one of his age & size, & probably his looks do not belie him.

Marcus R. Stevenson—Age 25

Born in Longmeadow, but has lived most of his life in Springfield in this State. Can read & write. Never learn'd any trade. Has work'd at almost every thing. Has run about the world a good deal and been very unsteady. In 1824 enlisted into the U.S. service. Was enticed by liquor. Says this step did more to ruin him than any thing else. Became habitually intemperate.

Says he is a singular kind of a Genius, and a considerable share of this genius runs to mischief. Knows it is very foolish & wrong, but liquor will lead to every thing. Says the people in Springfield are afraid of him. They think him very ingenious in villainy. Hopes he shall live to get out & do better. Intends to conduct well here.

Was sentenced in Springfield in Sept last, for life, to this prison for Burglary.

His reputation stands pretty high as a rogue.

JOHN STEVENS—AGE 23

Home, Portland, Maine. Born & brot up there. Education as good as common. His mother is still living. Father has been dead for several years. When young, work'd with his father in a Woollen factory. Has workd some at farming. Was steady & industrious till within 4 or 5 years, then went to Sea. Became rude, unsteady, & somewhat intemperate. Was convicted in Boston, of Larceny in October last and sentenced 2 ys. Says that he has never thought much till of late. Now see how foolish he has been. Thinks he shall live differently if he ever goes out from this place. Not much sensibility, tho I hope he feels some.

THOMAS SANDERSON—AGE 33

Home Waltham.[60] Education pretty good. Habits good till within a few years. Went to Sea. Had rather hard luck. Got to drinking to excess. 2d Comer. Here first time 3 ys. Out 3 ys. Returned last November. Sentenced for 2 ys—Larceny. Ascribes his misfortunes to DRINK.

Is pleasant, sensible man, and talks well. What horrible ravages Rum is making!!!

Says he reads his Bible a good deal. Hope he may be benifitted by it.

[60]Possibly Thomas Sanderson, the son of Thomas and Mary Sanderson, born in Waltham, Mar. 23, 1796. *Vital Records of Waltham, Massachusetts, to the Year 1850* (Boston, 1904), 80.

Abner Sheple—Age 44

Born & brot up mostly in Groton.[61] Education decent. By profession, a bricklayer. Has work'd at his trade in almost all parts of the U.S. Been rather a wanderer. Married early. Got a loose bad woman as he says. Left her & has never liv'd with her much. Says he has not been intemperate, but has drink'd his allowance. Convicted in Cambridge in Novr last of Larceny and sentenced for 2 ys.

Is a very strange sort of a being. Stupid & cares no more about his accountability to God or an hereafter that for the earth on which he treads. Is utterly regardless of every thing beyond this life, and I should think of this life too.

In fine, should think him a thoughtless, drinking character, not reckoning himself above the brutes that perish.

Sam[ue]l Stevens—Age 53

Born & brot up in N. Hampshire. Lived on the farm on which he was born till he was near 40. Says he was cheated out of his property which led to his subsequent misfortunes. Education poor. 3d Comer. First time 4 years. Out 9 months. 2d time 1 year. Additional sentence as 2d comer 6 mo. Out 19 months, & last fall Sentenced 3 ys for Storebreaking of which he says he was not guilty. Has a family in N Hampshire. Converses very well, & does not appear hardened like many others, but probably has given up trying ever to be anything but a wicked sinner.

[61] Abner Sheple, the son of James and Deborah Sheple, was born in Groton, Jan. 9, 1786. On July 8, 1806, he married Eunice Varnum of Pepperell. He died of dropsy on Mar. 20, 1849, age 63 years, 2 months, 13 days. *Vital Records of Groton,* 1:221, 2:267; *Vital Records of Pepperell, Massachusetts, to the Year 1850,* comp. George A. Rice (Boston, 1985), 222.

April 16, 1830

THOMAS STRATHERS—AGE 21

Born & brot up in N York. Father dead. Mother is living. Has been a wild boy. Education poor. Left his mother 2 or 3 ys ago & went to Sea. Intemperate & ran after bad women. Convicted in Boston 8 months ago of Larceny & sentenced for 4 years. Had just come to Boston from a West India voyage. Got into bad Company. Says he took a watch to Sell, which was a stolen one as it afterwards proved.

Is in Sab[bath] School. Not much feeling.

May 20, 1830

JAMES THOMAS—AGE 47

Born & brot up in Maryland. (Black-man) Born a Slave, but became free at a certain age. No learning at all. After leaving Maryland, followd the sea some. Learn'd to play on the fiddle, told fortunes &c &c.

Is now in this prison a 4th time.

1st time 1 year. Out about 6 mo.

2 time 3 ys. Out about 3 mo.

3d time sentenced for 3 years—and for being a 3d comer, had an additional sentence for life. Was here 11 years & then pardoned. About a year after this convicted again at New Bedford & sentenced for 2 ys. On his way to the prison escaped from the man who had him in custody & went to N. York where he resided till last fall, when he was taken and brought here on the sentence pass'd 2 ys before.

Two first times, says he was guilty. Two last times, innocent.

Is a very good convict in prison. Orderly and industrious.

Appears clever enough in conversation. Is probably better off here than out. Has been a sort of wandering planet when at large, & in all sorts of company.

THO[MA]S WHITNEY—AGE 26

Born & brot up in Northborough.[62] Early education Good. Friends respectable. His grandfather was minister of Northborough,[63] & he has an uncle who is a minister at Quincy.[64] Learnd the trade of a printer. Serv'd his time in Worcester. Since out of his time, has workd some in Boston & some in N.Y.

Before out of his time, became somewhat unsteady. Drink'd too freely. This habit grew upon him & occasiond his ruin. Came here in July last for 3 ys. Crime stealing some money at a public house in Boston.

Says he thinks his coming here will be the means of saving him from utter ruin. Intends hereafter to live a very different life.

Is a pleasant young man. Has good sense, & is a good prisoner.

May 21, 1830

SIMION TOWN—AGE 57

Born & brot up in Andover. No Education. Says he has been a man of property and respectable for character. Has sometimes indulged too freely in drinking.

---

[62] Thomas-Lambert Whitney, the son of Thomas-Lambert and Mary Whitney, was born in Northborough, Jan. 25, 1804. *Vital Records of Northborough, Massachusetts, to the End of the Year 1850* (Worcester, 1901), 68.

[63] Peter Whitney (Harvard A.B. 1762). See *Sibley's Harvard Graduates,* 15:334–338.

[64] Peter Whitney (Harvard A.B. 1791). Harold Field Worthley, comp., "An Inventory of the Records of the Particular (Congregational) Churches of Massachusetts Gathered 1620–1805," *Proceedings of the Unitarian Historical Society* 16(1970):503.

2d Comer. 1st time for burning a barn—6 ys. Says the Barn was his own, but it was mortgaged & he did not want the man to have it. Serv'd his time out, & was out 5 ys.

About 6 months ago was sentenced again for 2½ ys for Adultery.[65]

Should think him to be a very stupid sort of man, & not very well supplied with common sense. Says he has always got along well in prison.

He says some people thinks him rather shatter'd & he does not know but he is. Thinks he ought not to be here.

ALBERT WHITE—AGE 27

Born & brot up in Wilbraham. Home is now in Thompson Con. His parents live there.

Education very poor. Can barely read. Cannot write. Never learnd any trade. Has work'd, principally, at farming. Has burn'd coal considerably.

Says he has been rather an unsteady sort of a man. Drink'd freely. Was sentenced in Septr last at Springfield for 10 years, for Larceny. Says he stop'd at a tavern & put up over night, drink'd too much, & stole a watch. Appears harmless, and I should think him rather *white-livered.* Perhaps, however, he may be wiser than he appears. Says he has got along well so far. Is in Sab[bath] School.

JOEL WRIGHT—AGE 44[66]

Born & brot up in Spring[fiel]d Mass. Early education good, & was well brot up.

Work'd at farming in early life. Has since workd Some at

[65]Simion Town, Jr., married Olive Wardwell in Andover, Nov. 9, 1794. *Vital Records of Andover, Massachusetts, to the End of the Year 1849* (Topsfield, 1912), 2:329.

[66]Possibly died in Spencer, Oct. 9, 1834, age 49. *Vital Records of Spencer, Massachusetts, to the End of the Year 1849* (Worcester, 1909), 276.

tending mill, & some at blacksmithing. Married when 27. Wife was 17 & knew very little about business. Has 5 children. Did not live happily with his wife at all times. This with some pecuniary difficulties, led him to drinking too freely. Says he has always been an honest man, & a hard working man.

Sentenced in Springfield for an assault on his wife with intent to kill, for 5 ys. Has not yet been here 1 year. Feels very bad. Weeps a good deal. Has not much humility or penitence. Has strong passions, & does not know how to submit to his fate. Behaves well here as a prisoner & I hope his trials may make a solemn, good man of him.

Drink has doubtless been his destroyer.

In early life habits good & usd to attend meeting on Sabbath regularly. Late years he's neglected public worship a good deal.

Denies having any knowledge of an intent to kill his wife. Supposes he must have been very crazy.

JONAS WHITE—AGE 63

Born in Lexington.[67] Serv'd in apprenticeship to the Blacksmithing business in Waltham. Has lived for a number of years past in Worcester County.

Education decent. Character & habits always good. Never intemperate. Comfortable property. Married at 20. Has now a second wife. Has had 12 children. 7 are now living.

Sentenced last October for 2 ys to this prison, for per-

---

[67]Jonas White, the son of Ebenezer and Betty White, was born in Lexington, Jan. 20, 1768. He married Susanna Sanderson of Waltham, May 26, 1789, and Sarah Clark of Waltham, Apr. 25, 1799. *Lexington, Mass.: Record of Births, Marriages and Deaths to January 1, 1898* (Boston, 1898), 87; *Vital Records of Waltham, Massachusetts, to the Year 1850* (Boston, 1904), 240.

jury. Says he is entirely innocent. Never entertain'd the most distant idea of swearing falsely. Appears very well. Weeps freely, & should think him much above the prisoners generally, in character & feeling.

May 24, 1830

John Wade—Age 23
Born & brot up in R.I. Education as good as common. Attempted when young to learn the trade of a Blacksmith, but owing to ill health, did not succeed. For the last 4 ys has been employd in driving stage. Says his habits were always good, & until the transaction which brought him here, his char[acter] stood fair & his integrity unimpeach'd.

Says he never had any propensity to be unsteady until about a fortnight before he committed the crime. Says it appears to him now as though he must have been partially deranged.

Ran away with a sum of money, entrusted to him to carry from a Bank in Boston to Providence $5100.

Went to Maine. Was there a few days. Felt very wretched. Determin'd to come back & give up the money. Came in a vessel. The Captain, when he got to Boston, heard of the business, & saw an advertisement, & charg'd him with it. He ownd it & deliverd himself up. Sentenced for 3 ys. Came here last summer. Appears very well indeed. Has much more feeling than common. Weeps much, & feels that he has destroyd himself.

I hope he may yet be honest & useful.

Charles Wallis—Age 17
Born & brot up in Cambridge. Parents died when he was young & he was thrown unprotected upon the world. Early

education poor. Soon became wild & vicious. Is a 2d Comer. 1st time 3 ys. Out 18 mo & has now been here about 6 mo. Sentence 1 year.

Says he feels that he has liv'd very foolishly & wickedly. Since here this last time has thought a great deal on the past & is resolvd, if he lives to get out, to live a very different life. Reads his bible all the time he can get. Appears serious & well dispos'd. Hopes he may be saved from utter ruin both in time & eternity.

Patrick Yore—Age 27
Born and brot up in Ireland. Educated a Calico printer. Been in U.S. 3 ys. Has livd mostly in State of N.Y. till within a few weeks before he committed the crime for which he was sentenced. Says he had always sustained a good character in his own country & in this. Has wife in N. York. Came on from Hudson in N.Y. to Lowel in this State & workd in a factory there at his trade.

After having been there about 8 weeks, he was solicited, one Sunday, to go & take a ride in a Chaise with another fellow. Did so, and although, as he said, he had always been temperate, yet on this occasion, he got high. So much so that he did not care what he did.

Says he was so much under the influence of liquor that he could not have perpetrated the crime even if no resistance had been made.

Attempted to commit a rape in the highway on a girl whom they met. His companion rode on & left him to manage for himself. Sentence 7 ys. Been here a part of a year.

Feels very bad. Says he has no one to blame but himself. Weeps and thinks he shall be wiser in time to come.

June 1, 1830

Leonard Foster—Age 29

Born & brot up in Carlisle in this State.[68] Early Education decently good. Says his parents brot him up to industrious & good habits. Farmer. Married when 24. Has wife & 2 Children. Says he was never intemperate, & has been accustomed to attend public worship on Sabbath. Sentenced in April last for passing a Counterfeit Bill—for 5 years. Thinks his sentenced a hard one. Acknowledges that he did very foolishly & very wrong—passing the Bill. Appears to be a very decent man, although he did not manifest as much sensibility as I should have been glad to see.

Aaron B. Cutter—Age 28

Born & brot up in West Cambridge.[69]

Sentenced in Concord in Apl last for 1 year. Larceny. Says he was innocent as a child unborn. Indicted for Stealing 2 muskets. Says they were brot to him to repair & he knew nothing of them being stolen property. Parents dead. Mother died when he was quite young. Father has been dead about 6 ys. Says he was tolerably well brot up. Work'd at farming till 14. Afterwards in shop at smith work machinemaking, and as a Millwright.

Has been married. Wife dead. No children.

Education decent. For a few of the last years of his life he

---

68 Possibly Leonard Foster, the son of Benjamin and Sarah Foster, born in Carlisle, May 26, 1798. He published his intention to marry Dorande Tufts of Littleton, Apr. 30, 1825. *Vital Records of Carlisle, Massachusetts, to the End of the Year 1849* (Salem, 1918), 16, 52.

69 Aaron Burr Cutter, the son of Aaron Cutter, was born in West Cambridge, Dec. 10, 1801. On Nov. 25, 1827, he published his intention to marry Mary Stone. *Vital Records of Arlington, Massachusetts, to the Year 1850* (Boston, 1904), 16, 66.

has been wild & unsteady. Drink'd some, tho not as much as some, but too much. Has liv'd a sorry life & would not for the world live it over again.

Was in Salem Jail till Apl. Says that he heard Wm White's death talked of before he was put in jail last winter. Says that George [illeg.] tried to get him to join him in murdering the old man, but he would not consent.

Does not seem to have any feeling. Hope he may be softened by his confinement.

ELISHA FLAGG—AGE 23
Born & brot up in Needham, Norfolk Co. Education good. Had the best of parents, & was brot up to good, industrious habits, & till he went from home to learn a trade was a member of a Sab[bath] School. Says that the man he liv'd with was a fine man. Was kind &c &c. Had a great many different men live with him & work for him. Sometimes had those who would have their grog, & when this was the case us'd to bring the Bottle to the Shop. By this means he got into the habit of tasting and finally of *drinking* till he became intemperate, & this led him to the crime for which he was sentenced.

Sentenced for forgery in April last for 6 ys.

Appears amiable, and manifests a good deal of feeling. Hope his imprisonment may be the means of saving him from ruin.

June 2, 1830

WILLIAM EVANS—SAYS HIS NAME IS NEVENS—AGE 44
Born & brot up in N. Hampshire. For the last 24 ys has liv'd in this State, in Marblehead, Chelsea, & elsewhere. In early life work'd at farming.

Has of late years follow'd fishing in the season of fishing. Parents brot him up to regular & good habits. Education decent, tho not very good. Has been married. Wife dead. Has a daughter 14 ys old. Says he was never intemperate, altho he acknowledges that it was for stealing Rum with another fellow, to carry out into the woods where they were at work, that he was sent here. Says he has generally been a pretty industrious & regular man. Not accustomed to profanity. Gerrish[70] was the man who led him to steal the Rum & who betray'd him and came here with him. Sentenced at Concord in April last for 1 year. Appears to have some feeling.

Enoch Gerrish—Age 26

Born & brot up at Marblehead. Mother died when he was a child, father was killd during the late war. Education as good as common. Was brought up, mostly by a Mr Bartlett till he was 19, then left him. Until this time was pretty steady & industrious. After this livd here & there, became unsteady, & intemperate, & it was this vice which brot him here. Was convicted of Stealing Rum. Says that Evans who work'd with him (see Evans, next preceding) was a great Rum drinker. Never before in any difficulty of this sort. Says he is exceedingly sorry for his offence & is resolved to do better hereafter. Gets along here as well as could be expected. Came here in Apl last. Sentenced for 2 ys.

Asaph Spaulding—Age 22

Born in Leominster.[71] Father lives there. Liv'd with father till 16. Well brot up & education good. At 16 went to Pep-

---

[70]Inmate Enoch Gerrish. See next entry.

[71]Asaph Spaulding, the son of Asaph and Betsy Spaulding, was born in Leominster, May 20, 1807. After his release, he married Martha Chase in Leominster, Apr. 22, 1835. *Vital Records of Leominster, Massachusetts, to the End of the Year 1849* (Worcester, 1911), 131, 260.

perell to learn a trade, that of Carriage making. Sustain'd a good character. Since he became of age has been rather unsteady. Got into bad company & was rather dissipated. Convicted of passing C[ounterfei]t money & sentenced for life. Says it was his first offence of the kind.

Appears a smart, sensible young man, and manifests a good temper & a good degree of feeling.

June 3, 1830

MATTHEW WARD—AGE 43

Born & brot up in Ireland. Education poor. Can read, write poorly. Been in U.S.A. since 1807. Never learnd any trade. Has always liv'd out to service, as he terms it. For a good many ys has been intemperate. Lov'd a high scrape now & then. Stole a coat and was sentenced in Concord in April last for 18 mo. Says drink has done it all & he hopes this will learn him some wit. Does not seem to feel much. Is doubtless pretty ignorant & has liv'd very thoughtlessly. Says he intends to try all he can to please his keepers.

JOHN FINEMORE—AGE 22

Color'd man. His father died in this prison last winter.

Can read, not write. Has lived here & there. No trade. Says he has not been very steady. Did not often drink to excess. Sent[ence]d in Northhampton, in Apl for theft, 2 ys. Should think him very stupid & that he felt about as well to be here as any where. Say he will behave well.

His father Liv'd in Amherst before he came to prison.

ASA WOOD—AGE 23

Parents live in Vermont. Large family. All have done well but himself, and he might if he had only taken the advice & harkened to the counsel of his friends.

Education decent. Always has a roving disposition. Has lived here & there, been unsteady, & *Intemperate.* It was intemperance which ruined him.

Seems to have some feeling & frankness and I hope may come to his senses. Sentenced in Worcester in April for 2 ys.

June 4, 1830

SAM[UE]L D. DYER—AGE 25
Born & brot up in Freeport, Maine. Livd with parents till he was 19. Education pretty good, & was well brot up. His father not having work for all his boys, he, at 19, went from home, & came to this State, where he has lived most of the time. For the last 2 ys has liv'd in Boston, & has been most of the time tending *stable.* Convicted in Boston in Apl & sentenced for 1 year.

Says he was never addicted to drinking to excess. Does not know why he was led to the crime for which he is suffering.

It seems to him now as though he must have been possess'd. Says a Stable is a very bad place to work in.

Appears as well as common, tho not a great deal of feeling.

THO[MA]S STEEL—AGE 35
Home in Charlemont in Franklin Co. Has a wife & 4 Children there.[72] Born & brot up in Farmington Ct. Has work'd a good deal at farming, but served 3 ys at working Tin plate. Education decent. Says his habits have been good. Never intemperate.

---

[72]Steel and his wife, Polly, had the following children: Josephine Rice (b. 1822), Rozetta Hollister (b. 1824), Emeline Plum (b. 1825), and George Freeman (b. 1827). *Vital Records of Charlemont, Massachusetts, to the Year 1850* (Boston, 1917), 75.

Convicted in April last for burning the Barn of his Brotherinlaw. Says he was not within a mile of the place at the time. Says the evidence was all circumstantial, & they proved that he knew something of the business. Sentenced for 4 years. Feels pretty bad, and Sheds some tears. Says that he & his Brother in law had had some little difficulty about property.

Sylvanus Butterfield

Born & brot up in Dummerston, Vt. Never liv'd much with his parents but has work'd out. Can read pretty well. Since 16, has lived mostly in this State, in many places. Never laid up any property. Has been Intemperate, & it was this that led him to the crime (Stealing) for which he now suffers. Says he was never before in any difficulty for crime. Sentenced in Worcester in April for one year.

Thinks this will cure him of drinking & of running about. Is resolv'd to behave well here & afterwards.

June 14, 1830

William Gay—Age 23

Home in State of N.Y. Did not state where. Parents still living. Left them about 4 ys ago. Advantages for Education poor. Lived a good ways from school. Says he was not very well governed, & of course, having his own head, became wild & unsteady. Had not been long in this State before his apprehension. Convicted in Taunton of Storebreaking in April last. Sentenced for 3 ys. Says that a man by name of Stewart, but who now goes by the name of Hall, was concern'd with him. (Stewart is the celebrated Hatch, who was discharged from this prison last fall, and is now in Jail, for the purpose of having him as a witness in the case of the Salem murder, before his trial for the Store breaking).

Says that he occasionally drink'd too much, gambled, & run after the girls. Says he never before got into prison. (Gay not his true name).

Most likely has been a wild, dissipated, vicious young man, & unless reform'd here, is ruin'd. Appears pleasant, very little feeling, thinks he shall be wise, & better hereafter. Says he did not regard the Sabbath as he ought. Works in the cooper's shop and is now in Sabbath School.

JOHN STANNARD—AGE 21

Home Springfield, Mass. Father has been dead 3 ys, mother 15 ys. Education decent. Brought up to brick making, & liv'd with his father till his death. Has lived some in the State of New York. Has been usually industrious, but liked a scrap now & then, and when he had a frolic, he sometimes got too much liquor into his head.

Sentenced in Springfield in April last, for Stealing for 3 ys. Says that after drinking with 4 or 5 others in a grocery, he became in a great degree insensible to what he did, and took some money.

Has some feeling, weeps, & expresses regret & sorrow for his fault.

Appears, on the whole, pretty well.

June 16, 1830

PERO MANN (COLOR'D MAN)—AGE 18

Born in Granby Con. Parents have been long dead. For the last 3 ys has liv'd mostly in Springfield, Mass., where he was convicted in Apl last & sentenced for 1 yr.

Charg'd with stealing a watch. Says he never saw it, nor knew any thing of it. Two fellows had quarrelled with him & sworn that they had seen him have such a watch as was lost, but declares positively that it is false. Can read a little.

Is now in our Sab[bath] School. Says he never had been devoted to vice, but had been as steady as usual. Was not intemperate.

Appears very mild & pleasant, & should think him far from being a hardened offender.

Amos Smith—Age 47

Belongs in West Springfield. Has a family there. Is a second comer. Was here the first time 19 mo. About 11 ys since he went from here. Was now sentenced at Springfield for 2 years in Apl last. Intemperance, he says, has been his ruin. Education decent. Says he can plainly see what a foolish & wicked man he has been, & how he has been bartering all that is valuable for that which is worse than nothing. Exhibits some feeling, & says he often feels very much in regard to his future well being. Is full of trouble & knows not what to do with himself.

Micah Herring—[Age 24]

Born & brot up in Chester, Hamp[shi]re Co. Has a mother living. Age 24. Education pretty good. Says he has generally been pretty steady & industrious. Has lived at a tavern a good deal & though he has two or three times in his life drink'd too much, yet he was not habitually intemperate. Us'd to drink something almost every day, though not too much. Sentenced at Northampton in Apl last for 2 ys, for Storebreaking. Says he was guilty. Was led away by another. Is a young man of sense. Says it is his first deviation from rectitude. Converses with great propriety & a good sense of feeling, & but few convicts appear as well. Says he gets along without any difficulty, & any prisoner can if he is dispos'd. Loves to work & says he is as faithful as though he was working for wages. Considers it a privilege that he may work.

John Reed 3d—Age 26
Home in Westminster, Vt. Has not been there for several years. Has been to sea some & has work'd here & there.

Says he was never intemperate, although his face tells a different story. Perhaps his face tells a lye. Education decent. Convicted in Essex Co. in May of passing C[ounterfei]t Money & sentenced 2 ys. Says it was a 2 dollar Bill & he came honestly by it & passed it honestly. Being a stranger & having no friends there, he was convicted. Looks like rather a hard character. Wept some & may be will do well.

Robert Blaney—Blackman—age 34
Belongs to Pennsylvania. Can read & write. Has been married, but wife is dead. Has 1 Child 10 ys old. Has been absent from home 4 ys, and during that time has been at Sea, excepting occasionally in Port. Says that wherever he has been or livd, he has sustained a fair character for honesty & industry. Never addicted to drinking so as to hurt him. Drink'd a glass or two a day like other folks. Convicted in Ipswich in May for stealing some money in Salem. Says he has just come in from sea, and has been out 3 or 4 nights running after girls, and it was this which led to the Act. Never stole any thing before, & thinks he shall never steal again.

Is frank & pleasant & on the whole appears pretty well.

June 17, 1830

John Emerson—Age 66
Born in Liverpool, Eng. Came to Nova Scotia when quite young. Never had any advantages for Education. Cannot read. Has been married, & settled in life in New Brunswick. Wife is dead. Has children in New Brunswick. Has been a

hard-working man, as he says & has generally followd the business of Lumbering & boating in the British dominions. Drink'd freely & became intemperate, & this led to the theft which terminated in his being sent here. Sentenced for 18 mo at Ipswich in May last. Never in any prison before as he says. Hopes this will be a good lesson to him & make him leave off drinking.

John Gibson[73]—Age 47

Born in Ireland. Been in this Country about half of his life. Follow'd the Sea most of the time. Can read tho his Education is poor. Has been Intemperate, and ascribes his ruin to intemperance.

Acknowledges that he has been in the Vt. St. Prison at Windsor. Was sentenced there for 10 ys. Was pardoned out last fall after having been there 5 ys & 3 months in consequence of his good conduct & industrious habits. Came to Boston. There fell into company with a fellow by name of Watson, who had been a convict in the Vt Prison. From Boston they went to Salem & while there went into a Grocery to get their bottle replenish'd, & unbeknown to him Watson stole a Watch from the Grocery, & he being in company was convicted with Watson & sentenced for 1 year.

Says that after the trial, Watson made oath that he (Gibson), know nothing of the transaction, & that the Judge & others had made out a Statement of the case & forwarded them to the Governor, & he expects to be pardoned. Intends to conduct well and when he gets his liberty to avoid drinking Rum. Tells a very fair story, but very likely not a word of truth in it.

---

[73] "John Gibson, 44 y, prisoner in State Prison, d. there Nov. 2, 1833." *Vital Records of Charlestown*, 2:274.

Charles Watson—Age 27
Home in Ohio. Parents live there. Has not been there himself for many years. Has no education. Has been a wild fellow. Follow'd the sea most of the time since he left home. Intemperate—(has been in Vt St. Prison, This fact I learned from Gibson. [illeg.] I did not ask Watson in regard to it lest he might be angry with Gibson.)

Has a bad face & does not appear to have much feeling. Fear he is a ruin'd man. Says he has got along well here.

Samuel Gilford—Age 20
Home in Danvers. Father died when he was 14. Mother is still living. Education decently good. Has not lived much as home since the death of his father. Has had his own way too much. Work'd 2 ys in Marblehead, part of the time at the Business of Blacksmithing. Became intemperate, & that led to Stealing, of which he was convicted in May last at Ipswich & sentenced for 2 years.

Manifests considerable feeling, & should think him an interesting young man.

June 18, 1830

Tho[ma]s W. Quimby—Age 32
Born & brot up in New Hampshire, but for the last 8 or 10 years has lived in and near Newburyport. By trade a Tanner & shoemaker. Education tolerably good. Has always been a hard working man & unfortunate. Has had a great deal of sickness himself & in his family. Says he was never what is called an intemperate man, altho when he work'd hard has drink'd considerable. Thot he needed it. Sentenced in May last for 18 months at Ipswich for theft. Says he found a

wallet with money in it & did not give it up as he ought. The temptation overcame him.

Says that he got a good deal into debt & his creditors threaten'd to put him to Jail, & he left home to avoid being plague'd, & has at last landed here.

Weeps freely. Seems to feel considerably & I cannot but hope that his confinement may make him a steadier & better man.

Wife & 5 children.[74]

George Larkin—says his true name is Lakin—[Age 17]

Born & brot up in Boston. Age 17. Father is a pilot. His mother is derang'd & lives in the country, & his father does not keep house. Has been most of his life at Sea. Can read poorly—not write. Like most sailors, rather wild—lov'd his grog—and is sensible he drink'd more than he ought. Was led away by others. Convicted in Boston of theft in May last & sentenced for 1 year. Probably has been a wild youth & has been left to himself without much parental care or instruction.

What certain ruin in such a place as Boston.

John Power—Age 35

Born in Ireland. Brot up a Waterman. Been in America 14 ys, mostly in Newfoundland. A year ago this Spring came to Boston, from thence. Has been on fishing voyage. Can read very poorly. Very intemperate & to this vice owes all his troubles.

In a state of intoxication robbed two ladies in that street,

[74]Thomas W. Quimby married Dolly S. Short in Newburyport, May 8, 1825. *Vital Records of Newburyport, Massachusetts, to the End of the Year 1849* (Salem, 1911), 2:398.

in Boston, one of her veil & the other of her Work Bag, and for these offences was sentenced in May last for 5 ys. Say he is very sorry indeed. Would no more have done it if he had been sober than he would have taken his own life. Says Rum is a dreadful thing and he will never have any thing more to do with it. Seems frank, and appears really to mourn over his misconduct.

June 22, 1830

George S. Murray—Age 22
Born & brot up in Providence, R.I. Parents live there now. Has not lived there himself for the last 3 ys. Has liv'd mostly in Boston. Is married. Wife in Boston. No children. Says his habits have always been good. Never intemperate. Accused of receiving stolen goods. Says he was not guilty, & if he had only been acquainted with the Law he should not have been convicted. Sentenced in Boston in May last for 1 year. Weeps pretty freely. Most likely he keeps his habits & course of life, of late years, out of sight. Says he has drink'd some spirits, tho not to excess.

James Jones—Age 25
Born in England.

By trade a cabinet maker & Joiner. Education good. Has been to school 14 ys. Parents are dead. Has been joiner on board a British vessel of War. Deserted at Halifax & came to Boston, where he was convicted in May last of Larceny & sentenced for 1 year. Had, as he says, become very intemperate, & could not have lived long in the way he was going on. Is glad he was arrested & placed in a situation where he has opportunity to look at his case. Thinks he shall reform wholly, & pursue a different course of life. Friends very respectable.

Appears mild & amiable. Looks very young, & his countenance very fair. Hope he may be benefited by his afflictions.

THO[MA]S BYRON—AGE 40
Born & brot up in Ireland. Left that Country 4 ys ago. Says he brough[t] a good character with him from the most respectable gentlemen. Wife dead. Has 6 children, 4 in & about Boston, & 2 in Ireland. No Education. Brot up a flax & Hemp dresser.

Says that for 2 ys past he has kept bad company & drink'd too much & the curse of God has follow'd him for it. Says a bad woman swore him here. Is very sorry. Weeps. Seems to feel for his children a good deal. Convicted of Larceny in Boston & sentenced for 2 ys. Been here 5 weeks.

Has probably been a hard working, hard drinking, & thoughtless man.

Thinks he shall let drink & bad company alone for the future.

BENJ[AMI]N BRAUN—AGE 46
Has been married. Wife been dead 16 ys. Born & brot up in England. Has children there. Has not seen them for many years. Was press'd into the British Navy, & taken from home. After several years Service came to Quebec. There deserted & came to U.S. & has since been 8 or 9 ys in the U.S. service. Very intemperate. Says this destroy'd him. Looks as though he were almost burn'd up with Rum. His face like a blaze of fire. Says he can now see his folly and madness, & hopes to be benefitted by being shut away from the world & temptation. Converses sensibly, but is probably, a ruin'd man. Convicted <*in Boston*> & sentenced for 2 ys in May last.

June 23, 1830

J.T. Torrey—Age 39
Born & brot up in Scituate Plym[out]h County. Early education good. Kept school one or two winters. By trade a ship-carpenter. Has 1 child. Wife dead. Early habits, as he says, good.

Ship business being rather dull went to trading & fail'd in consequence of being defrauded by some men in Boston as he says, & to be revenged on them & to get a part of the property back told them he was building a Brig at the east & got trusted for the sails, rigging &c to the amount of about 1000 dollars. But he told a lye, as he had no Brig. For this was arrested & prosecuted for Swindling & sent to this place for 3 ys. This was near 8 ys ago.

Since his discharge has work'd in various places. Says he was never intemperate. Convicted in May Last in Plymouth for Larceny & sent here for 1 year. Says he is not guilty. Was convicted because he had been here before, merely on suspicion.

Is an intelligent man & I doubt not a shrewd one. Says the state of things was horrible here when here before. Very different now. Could then get into the prison through the officers, just what he wish'd. Thinks some of the officers were as bad as the prisoners.

George White—Age 62
Born in Taunton. Education rather poor. Learnd trade of Blacksmith. Says he was pretty steady till he was 24 or 25 years old. Since that time has run a strange race. 3d Comer, to this prison & says he has been once in the S. Prison at N. York several years. Has been in Prison as he says between 20 & 30 years.

Has a very bad face, & from his life, it does not belie him. Says he is not guilty of the crime for which he is sentenced, horse stealing. Bought the Horse.

Says he was none of your common every day tipplers. Us'd every now & then to have a real *blow out* & then let liquor alone for some time.

Convicted in May last & sentenced for 1 year. Is, I doubt not, a finish'd scholar in his line of business.

Elisha Dillingham—Age 68

Born & brot up in this State. Education pretty good, & his habits were pretty good till he went into the Army in the time of the Revolutionary War. Since that time has been irregular in his habits. Been 3 times in State Prison in all 12 or 15 ys.

Says he has not been a drinking man, but very temperate. Face looks like a drunkard's face. Says it is a natural humour.

The old man is in a perfect agony of feeling. Rarely have seen a man who has been in prison so much, who feels more the misery & degradation of his situation. Says he never has felt so before when in prison. Feels how dreadfully he has lived how he has abused God's goodness. Intends now to seek something better than the fruits of sin. Weeps violently so that his whole frame is agitated.

Edmund Murdock—Age 48

Born & brot up, & has liv'd mostly, in this State.[75] Carpenter. Never married. Gone from place to place. Education poor. Sentenced in Plymouth in May for passing Counter-

[75] Edmund Murdock, the son of Andrew and Meribah Murdock, was born in Carver, Sept. 11, 1782. *Vital Records of Carver, Massachusetts, to the Year 1850* (Boston, 1911), 46.

feit money. Says he thinks it would be better to earn money than to get it in this way. Says if he had settled down in early life he should probably have avoided getting into prison. Should then, most likely, have been a steady man.

Sentenced for 18 months.

June 24, 1830

Green Lawrence—Age 30

Belongs in Pepperell. Wife & family. Learnd the trade of a Shoemaker & has work'd at it some. Has also work'd at coopering. Education as good as common. Habits in early life regular. Says he has been temperate, that is, he has never drink'd too much. Has usually drink'd about *3 times* a day. (It seems men call themselves temperate if they do not get drunk, though they drink ever so much.)[76]

Convicted in Plymouth in May last of passing C[ounterfei]t money & sentenced to this prison for 2 ys. Says he lay in prison before trial about a year.

Left home in May 1829, on Saturday & on Tuesday of the next week was apprehended & committed to Jail just after the Session of the Court, & had to wait till this Spring for Trial, the court sitting but once a year in that County. Says it is his first attempt at passing bad money & he intends it shall be his last. Can now see clearly that it is a ruinous as well as wicked business.

Is determined to be industrious & orderly while here. Appears pretty well on the whole.

Antonio Guy

Is a Spaniard & cannot talk English much. On this account did not attempt to say much.

---

[76]Close parenthesis supplied.

Samuel G. Hale—Age 22

Born & brot up in Dunstable N.H. Parents live there now. Was brot up to farming, and was well brot up in good & industrious habits. Education decent. Liv'd at home till 21. Convicted at Plymouth, in May last, of passing Counterfeit money, and Sentenced for 10 months. Says he was riding in the Stage with G. Lawrence the individual named on page 140,[77] who had Considerable bad money & Green got him to take a Bill & offer it, which he did. Says this is all he ever had to do with Bad money. In consequence of his former good character & certificates from the Selectmen of the Town where he belonged he got a short Sentence. Appears very well, & should think he intended to behave well & do well. Says he was never intemperate.

William P. Bunker—Age 28

Home in Falmouth, Barnstable Co. Has wife & 3 children.[78] His father is living. Is a seafaring man, and is now at Sea, ignorant of his situation. Education pretty good, and until 18 ys old, was very steady. After going to Sea, got into the habit of drinking & before his conviction had become very intemperate. This habit led him to the theft for which he is suffering in this prison. Has followd the Sea for a number of years past, part of the time fishing, & part of the time in the merchant service.

Says he thinks it will be a good thing for him that he is here. Is resolv'd to overcome the habit of drinking.

Appears very well. Convicted in Barnstable in May & sentenced for one year.

---

[77] See inmate Green Lawrence, above, p. 209.

[78] William P. Bunker's marriage to Cloe Baker was registered in Falmouth, May 11, 1823. *Vital Records of Falmouth, Massachusetts, to the Year 1850*, comp. Oliver B. Brown (Warwick, R.I., 1976), 140.

June 25, 1830

LYMAN BOOTH—AGE 22
Mulatto. Born & brot up in Wmstown Mass.

Can read, but not write. Has for a considerable portion of his life been moving here & there on one kind of business & another. Has tended stud horses, driven droves &c &c. Drink'd some though not very hard, & been at times rather rude. Work'd some at blacksmithing with [illeg.] his father. Sentenced in Berkshire Co in May last for 2 ys. Convicted of Theft. Says he was led to it by getting into bad company. Says it was his first offence & he intends it shall be his last. Has been in some trouble here, been punish'd for quarrelling. Says he is sorry & intends hereafter to govern himself in an orderly manner, & do well.

MARTIN BARBER—AGE 23
Born & brot up in Sand Lake, Renssallaer Co. N.Y. Father died when he was 3 ys old. His oldest brother kept the family together a good while. There were 8 boys. Education decent. His father being dead, he was under very little restraint. Had his own head, & ran wild. Contracted ruinous habits, at the head of which was that of Intemperate drinking. This finally led to this prison. Convicted in Berkshire Co. in May last. Sentence 18 months. Says he sometimes, but rarely attended meeting on the Sabbath when he was a boy. Of late years, not at all. Has neglected every thing of a religious nature. Should think he has not much feeling. Wife and one child.[79]

---

[79]Martin Barber's marriage to his wife, Achsah, was registered in Medway, Apr. 5, 1828. *Vital Records of Medway, Massachusetts, to the Year 1850* (Boston, 1905), 151.

CHARLES POTTER—BLACKMAN—AGE 23

Born & brot up in Dutchess Co. N.Y. Father is living. Mother dead. He's follow'd farming mostly, but has been employ'd in Boating some up & down the North or Hudson River.

Last fall, went to N.Y. & since that time has follow'd the coasting business. Came in a Schooner to Boston & there Stole some money from the vessel, for which he was sentenced for 2 ys to this prison.

Came here the present month of June from the Municipal Court in Boston. Can read & write. Says he was not addicted to drinking to excess. Means this shall be the last of his committing crime.

JAMES MOORE—AGE 22

Born & brot up in New Hampshire. Supposes his parents are still living there. Has not heard from them for 2 ys. Can read. Left his parents 9 years ago, since which, he has lived here & there, been unsteady & wild. Has follow'd the Sea for 3 years past. Became very intemperate. Came into Boston, got high, stole a watch in a drunken scrape. Was convicted, & sent to this prison from the municipal court this present month of June. Sentence 2 ys.

SILAS RIPLEY—AGE 29

Born in Easton (Mass).

His parents moved into N. Hampshire when he was young. Has not lived with them very much. Has lived in various places, for a number of years in Boston. Been to sea some. Education decent. Says he never drink'd much. Is not guilty of the theft of which he was convicted. Says a man came across him in Boston and got him to assist in moving some broken Anchors. They were taken to Long

Wharf where the man sold them & gave him for his troubles 25 Cts. Did not know the man. Was apprehended as the thief, because he was seen moving the anchors, & as the other man was gone, he had to suffer. Sentenced for 1 year. Wept very freely. Hope he may learn a valuable Lesson, whether his story be true or false.

June 29, 1830

Robert Douglass—Age 30
Born & brot up in Scotland. Has lived, the latter part of his life, for 8 or 10 ys in Edinburgh. Clerk in a Store. Education & parentage good, & as he says, character always fair. Was persuaded by an acquaintance to come to the U.S. who told him he could get better wages. Accordingly came to Boston in March last. Convicted of Larceny & sentenced for 2 years.

Says he found a pocketbook which a gentleman had dropped & instead of making the fact known & giving up the Book as he ought, he concealed it, although it was advertised & a reward offered for it.

Is intelligent & appears dispos'd to conduct well.

W[illia]m F. Dix—Age 30
Sentenced in Boston for Larceny, the present month of June, for 2 ys. Is a man of good Education. Born & brot up in this State, but has lived mostly for a few years past in Providence R.I. Wife & 3 children. Lost his father in early life, & was left very much to himself. Was not properly governed. Begun business for himself when 19. Succeeded very well. Is a joiner. Before he was of age, was chosen an officer in the Militia. All these things raised him above his level. As he was prospered, he did not anticipate days of adversity. But they came. His property went, & from one thing

to another he has finally landed here. Says he never drink'd to excess.

From some things I have learn'd, I suspect he has been very wild & vicious for a season back.

Has left his family & lived with a bad woman.

He denies it and says it is false.

Hope he may repent.

JEZANIAH COOK—[AGE 45]

Born & brot up in Cambridge.[80] Education pretty good. Has follow'd butchering & marketing for a livelihood. His father was of the same business and for many years supplied Cambridge College[81] with Meat &c. Wife dead. 6 children. Oldest a son 17, the rest daughters. His son follows marketing, & goes to Boston every day with poultry &c. Name Oliver.

Says he has very little property of his own.

Children had some land left to them.

Has of late been rather unsteady. Got into bad Company and led to crime. Sentenced to this prison in Boston the present month of June, for 2½ years.

Does not seem to possess very much sensibility. Says he was not what might be call'd an intemperate man. Drink'd some.

August 4, 1830

WILLIAM TAYLOR—AGE 43

Born St Domingo. Been in this country 25 ys. Can read, write very poorly. Says he understands various kinds of

---

[80] Jazeniah Cook, the son of Ephraim and Hannah Cook, was born in Cambridge, Feb. 25, 1785. He published his intention to marry Elizabeth Hall, May 24, 1806, and died in Cambridge, Nov. 27, 1846, age 63, of consumption. *Vital Records of Cambridge*, 1:155, 2:87, 512.

[81] Harvard College.

Mechanical business, such as carpentering, basket making &c &c.

Says he has always been industrious & steady. Not intemperate. Sustaind a fair character.

Had a bad wife, who us'd to get with another man. Caught her in the act. Struck her & she went off home & died not long after. Says he knows that the blow he struck her did not kill her. Was tried last year, & the Jury could not agree. Again tried in July last. Convicted of man-slaughter & sentenced for 2 ys. Barnstable. Says he fears God and it is his desire to serve him. Intends to behave well here. Is satisfied that it is the will of God that plac'd him here & he submits quietly.

September 20, 1830

CHARLES EASTMAN—AGE 22

Born & brot up in Concord, N.H.[82] Mother died when he was a child. Father died when he was 7 ys old. After that, lived with his Uncle, a very respectable man & president of the Bank.[83] Education good. Has kept school several winters. Has driven stage some.

Sentenced in Boston in July last for Larceny & sentenced for 1 year. Says he was not guilty of the offence. Says no stain was ever on his character before. Do not think he manifests much humility or feeling, but perhaps he feels more than he appears to. But I fear he has not all that feeling which he ought to possess.

---

[82]Charles Eastman, the son of Charles and Persis Eastman, was born in Concord, N.H. Nathaniel Bouton, *The History of Concord* (Concord, N.H., 1856), 648.

[83]This may be Richard Bradley, a director of the Concord Bank. The first wife of the inmate's father was named Sally Bradley. *New Hampshire Register . . . 1817* (Exeter, 1816), 85; *New England Historic Genealogical Register* 92 (1938):277.

JOHN TURNER—AGE 27
Englishman. Has follow'd the sea all his life. Can read, but not write. Sentenced for 1 year in Boston in July last for Larceny—stealing some rope from a vessel. Says he did not steal. Had drink'd too much, & went on board the vessel to lie down, & that was all. Says he has not drink'd any before for a year.

A real sailor. Rum—Rum—Rum. Says he will not drink any more. Cried at Judeus Apella!!

September 27, 1830

SAMUEL HICKMAN—AGE 26
Born in Pennsylvania. When quite young, workd on farm when not at school. Education decent. Has followd the Sea most of his life. For the last 4 years, has been mate of a vessel, & has of late saild out of Boston.

Has a wife & 2 Children in N. Jersey. Says that he had been in the habit of carrying out ventures, & the proceeds of these <*vessel*> ventures he usd to smuggle into the port on his return. Was inform'd against & in order to get revenge, did that which brought him here. Sentenced in July last in Boston for Larceny for 1 year. Says he has got along well. Time runs away very heavily.

Early habits good. Never intemperate, as he says. Does not seem to be very frank. Says he believes the Bible to be the word of God.

JOSEPH <*William*> KING—AGE 31
Blackman. Born in Rio Jeneiro, Brazil, S. America. Talks very broken English. Sentenced in Boston in August last for 2 years—for Larceny. Has followd the sea most of his life. Has wife & 2 Children in S. America. Says he us'd to get drunk sometimes. The reason of his getting here as he

says, was that he refus'd to go back to South America with the Captain he came with, and engaged aboard with another vessel. The Capt. owd him 2 months wages & would not pay him, & to get his pay he took the Compass, as he says, before the Capt's eyes & carry'd it off, with some other articles & was prosecuted for theft.

October 5, 1830

LYMAN DUREN—NAME, AS HE SAYS, IS DURRIN—[AGE 38]

Born & brot up in Southington, Con. Had good parents. Education decent. In early life, habits good. Says the occasion of his going astray was that his Step Mother cross'd him in regard to marrying a young woman whom he loved. Went away from home, enlisted into the U.S. Army, & became unsteady although, as he says, he was never given to drinking to excess. Age 38. Has a wife in N. York. Came from City of N.Y. to Boston, with a very bad man, by name of Farrell, or Carroll, not long before his conviction. Says he believes the fellow has once been in this prison by name of Carl. Says George Lynds of Cragies Point made false keys for Farrell, and from his connection with this fellow got into his present troubles.

Says his wife told him, before he left home that if he came off with that fellow, he would get into trouble, & he finds her words true. Is a Shoemaker by trade. Weeps freely, appears frank, & feels that he has got into a bad Box. Convicted on 3 indictments in Boston, for Larceny in Sept last. Sentence 5 ys. (Different [illeg.] notices in A[uburn] S[tate] P[rison].)

WILLIAM REA—AGE 18

Born & brot up in Boston. Has a pious good mother there. Has been a wild boy & given her a great deal of trouble. Sentenced in Boston for Larceny, for 18 months, in Sept last.

Appears rather shy, & does not incline to say much. I think he felt more than he was willing to shew.

October 6, 1830

ARTHUR E. THOMPSON—AGE 18

Born & brot up in City of N. York. Father is now living there, a ship carpenter, & in tolerably good circumstances. Habits good till he went to sea. Education good. Has follow'd the sea since 13 ys old. Says he has been an officer for a year or two past.

Convicted in Boston in Sept Last, & sentenced for 3 ys. Says that he was ruined by gambling. Never gambled much till he came to Boston. Has been after bad women some, tho not much. Says he never drinkd a glass of spirits in his life. Says he had good parents & if he had followd their advice he should not have been here. Has not been home for two years, & his father does not know where he is, & he does not wish him to know.

Says he thinks this will be a good lesson, & he trusts it will cure him of his bad habits. Seemd frank & manifested some feeling.

October 12, 1830

W[ILLIA]M WHITE—AGE 25

Home, Boston. By trade a printer. Began his apprenticeship when 13. Education good. Since of age has been to Sea 2 years & more. Says he was never intemperate or addicted to Bad habits. Convicted in Boston, in Sept last of Larceny & sentenced for 2 years. Declares in the most solemn manner that he is entirely innocent. Says he purchas'd, fairly, the goods which he was accused of stealing.

Says his brothers and sisters are christian people—members of Mr. Bennets Church in Woburn.[84] His father lives in Methodist Alley, Boston.[85] Says he was to have been married next Thanksgiving.

William Vanner—Age 18

Home—Waldoborough, Maine. Has a mother living there. Father is dead. Education decent. Brot up to farming. Habits regular & good. Has follow'd coasting some. Came on to Boston, got into bad company, and in Sept last, convicted of crime & sentenced in Boston for 3 ys.

Diffident & not inclin'd to say a great deal.

October 21, 1830

William Johnson—Age 41

Home Westfield. Has wife & 7 Children. 2d Comer. Left the prison about 7 ys ago. Served 3 ys for passing C[ounterfei]t Money. Says he was well brot up, & to industrious habits. Never intemperate. Education, decent. Convicted in Septr last in Springfield of the crime of Adultery & sentenced for 2 years. Says he was guilty, although the principal testimony in which he was convicted was false. Says that until this transaction his conduct since leaving the prison had been good.

When here the first time, made a profession of Religion, & was baptized.

---

[84]Rev. Joseph Bennett (Harvard A.B. 1818) was minister of the First Church in Woburn from 1822 until his suicide in 1847. Samuel Sewall, *The History of Woburn* (Boston, 1868), 462–468.

[85]Methodist Alley, now Hanover Avenue, ran between Hanover Street and Ann Street. *Boston Directory* (1829), 11.

Says he was sincere, although he may have been & probably was deceiv'd. Did not intentionally play the hypocrite.

FRANCIS WILLIAMS—AGE 31
Color'd man. Home in Westfield. Born there. Has a mother in Springfield. Work'd at farming till within 3 ys. Since that time has been to Sea. Cannot read at all & of course brough[t] up in great ignorance. Says he was never intemperate. Probably was like most negroes—unsteady & fond of frolicks. Convicted of Larceny at Springfield in Sept. last & sentenced for 1 year. Says he did not steal the goods. A fellow brought him 3 new axes & wishd him to keep them. Suspected the fellow did not come honestly by them. Appears pleasant. Says he gets along well & intends to behave himself in all respects.

November 1, 1830

HENRY BURT—AGE 35
Born & brot up in Springfield, Mass., and convicted there in Sept last of Larceny & sentenced for 5 ys. Has wife & 5 children. Says he was never in a like difficulty before. Acknowledges that he has drink'd more than he ought for many years, & for the last six or seven years, has neglected public worship & disregarded the Sabbath. Is in the Stone Shed. Says he gets along well & intends to behave well.

November 17, 1830

HORATIO HILL—AGE 27
Born & brot up in Lebanon, Con. Parents live there. Says they do not know of his situation. Education good. Brot up to farming. Had been to work in the Canal in Hampden

County. Convicted <*of Larceny*> in Springfield of Burglary & sentenced for life in Sept last. Intemperate, gambled, & Intemperance ruind him. Can now realize the dreadfulness of the habit.

Erastus Goodell—Age 26

Born & brot up in Amherst, Mass. Mother is now living there. For the last 8 or 10 ys has workd at Carriage making & trimming. Education as good as common. Has not livd with his mother for a long time. Says his early habits were in general good. Occasionally, on public days would drink more than he ought. Convicted at Spring'd & sen'd 1½ ys in Sept last. Is pleasant & intelligent.

James Wilson—Age 27

Born in Rhode Island, but for a number of years past has lived in State of N.Y. Parents dead. Education not good, but can read & write. Has wandered about the world a good deal. Has been in the U.S. Army. Pretty early in life became intemperate—late years very much so. To this habit owes all his troubles. Says he was never in any similar trouble before. Convicted in Springfield, of Larceny in Sept. last, and sentenced for 2 ys. Feels bad. Weeps freely. Says he gets along well and intends to do well. Should think him a man of not very much mind.

William Stoddard—[Age] 27

Black-man. Born in Canada. But has lived most of his life in the State of N.Y, & in this State. For the last 10 or 12 years has liv'd in this State in Sheffield, Barrington, & West Stockbridge. Has a wife & 3 children. Has no learning. Is learning to read in our Sab[bath] School. Convicted in Lenox, in Sept. last, of stealing a peck of potatoes, & sentenced for 1 year. Says he us'd to drink some. Thinks it very hard to come to S. Prison for so trifling an offence, & when, as he says, another Negro took the potatoes & he was only carrying them for him. Appears clever enough. Hope he may learn wisdom.

Nicholas Nichols—[Age] 23
Born in Barnardston in the County of Franklin. Left there when he was quite young. Education poor. His Brother took him away from home into the Black River country. After a while left there, & wandered about, got unsteady, became intemperate, and has lived a sorry life. Convicted at Lenox, of Stealing a Jack-knife, & sentenced for 1 year, in September last.

Dixit se finisse in carcere Nov. Ebor.—apud S.S., 5 ys. Rel. in Mens. Jan. ult.[86]

Most probably has been a very wild boy & it is to be fear'd that he is ruined. May he repent & become a good man.

Seth Hamilton—Age 28
Born & Brot up in Stockbridge, Mass. Advantages for Education, good.

The Chaplain has know him from a boy. His father was almost entirely deaf & could not, of course, watch over him very well. His mother a *bad woman* & not fit to have charge of any child. This boy always has his head, & many of his acquaintance prophecy'd as to what his end would be. He is married, & has a handsome property, but he lacks moral principle. Sentenced in Lenox, in September last, for 2½ ys

[86] He says that he finished in prison New York at [Sing Sing?]. 5ys. He was sent here last January.

for forgery. Hope this affliction may teach him wisdom. Behaves well here so far.

November 26, 1830

JOHN NORMAN—AGE 51

Born in Portsmouth N.H. Has followd the sea since he was 11 ys old. Has been married. Says that his wife & 3 children, all that he had, died of the yellow fever in N. York, when he was absent on a voyage. Came home & found them all in the grave.

Can read & write poorly. Says he has been intemperate & wicked like most sailors, & has lived a sorry life. Never in prison before for crime. Convicted of Larceny at Northampton in Sept last & sentenced 1 year. Looks like a sun burnt & rum burnt old sailor.

JOHN WILLIS—AGE 29

Born in Pennsylvania. <*A*> Colored man. His mother died when he was young. Went away from his father when about 12. Can read some. At 13 went to sea & has follow'd the Sea ever since. Has been wild & giddy. Intemperate, & when ashore, has run after bad girls. Says he has livd wickedly & is very sorry for it. Has not been into a Church or a Christian assembly, that he recollects, for 20 or 25 ys until he came to this prison. Says he hopes it will do him good. Sentenced in Boston for Larceny for 2 ys. Shed some tears.

December 21, 1830

JOHN RINE OR O. RINE—AGE 47

Born in Ireland. No Education. Convicted in Worcester in Oct last of Larceny, & sentenced for 1 year. Has been either a soldier or sailor most of his life. Has been very intemperate. Says he was once in the house of Correction for one month in Boston. Otherwise was never in Prison till this transaction. Intends to do well & behave well.

March 29, 1831

EDMUND SHATTUCK—AGE 28

Home in Townsend, M[assachusett]s. Parents live there. Education decent. Says he has always been industrious & of good habits. Has been in the habit of regularly attending public worship on Sabbath. Not intemperate, though he sometimes drank some but not to *feel it.* Has d[r]ove a team a good deal. Sentenced in Oct. last at Cambridge for 1½ year for passing C[ounterfei]t money.

Says he took it honestly & had no suspicion of its being bad money. Calls God to witness the truth of what he says. Character always fair where he has lived & been known. Believes the Bible & knows how important it is to seek first the kingdom of God &c.

Should think him a tolerably fair minded man, and not hardened as many are.

STEPHEN RANDALL—AGE 42

Born & brot up in Roxbury.[87] His home is there. Wife & 9 children. Carpenter by trade. Had good parents, & was as well educated as most young men, and nothing particularly bad in his habits. Does not enter very freely into the History of his life. Says he has had a good deal of sickness & hard fortune and although he has made use of spirits, yet

[87] Steven Randel, the son of Abraham and Zibiah Randel, was baptized in Roxbury, Aug. 30, 1788. He married, first, Sarah Ann Warren, on Sept. 2, 1810. She died Dec. 1, 1814. He married, second, Rachel Tirrell, May 12, 1816. He died of cancer, Apr. 16, 1847, age 58 years, 8 months. *Vital Records of Roxbury, Massachusetts, to the End of the Year 1849* (Salem, 1925–1926), 1:289, 2:333, 620.

not to excess as he thinks. Convicted of Burglary at Dedham Nov last & sentenced for life. Never before convicted of crime. Believes the Bible to be the word of God. For 4 ys past has lived a good ways from meeting & has not attended worship very regularly. Does not seem to possess very much feeling. Hopes his friends may yet get him pardoned. Works at Brickmaking in the prison & gets along as he says, very well.

WINSLOW AMES—AGE 25
Born & brot up in Brookline, N.H. Has of late years, lived in Pepperell, Mass. Education pretty good, & has been for years in a Store. Never intemperate. Says he has not for several years kept the Sabbath as he ought. Used generally to post Books &c &c on that day.

Has Gambled some. For some time previous to his conviction had been in the habit of dealing in C[ounterfei]t Money. For this offence he was convicted in Boston in Nov last & sentenced to this place for 5 ys.

Ames is a man of sense, converses well, is frank, has a good deal of feeling, & weeps freely.

He confesses his crime & his follies & says he sincerely hopes that this trial will work for his good.

April 8, 1831

ROBERT H. JONES, COLORED MAN—AGE 23
Born & brot up in Baltimore. Parents live there now. Never a slave. Can read pretty well. Was taught mostly in the Sab[bath] School. Never before in any difficulty as he says. Appears frank, is intelligent, mind tends on religious Subjects, and appears very well in the Sab[bath] School. Think much better of him than of most of his fellows.

Sentenced in Boston in Nov for Larceny & for the term of 1 year.

THO[MA]S B. ROTCH—[AGE 35]
Home in Portsmouth N.H., age 35. Convicted in Salem in Nov last as a common cheat & sentenced for 6 months. An intelligent man, but has led of late years a very sorry life—drinking &c &c &c.

Says he has commonly when he could get it drink'd a quart a day. Wife & children.

Not much feeling. Says he will never drink any more, but I have no faith in him.

April 11, 1831

CHARLES DAVIS—AGE 24
Born & brot up at Fall River. Lost father at 12 & mother at 15. Went into a factory to work when 9 ys old. Education poor. Can read but not write. For the last 8 ys has been at Sea almost constantly, and of course has had very little religious instruction. At Sea contracted the habit of drinking to excess. This it was that led to the crime of Larceny for which he is now suffering. Convicted at N. Bedford in Dec. last, & sentenced for 1 year. Says he believes the Bible to be the Word of God. Knows he has not lived as he ought. The Register of the Prison calls him a 2d Comer.

This he absolutely denies. Says he never saw this place till he came here this time. Appear'd frank, & sensible of his folly.

GUILFORD BROWN—AGE 41
2d Comer. Home in Taunton. Has wife and a large family of children.[88] Ed[ucatio]n poor. Has some feeling.

---

[88]Guilford Brown registered his marriage to Charity Adams in Taunton, Nov. 30, 1809. He died of consumption in the Taunton almshouse, Nov. 10 or 11, 1840, age about 50. *Vital Records of Taunton*, 2:71, 3:37.

April 12, 1831

JOHN PEDRICK—AGE 40
Convicted in New Bedford in Dec last. Sentenced 1 year. Born in Marblehead. Follow'd the Sea most of his life. Education decent.

A *Rum drinker* & the rest need not be told. Stupid.

SAM[UE]L SPENCER—(BLACK)—AGE ABOUT 45
Born & brot up in Ashford Con. For many years past has liv'd in and about N. Bedford. Sentenced in New Bedford in Dec last for passing a Counterfeit Bill. Says he is perfectly innocent. Took it of a woman to buy her a pr of Shoes at her request, & was apprehended. &c.

Says he has always lived honestly. Rather stupid. Sentence 1 year.

A. TWOMBLEY—AGE 27[89]
Born & brot up in Madbury N.H. Mother lives there now. Tanner & Currier by trade. Has workd 7 years with the Tufts, in their Tannery in this Town.[90] Education as good as common. Got into the habit of drinking to excess, & that ruined him. Sentenced at Cambridge in Dec. last for an attempt at rape & sentenced for 5 ys. It was expected he would have been convicted of *Rape* & of consequence be hung, as there is very little doubt of his guilt. The act was committed in a fit of intemperance on the person of a young girl whom he met in the highway.

---

[89]Possibly Alfred Twombly, who married Susan Norton in Charlestown, Apr. 20, 1825. *Vital Records of Charlestown*, 2:374.

[90]The Tufts family was among the most prominent in Charlestown. Several members operated tanneries. Curtis may be referring to Nathan Tufts and Co., tanners. Timothy T. Sawyer, *Old Charlestown: Historical, Biographical, Reminiscent* (Boston, 1902), 39, 160–170.

Has some feeling, though far less than he ought to have. Hope he may be brought to repentance for this and all his sins.

April 18, 1831

EDMUND BEAN—[AGE 26]
Has been here 5 ys. Is to be discharg'd on the 22d Inst. Age 26. An atheist in sentiment, or at best a confirm'd Infidel. Had a long talk with him and warn'd him in the most solemn manner of what his sentiments must lead in time & in Eternity.

April 19, 1831

CHARLES FOLSOM—AGE 22
Not. G. Education good. Appears pretty well. Says his character has been good. Carpenter & Joiner. Convicted of Stealing a Watch at Lowel. Sentence 1 year. Came to prison in Dec last.

WILLIAM RILEY, AL[IAS] BENNET—AGE 50
2d Comer. Ireland. Drink ruins him. Says he has learn'd more and *felt* more since he came here the last time in Decr last, than in all his life.

Is now resolved never to drink another drop. Education very poor. Cannot read. Is in the Sab[bath] School. Is a peaceable, orderly fellow.

CHARLES FARRAR—(BLACK)—AGE 40
No learning. Seaman. Intemperate. 2d Comer. Out about 6 ys. Says *Morris*, a blackman now here,[91] was the means of

[91] Curtis did not include an entry on any inmate with the surname Morris.

getting him here. Has a wife & family. Is in our Sabbath School.

FRANCIS NICHOLAS

Color'd man. Belongs in Penn. Seaman. Can read, not write. Appears frank, tho not much feeling. Sentence 2½ ys for Larceny in Boston. Drink'd some thought not hard.

EDWARD PURRINGTON—AGE 17

Philadelphia. A beautiful & interesting lad. Reserved as to communicating much in regard to himself. Has a mother & brothers, who are respectable. Education good. Came on to Boston last fall where he got into trouble. Sentenced for 2½ ys. Larceny, in Dec last.

I fear he has not much sensibility. Says he was never vicious.

W[ILLIA]M SAWYER—AGE 18

Baltimore. Says he has no parents. A very interesting youth. Came here with Purrington (vid supra). Been Clerk in Store at N.Y. Says this is his first offence. Ed[ucation] Good. Sentenced in Boston in Dec last for 2 ys.

APPENDIX

In addition to the regular entries in Jared Curtis's memorandum book, on the six final pages of Volume I he included notes on meetings with prison inmates. Although some of these jottings are now completely illegible, and only one approaches a polished entry, the portions that can be recovered provide additional information on the population of the Massachusetts State Prison at Charlestown.

COLE[1] wishes for a Bible with plainer print than the one he has. Apl 11.

JOSIAH HARRIS. Wishes me to write to Selectmen of St. George, State of Maine. Wishes them to send a recommendation & get such other necessaries they may think would be useful. Says they all know him in the town & know that his character has been good. [T]his he wants to aid him in getting a pardon. Been here [15?] months. Sen. 5 ys.

Direct Letter to Joel Williams, Esq., Chairmen of Selectmen.

---

[1]Presumably Elijah Cole. See above, p. 69.

Abel Parker,[2] of Douglass Worces. Co. to get & forward a copy of his Indictment also a petition of the Citizens in his behalf & send them on in season for the May session—for George W Watkins.

Freeborn, lying at the point of death, wishes, when he is dead that I would send what money is due him on the Books of the prison to his sister, Sarah Dick[3] of Dartmouth Bristol County.

J.A. Pomeroy, Coventry Con.
Post Master—Rand who here in prison stole the mail from him—was afterward convicted of another offense in Jersey & sentenced to NJSP[4] for 6ys. escaped and is now here.[5]

Think to inquire of Mas. Prison in regard to the manner in which the prisoners now obtain tobacco.

Whitmarsh—Sentenced in Taunton for C[ounterfei]t Money 3 ys ago next Oct. Says that another man who was indicted for the same offence at Dedham & fled was the man who led him astray & has led many others astray in the same way & has been the means of getting several into the State prison. Says that man went through the prison yesterday as a visitor, & he learns now lives in Boston. True name Warren A Field. Goes now by the name of Warren. Is a

---

[2]Abel Parker and Sally Darling registered their intention to marry, Sept. 10, 1826. *Vital Records of Douglass, Massachusetts, to the End of the Year 1849* (Worcester, 1906), 133.

[3]Sarah Freeborn and Ebenezer Dick, both of Dartmouth, registered their intention to marry, Jan. 6, 1809. *Vital Records of Dartmouth, Massachusetts, to the Year 1850* (Boston, 1929–1930), 2:186.

[4]New Jersey State Prison.

[5]Rest of entry indecipherable.

large, fleshy man, weighs near 200. Makes it his business to go back & forth to Canada & Vermont & brings back large supplies of bad money. June 26.

A. Crosby—Leverett nearby[6]

Nehemiah Hughs wishes me to write a letter to his sister, Sally Gile, town of Walpole, Norfolk Co. Wish Mr. Gile to come and see him, & if father & mother have moved out of Walpole to write & let him know it & where they have gone. Should be glad to have something done to get off pt of his time. July 3

Josiah Harris wishes me to write a Letter to Francis Hall Boston, his cousin, & inform him that he is here, the reason etc & his conduct once here.
(see his ¶)

Alfred Clark—Age 45
Sick in the Hospital. Has been in prison about 2 mo. Sentenced in the County of Hampden for Stealing, for one year. Has long been feeble, & in the Hospital ever since he came here. Has wife & eight children. Belongs to Granby. His family is now in Chester. Wifes name Sally.

His parents live in Granby. Fathers name Joshua. Wishes me to write to him, stating his situation. Says he fears that he has been the means of hastening their gray lives to the Grave. Early life temperate. Late years, drink'd too much. Wife drinks. Letter to care of Israel Clark Junr. East Granby.

---

[6]Rest of entry indecipherable.

ACKNOWLEDGMENTS

Nothing races a scholar's pulse more than coming upon a hitherto unknown source of major significance. Hence, my excitement in 1998 when my friend Doug O'Dell, proprietor of Chapel Hill Rare Books, showed me two manuscript volumes that he recently had purchased. They consisted of handwritten biographies of hundreds of prisoners in the Massachusetts State Prison in Charlestown in the early nineteenth century, recorded by a prison chaplain. I immediately realized the importance of these manuscripts to our understanding of the demography of a large state prison population, and to antebellum reform institutions in general. Adding to the courtesy and generosity that Doug and his wife (and co-proprietor), Maureen, had shown me over the years, they permitted me to take the books to my office to evaluate and transcribe them, and, if I wished, to write about them.

This volume is the result, a project that went quickly and smoothly because of the assistance I had on it from the beginning. Laura Mielke, then a budding graduate student and now completing a dissertation under my direction, performed the heroic work of initial transcription. A Peterson Fellowship at the American Antiquarian Society in the summer of 1998 allowed me to fill in my knowledge of the Massachusetts State Prison during the years in which

Jared Curtis, the prison chaplain, interviewed its prisoners and recorded their life stories. Among the Society's superb staff I wish to single out Joanne Chaison and Caroline Sloat, always willing to answer my queries, even after my residency had ended. John White and Tim Pyatt of the Southern Historical Collection at the University of North Carolina at Chapel Hill, which serendipitously holds correspondence between Curtis and his son Moses Ashley, a botanist of considerable importance, expedited my work in those papers.

At some point I realized that I would strengthen any interpretation I gave these materials if I could publish the entire manuscript. I immediately thought of the Massachusetts Historical Society, with its long and distinguished record of making available valuable primary sources, and indeed they were interested. Conrad E. Wright jumped at the project, supported it fully as I envisioned it, and himself did the tedious work of preparing a final copy of the memorandum books. Along with his then colleague Ed Hanson, Conrad also helped greatly with the annotations. Ondine Le Blanc moved the volume smoothly through production and, along with Sally Pierce at the Boston Athenæum, located much of the illustrative material that makes the volume even more valuable. Finally, Bill Fowler did what any first-rate director of a major historical society would do: he added these priceless volumes to the Society's permanent collections.

As I worked on this volume I realized that I had been introduced to the subject over twenty-five years earlier, when I first had read David Rothman's *The Discovery of the Asylum* (1971). His portrayal of the way the United States struggled to understand and rehabilitate those who did not fit seamlessly into a society driven by the market revolution made an indelible impression on me. I yearned to find out more about the individuals who had been placed in the asylums, prisons, and reformatories, even as I understood that for the most part such individual stories were forever lost to history. Then came Reverend Curtis's memorandum books. I offer them to the public not only because they give voice and life to a hitherto silent and anonymous population, but also so that we might honestly continue to reflect on what we continue to consider "deviant," and why.

PHILIP F. GURA
Chapel Hill, N.C., 2001

INDEX